W9-CRH-651

PAIN AND POSSIBILITY

Writing Your Way Through Personal Crisis

Gabriele Lusser Rico

JEREMY P. TARCHER/PERIGEE

Jeremy P. Tarcher/Perigee Books
are published by
The Putnam Publishing Group
200 Madison Avenue
New York, NY 10016

Library of Congress Cataloging-in-Publication Data

Rico, Gabriele L.
    Pain and possibility: writing your way through personal crisis/by Gabriele
Lusser Rico.
      p.   cm.
   ISBN 0-87477-642-2   ISBN 0-87477-571-X
          1. Suffering.   2. Pain—Psychological aspects.   3. Authorship—
Psychological aspects.   I. Title
BF789.S8R53   1991   91-9505
158 ' .1—dc20   CIP

Copyright © 1991 by Gabriele Lusser Rico

All rights reserved. No part of this work may be reproduced or transmitted in
any form by any means, electronic or mechanical, including photocopying and
recording, or by any information storage or retrieval system, except as may be
expressly permitted by the 1976 Copyright Act or in writing by the publisher.
Requests for such permissions should be addressed to:

Jeremy P. Tarcher, Inc.
5858 Wilshire Blvd., Suite 200
Los Angeles, CA 90036

Illustrations by Gabriele Lusser Rico and Janée Proctor

Manufactured in the United States of America
10   9   8   7   6   5   4   3   2

For Parviz,
who sees possibility all around him
and
for my daughters, Stephanie, Suzanne, Simone,
from whom I continue to learn about the life of feeling,
and
for philosopher Susanne Langer,
whose life's work on the forms of feeling
served as a catalyst for my own.

In the spent of one night he wrote three propositions:
That nothing lasts. That hell is the denial of the ordinary.
That clean white paper waiting under pen
is the gift beyond history and hurt and heaven.

JOHN CIARDI
''THE GIFT''

Human feeling is a fabric, not a vague mass. It has an intricate dynamic pattern, possible combinations and new emergent phenomena. It is a pattern of organically interdependent and interdetermined tensions and resolutions, a pattern of almost infinitely complex activation and cadence.

SUSANNE LANGER
PHILOSOPHICAL SKETCHES

Everything we name enters the circle of language,
and therefore the circle of meaning.
The world is a sphere of meanings, a language.

OCTAVIO PAZ
ALTERNATING CURRENTS

The author would like to thank the following for permission to reprint.

Natalie Babbitt, from *Tuck Everlasting*. Copyright © 1975 by Natalie Babbitt. Reprinted by permission of Farrar, Straus & Giroux. John Barth, from *The End of the Road*. Copyright © 1958 by John Barth. Reprinted by permission of Avon Books. Wendell Berry, "I Go Among Trees." From *Sabbaths*. Copyright © 1987 by Wendell Berry. Reprinted by permission of North Point Press. Wendell Berry, "To Know the Dark" from *Farming: A Hand Book*, copyright © 1967 by Wendell Berry, reprinted by permission of Harcourt Brace Jovanovich, Inc. Wendell Berry, "Song(4)." From Collected Poems: 1957–1982. Copyright © 1985 by Wendell Berry. Reprinted by permission of North Point Press. Ray Bradbury, from *Dandelion Wine*. Copyright © 1978 by Ray Bradbury. Reprinted by permission of Alfred A. Knopf, Inc. William Bronk, "I Am." From *That Tantalus*. © 1971 by William Bronk. Reprinted by permission of William Bronk. John Ciardi, "The Gift." From *Live Another Day*. Copyright © 1949 by John Ciardi. Reprinted by permission of Twayne. Emily Dickinson, "Surgeons must be very careful" and "After Great Pain." Reprinted by permission of The Belknap Press of Harvard University Press, Cambridge, Massachusetts. © 1951, 1955 by the President and Fellows of Harvard College and the Trustees of Amherst College from Thomas H. Johnson editor. Joan Didion, from *Play It As It Lays*. © 1970 by Joan Didion. Reprinted by permission of Farrar, Straus and Giroux. Otto Dix, "Lens Bombed," etching and aquatint. Courtesy Philadelphia Museum of Art. Alan Dugan, "Morning Song." From *New and Collected Poems, 1961–1983*. Copyright © 1961, 1962, 1968, 1972, 1973, 1974, 1983 by Alan Dugan. First published by The Ecco Press, 1983. Reprinted by permission. Stephen Dunn, "Loneliness." From *Between Angels*. Copyright © 1989 by Stephen Dunn. Reprinted by permission of W. W. Norton Company, Inc. Edward Field, "The Tailspin." From *Variety Photoplays*. Copyright © 1967 By Edward Field. Reprinted by permission of Maelstrom Press. Richard Frost, "Some Important Advice." From *The Circus Villains*. Copyright © 1965 by Richard Frost. Reprinted by permission of the author. J. Ruth Gendler. Excerpts from *The Book of Qualities*. Copyright © 1988 by J. Ruth Gendler. Reprinted by permission of HarperCollins Publishers. Sandra Hochman, "Postscript," copyright © 1969, by Sandra Hochman, from *Earthworks* by Sandra Hochman. Used by permission of Viking Penguin, a division of Penguin Books USA Inc. Edward Hopper, "Nighthawks," oil on canvas, 1942. Photograph © 1991 The Art Institute of Chicago. All Rights Reserved. David Ignatow, Poem 23 ("Witness") Reprinted from *Shadowing the Ground* © 1991 by David Ignatow, Wesleyan University Press by permission of University Press of New England. James Joyce. From *Portrait of the Artist as a Young Man*. Reprinted by permission of Viking Press. Galway Kinnell, from "The Still Time." From *Mortal Acts, Mortal Words* by Galway Kinnell. Copyright © 1980 by Galway Kinnell. Reprinted by permission of Houghton Mifflin Co. Maxine Kumin, "Address to the Angels." Copyright © 1978 by Maxine Kumin. Stanley Kunitz, "Change." From *Selected Poems 1928–1958* by Stanley Kunitz. Copyright 1929, 1930. By permission of Little, Brown and Company. Stanley Kunitz, "The Scene." From *Next-to-Last Things*. Copyright © 1985 by Stanley Kunitz. Used with permission of Atlantic Monthly Press. Reprinted by permission of Penguin Books. Frances Lear, "Color Me Blue." Copyright © 1989. Reprinted by permission of Lear's Magazine. Osip Mandelstam, "Stone." Copyright © 1981 by Osip Mandelstam. Reprinted by permission of Princeton University Press. Peter Meinke, "The Heart's Location" and "Because." From *The Night Train and the Golden Bird* by Peter Meinke. Copyright © 1977 by Peter Meinke. Reprinted by permission of the University of Pittsburgh Press. Michelle Murray, "Death Poem." From *The Great Mother and Other Poems*. Copyright © 1974 by Michelle Murray. Reprinted by permission of Universal Press Syndicate. Sharon Olds, "The Blue Dress" and "I Go Back to May, 1937." From *The Gold Cell* by Sharon Olds. Copyright © 1987 by Sharon Olds. Reprinted by permission of Random House. Linda Pastan, "Helen Bids Farewell to Her Daughter Hermione." From *Waiting For My Life*. Copyright © 1981 by Linda Pastan. Reprinted by permission of W. W. Norton Company, Inc. Linda Pastan, "Last Will." From *A Fraction of Darkness*. Copyright © 1985 by Linda Pastan. Reprinted by permission of W. W. Norton Company, Inc. Alastair Reid, "The Spiral." From *Weathering*. Copyright © 1978 by Alastair Reid. Reprinted by permission of the author. Theodore Roethke, from "The Waking." From *The Collected Poems of Theodore Roethke*. Copyright © 1964 by Theodore Roethke. Reprinted by permission of Doubleday. William Stafford, "How to Build an Owl" and "Any Time." From *Allegiances: New Poems*. Copyright © 1970 by William Stafford. Reprinted by permission of the author. Wallace Stevens, from *The Collected Poems*. Copyright © 1982 Reprinted by permission of Random House. Kurt Vonnegut, from *The Sirens of Titan*. Copyright © 1977 by Kurt Vonnegut. Reprinted by permission of Delacorte Press. David Wagoner, "The Other House." From *First Light*. Reprinted by permission of the author. Alice Walker, "Good Night Willie Lee," copyright © 1975 by Alice Walker, from GOOD NIGHT WILLIE LEE, I'LL SEE YOU IN THE MORNING by Alice Walker. Used by permission of Doubleday, a division of Bantam Doubleday Dell Publishing Group, Inc. Miller Williams, "Sale," from Halfway from Hoxie by Miller Williams. Copyright © 1973 by Miller Williams. Reprinted by permission of Louisiana State University Press.

CONTENTS

Acknowledgments

"Only connect!" wrote E. M. Forster. If the small word *for* is a connecting word, here, then, are the most immediate human connections to the writing of this book.

For Parviz, without whom, still not.

For my daughters, Stephanie, Suzanne, and Simone, who have grown into healthy expressions of both pain and joy.

For my three sisters and brother who, I'm sure, have their own versions of the story, and in memory of Tobias Grether who kindled a life-long passion about the role of time in human consciousness.

For colleagues and friends:

* Hans P. Guth, whose passion for projects continues to push me to "plow ahead."
* Joseph Bogen, M.D., for permitting me ongoing glimpses into the adventure of the brain's mysteries.
* Scott Rice, my office-mate and perpetrator of the Bulwer-Lytton Contest, eliciting the world's worst opening sentences to the world's worst novels.
* Scott Hymas, who made me aware of the power of polarities in literature.
* James Conner, University president and master speech writer—for his wisdom, passion, grace.

For special friends:

* Mary Naylor, whose forthrightness and sense of humor in the face of life's crises make me smile.
* Una Nakamura, Maureen Girard, and Nancy Wambach, first students, then peers, who are not afraid to grow again and again.
* Karen Seale, who can, and does, and will.

For the nuts-and-bolts people, without whom no manuscript would ever see daylight:

* Allyn Brodsky, my editor with a vision and a deeply intelligent grasp of what I was struggling to put into words.
* Mary Ellen Strote, second reader, for keeping my sometimes errant flight of words on course.
* Daniel Malvin, simultaneously mediator, tightrope walker, voice of reason.
* Jennifer Boynton, production editor, whose thoughtful tackling of the many layers of production involved in this kind of book, helped me see it through.

For those at a greater distance, who have influenced my work and reenforced my thinking:

* Edward P. J. Corbett, the very model of Rhetoric, who also knows about suffering—yet remembers to laugh.
* Donald Murray, who hypothesized that "all writing is autobiography."
* Peter Elbow, whose *Writing without Teachers* struck a nerve.
* The many, many recent writers in fields as diverse as literature, physics, and psychology whose work I've read and from which I have distilled so many quotations influencing my thinking, but especially Susanne Langer, Marilyn Ferguson, M. C. Richards, Jean Houston, Sam Keen, John Briggs, David Peat, James Gleick, David Loye, Sheldon Kopp, Octavio Paz, Ken Wilber, and Charles Johnston.
* All poets, those wordsmiths of the life of feeling, whose words are part of the fabric of my life.

And last, but significantly, for the ongoing privilege of interacting with:

* My students, who, over the years, have been a rich source of insight about writing, learning, teaching.
* My workshop participants, all, for their desire to be there and their willingness to risk.
* The many educators across the United States, who sense that, in order to stay vital in the classroom, they must be life-long learners.

Preface

When I was small, I read a fairy tale about a princess who was born with a glass heart. One early spring day, grown into a lovely young woman, she leaned far out over a window sill in the castle, feeling joy at the sight of the first crocuses in the palace garden below. The pressure on her fragile heart proved too much. There was a tiny sound, like glass breaking, and she fell as if dead. When the confusion settled, the court doctor discovered her heart was not broken after all but it had a long, slender crack in it. The story evolves from there.

What is most vivid in my memory is my childhood amazement that she lived to be very old and, even more amazing, that she continued to find deep pleasure in her life. I remember puzzling, "How can she run and play? How can she be happy and not be afraid every minute of every day?"

My mother died in a bombing raid three weeks before the end of World War II. It left our family vulnerable, confused, afraid, and in great pain. I pictured a long, jagged crack across my small heart. I felt fragile as glass, and I wondered if glass could ever heal. Then I recalled the princess's words: "What survives a crack and doesn't break on the spot will be all the stronger for it."

At seven, I did not believe it. Now I do. Although not a single one of us is exempt from pain—in fact, we are all damaged somehow, somewhere, somewhen—the real issue is not whether, but *how,* we learn to deal with our damage. That makes all the difference.

This book is based on a profoundly simple premise: empowerment of self. As we follow the unpredictable paths our lives take, we need tools to mediate our unease, uncertainty, sadness, imbalance, confusion. Empowerment does not lie in trying to escape these unpleasant states, but rather in learning to transform our suffering. Running away from suffering intensifies it; denying suffering intensifies it; wallowing in suffering intensifies it; blaming our suffering on others intensifies it. Anesthetizing it will work for only so long. And emotional shut-down is ultimately destructive to mind and body. I know. It happened to me.

What helps is to direct your pain into constructive acts, thus transforming it. Writing is one of these acts. Writing gives shape and form to your feelings. Writing opens the wilderness of feelings for exploration, and the emerging patterns in your writing lead to gradual insights, occasional life-changing epiphanies, but mostly a wary grace.

"But I can't write," you say.

I say, "Of course you can—language is your birthright."

"I would not know *what* to write," you say.

I say, "Trust your natural inner voice, and it will find its way into the tangled feelings of your unease."

"But it's too painful," you say.

I say, "Spilling your pain onto the page is healing; holding it in is as unfruitful as holding your breath. Letting go leads to life."

"I don't know where to begin," you say.

That is why I have written this book. It represents a natural evolution of the ideas developed in my 1983 book, *Writing the Natural Way.* In the course of giving innumerable workshops over the past fifteen years, in the letters I received from so many of you describing your awakening to your own need to express yourselves, and in writing through my own extended and terrifying crisis, I became aware of the depth of human pain, the human hunger to make connections, of the intense imperative for expressing long-buried feelings. I saw that giving a name to feelings—what I call naming and framing—is empowering. I noticed that an increasing sense of empowerment helped people shed a sense of helplessness, enabling them to become open to feelings and receptive to their pain instead of denying, fighting, or ignoring it. Such a shift allowed them to move into—and through—their pain, to get on with life instead of feeling stuck, victimized, helpless.

Learning to express our all too often amorphous mass of feelings is a constructive, creative act. It taps your potential for regaining balance; it allows for the emergence of patterns of feeling. It alerts you to the power of change coming from

Wisdom is the courage to live in the moving resonance of the present.

SAM KEEN

within, leading you from hurt to health, from numbness to vitality, from pain to possibility.

I learned early to deny my feelings. It was many years before I unlearned that impulse. As an adult I thought, "If only I try harder, work longer, pretend I'm not having bad feelings, I can contain them." In fact, I was so out of touch with my emotions, I believed I could actually avert crises. So I denied. I denied how I really felt about a multitude of things for years, again and again, until I no longer knew how to disentangle my real feelings from my pretend feelings. The more intense my moments of high emotion, the more energy I spent suppressing them.

What I finally learned seems obvious in retrospect. Feelings are signposts; you are supposed to pay attention to them. To deny them is to deny your self. I learned you can neither run away from your feelings nor from the problems that have generated them. A time came—as it had to—when the deeply buried problems and the denied feelings of many years hit me like a tidal wave.

I almost drowned.

Out of desperation and pure instinct to survive, I began to use a gathering process I named *clustering*, developed in my doctoral thesis in 1975, to tap these buried emotions. Whenever the chaos engulfing me became too frightening, I wrote. Gradually, I began to see patterns of meaning in the little vignettes pouring onto the page. They were rarely long, written in bursts of two to ten minutes. Through this process I began to rediscover unacknowledged feelings, to learn how to feel all over again, to confront instead of repress. From confronting I learned I wouldn't crumble. I began to trust flexibility instead of iron control. I discovered that the impetus for genuine personal change comes from within.

This book speaks to that impetus, to the inner voice that finally wants—needs—to be heard. Only when we become receptive to that vital impulse can we begin to express our feelings. Expressing what moves us liberates us. Given shape and form on the page, our feelings begin to take on recognizable patterns, letting us shift from outworn beliefs and attitudes to more appropriate ones that serve us in a new time and a new emotional space.

When we struggle with feelings such as grief or anger, we tend to forget that, although we seem to be paralyzed by crisis, unable to engage in our normal day-to-day activities, we can still experiment with self-expression.

To stop functioning during a crisis is normal—for a while—but ultimately, we must permit ourselves to explore our feelings in order to move beyond stuckness. Philosopher Sam Keen writes that "depression is repression." Repression may act as a safety valve for a time, but it won't work for long. Conversely, a headlong plunge into frantic, almost compulsive activity to avoid the feelings raging against the barred windows of our psyche is just as useless. At some point, denial is no longer an option; facing becomes an imperative. In doing so, you will gradually discover a way through the crisis, uncover purposes you didn't know, rediscover an evolving self, and achieve the new equilibrium which comes with empowerment.

The best anti-depressants are expression and action. That way our depression is not an end but a meaningful beginning.

MARILYN FERGUSON

We can only begin where we are. We all have stories to tell, big or small. We *are* our stories, as poet Linda Pastan tells us.

Our problems in world crisis may be soluble only creatively—that is, by a profound and thorough alteration of our inner life and of the outer forms in which life finds expression and support.

BREWSTER GHISELIN

> There is time
> to tell you
> the only story I know
> A youth sets out,
> a man or woman returns;
> the rest is simply incident
> or weather.
>
> And yet what storms
> I could describe
> swirling
> in every thumbprint.

Our stories are simultaneously the same *and* different. My story will be different from yours, yet the underlying feeling patterns of both will reveal striking similarities. Precisely because our stories are both the same and different, the expression of your story can only come from you. Your experience is unique to you and only you can truly get in touch with its patterns. Expecting someone else to do it for you is like asking someone else to chew your food.

When at last we can explore our pain or despair through language, we see ourselves in a new light. Best of all, we discover the enormous satisfaction that comes from putting our feelings onto the clean white page of healing.

The princess of my childhood fairy tale could not wish away the crack in her heart, just as we cannot wish away past or present pain. But she did learn how to live her life in joy—despite the damage. I have learned how; so have many, many others. You can, too. That is the promise of this book.

I know of no trouble in life which does not stand as a counterpart to some positive capacity. Let us rejoice in our sufferings, knowing them to be symptoms of our potential health. Pain is a script, and as we learn to read it, we grow in self-knowledge.

M. C. RICHARDS

The Motive for Writing: Naming and Framing

This book came into being because of my own terrible downward spiral into crisis, before I had tools to sustain me. I couldn't move into an upward, healing spiral, until I had discovered the consequences of being afraid to grow: emotional denial, chronic anxiety, acute panic attacks, and, finally, physical illness. At the bottom of the spiral my customary self-control gave way. Reconnecting with my feeling self became a condition of survival. My iron control no longer worked; running away no longer worked; reading *about* what would work no longer worked. (I had devoured books on stress and anxiety—all of which only made me feel worse.) How-to-get-well advice or someone else's "Five Steps to . . ." only made me more afraid.

One day it hit me: to look outside myself was useless. I had to look inside. I was able to shift gears from without to within only by putting words on a page. I wrote—out of desperation—to discover where I was, who I was, what I was, what I was feeling, and what I had *not* been feeling.

Writing quick word sketches when the pressure became unbearable brought me small moments of discovery, occasional leaps of insight, and gradually, personal transformation.

The very act of putting pen to paper began to relax my emotional rigidity, generating an unfamiliar sense of flexibility. Ultimately, writing enabled me to negotiate the downward spiral, explore who the "I" was at its still center, and then, finally, begin the spiral upward into healing. My key discovery was that insights cannot be forced: they can only be evoked; they cannot be tackled directly, they can only be elicited indirectly and metaphorically.

WHY WRITE ABOUT PAIN?

If you cannot find it within yourself, where will you go for it?

CONFUCIUS

The very fact that a thing—anything—can be fitted into a meaning built up of words, small black words that can be written with one hand and the stub of a pencil, means it is not big enough to be overwhelming. It is the vast, formless, unknown and unknowable things we fear. Anything which can be brought to a common point—a focus within our understanding—can be dealt with.

LARA JEFFERSON

This book is about pain and about how to transform it into possibility for personal growth using your own words on a page. It is about tapping your untapped feelings and giving them shape in a medium you already have at your command: language. It is also about words; more specifically, it is about the power of language—*your* words, my words. It is about expressing feelings. It is about learning to confront—using the safety net of words—the echoes of your past, the vague, tangled images of some uncertain future, the seemingly inarticulable feelings of the present moment. Most of all, this book is about creating rather than stagnating or self-destructing.

No one is immune to pain, but I know many who let pain fester and take charge of their lives. I know from my own experience that it is possible to *dis*charge that pain and become *re*charged. Discovering your own meanings in your own words transforms potentially self-destructive feelings into creative acts, lets you become a do-er, instead of a passive victim. Your pain becomes manageable, explorable, transformable into unexpected patterns of meaning.

> The pain is the aversion. The healing magic is attention. Properly attended to, pain can answer our most crucial questions, even those we did not consciously frame. The only way out of our suffering is through it. Conflict, pain, tension, fear, paradox—these are breakthroughs trying to happen. Once we confront them, we realize that the reward is worth the scariness of the unanesthetized life. The release of pain and the resolution of conflict make the next crisis easier to confront.

I first read Marilyn Ferguson's words in a time of great personal turmoil. I knew they were important, but what I didn't have were tools—ways to grapple with the pain. So I tried to outrun it. Years of chronic denial led only to the numbing of my feelings. Since feelings merely go underground, they inevitably bubbled to the surface as ominous anxiety symptoms, then escalated into debilitating panic attacks, and finally into feelings of utter helplessness. Something had to give—in this case, my body. I was diagnosed with cancer. The emotional slicing-through the ice of control that followed nearly destroyed me. Almost too late did I learn that there are other, less devastating ways to move through crisis.

Crisis: By definition, the word suggests a state of instability. From the Greek and Latin *krisis*, meaning 'decision,' it names a turning point. The Chinese ideogram for *crisis* clarifies this ambiguity:

Figure 1.1   Chinese ideogram meaning *crisis*

The first character means danger; the second, opportunity. Taken together, the two figures signify crisis, pronounced "Wei Ji" in Mandarin and "*Ki* Ki" in Japanese. And that is the crux: A crisis is the signal not only of danger but also of promise. I read only danger. Thinking of myself as a sort of superwoman, I felt worthy only when I produced—which meant working harder, running faster, juggling more and more balls—and almost always denying: denying a hunger for something, denying emptiness, denying anger, denying pain. Denying opportunity.

The key to expanded awareness is surrender.

WILLIAM JAMES

The Tailspin
Going into a tailspin in those days meant curtains. No matter how hard you pulled back on the stick the nose of the plane wouldn't come up. Spinning round, headed for a target of earth, the whine of death in the wing struts, instinct make you try to pull out of it that way, by force, and for years aviators spiraled down and crashed. Who could have dreamed that the solution to this dreaded aeronautical problem was so simple? Every student flier learns this nowadays: You move the joystick in the direction of the spin and like a miracle the plane stops turning and you are in control again to pull the nose up out of the dive. In panic we want to push the stick away from the spin, wrestle the plane out of it, but the trick is, as in everything, to go with the turning willingly, rather than fight, give in, go with it, and that way come out of your tailspin whole.

EDWARD FIELD

The day came, as it had to, when I lost the control on which I had depended. To my terror, my automatic denial strategy suddenly didn't work anymore. I had a panic attack. And another. And another. As yet, I had no name for what was wrong. I only knew that something said, "I quit," by giving out, like nonfunctioning brakes frantically floored as the car spins out of control. The sense of lost control was utterly terrifying. Improvisation became an imperative.

Coming out of such a tailspin whole is also what this book is about. With simple word tools you will learn to move *through* your crisis instead of struggling uselessly to avoid them, to be an active participant in your own changes instead of their victim, to be a creator and *re*creator of your self, to grow into possibility. In short, the most constructive response to crisis is moving into and through pain to a new sense of wholeness.

This process of finding your own words will help you see new patterns of meaning—your own patterns. Since your own words are your best healer, you can learn to turn your emotional dross into gold. *Naming* your feelings through writing will *frame* the hidden patterns of your invisible, elusive, often fearful, emotional life. Each naming and framing moves you toward getting unstuck, toward turning desolation, meaninglessness, anarchy, into possibility.

What can you expect to gain from writing your way into and through your pain? A better handle on your problems, sudden awareness of options, and a profound satisfaction in knowing that the impulse toward healing comes from within yourself. You can break through emotional barriers, become involved in creative acts of growth, explore your own inner voice, confront your feelings as they are, not lock them into what they *ought* to be, and know that if you get lost again, you have strategies and tools to enable you to find your way—again, and again, and again.

These techniques actively engage you in your feelings and your own healing, in moving from emotional hurricanes to emotional responsiveness and in learning to experience emotional flexibility instead of rigidity. It helps you discover that feelings are natural—all feelings, not just the "good" ones—and that acknowledging them is a healing act. Risking is far superior to avoiding; you cannot learn any other way. Giving voice to patterns of feelings is a way of triggering change. Lives are not fixed but a flow of possibilities and your own words, given form, empower you. Listen to the voice of a workshop participant, Robin Rector Krupp.

My Writing

Secret, silent,
my writing
is a quiet buddy wanting to come home.
My writing
doesn't want to go on vacation,
doesn't want to go away.
My writing is honey, elixir in my blood.
Don't turn away.
Look it in the face.

Writing is a way of cutting away at the surface of things, of exploring, of understanding.

ROBERT DUNCAN

Only unfelt emotions distort the mind. Emotions are only blind when they are blocked.

ARTHUR JANOV

THE LESSONS OF PAIN

Clearly pain has a function in our lives. Physically, it warns us of danger to our bodies, pressing us to act. Psychically, it lets us know when we are out of balance. Yet, because too many of us have learned to ignore the signals; we are out of touch with the very feelings that let us know something is wrong. We cannot hear the message.

Milton Ward, in *The Brilliant Function of Pain*, describes what we know in our gut: that we will do almost anything to stop pain. He argues that we pay an enormous price for our avoidance attempts, because we miss what needs attending to. In listening to our pain, we tap into its wisdom and thereby move toward the mental, emotional, and physical equilibrium we naturally seek. Pain's own logic and messages are astounding when we become receptive.

- Pain is a guide, not an enemy. Follow it.
- Pain tells you something, you do not tell the pain. Listen to it.

- Rationalizing your pain will distort your response to it. Face it.
- Fearing pain, fighting it, avoiding it, or ignoring it only increases it. Flow with it.
- The best way to respond to pain is simply to allow yourself to feel it deeply and to respond to those feelings—and in that way, pain becomes self-limiting. Take time for it.

Emotional pain runs the gamut from mild distress to utter despair; it manifests itself in our feelings, our bodies, our spirit, or all three at once. At best, we feel malaise or discontent; at worst, desolation, anguish, agony, torment.

Philosopher Sam Keen says pain is nature's way of getting our attention. Most people, he insists, deny the bulk of their feelings or are totally unaware of them; as he puts it, "You are caught by what you are running from." It is time to stop running and redirect that energy into naming and framing what we are afraid of facing.

You may ask: "Why is it so essential to undertake this journey—at best uncomfortable, at worst agonizing—into my most painful feelings in the first place?"

An answer: "Because avoidance works only for so long; the longer we run away, the harder the pendulum swings back, and then it knocks us for the proverbial loop."

We cry out for help only when we are desperate enough to be forced into listening to our pain. Out of touch with our feelings, the body will magnify them in physical ways.

According to University of Texas psychology professor Blair Justice, "psychoneuroimmunology" (PNI) has been suggested as the name for a new field of medicine that deals with the connections between our immune system and our emotions. A fundamental premise of this field is that prolonged suppression of emotions leads to suppression of the immune system. Accordingly, the constructive/destructive role of the emotions in immunology is at the heart of this research. Explored at length in Dr. Justice's *Who Gets Sick?*, this research points to built-in self-healing capacities of which our emotions are a kind of barometer.

THE POTENTIAL WITHIN PAIN

As the orange already exists as potential in the orange blossom, so possibility already lies within our pain. When we relearn to face pain, we discover choices we didn't know we had. If we deny it, emotional confusion can quickly become utter anarchy; if we learn to be receptive, it becomes absolute potential.

I've learned that naming and framing pain becomes a way to look at the other side of the coin—the awareness that pain and possibility are interdependent. Seeing them as the extremes of a single continuum instead of opposites, we begin to see the potential for growth inherent in pain.

Potential. Its Latin root is *potere* 'to be able; able to act, do.' Possibility. Its Latin root is *poss* 'power.' Empowerment leads to the surmountable, the imaginable, conceivable, attainable. Pain's potential lies in a new grounding for choices, new confidence. Pain is a signal that change is required. Given the tools we can, by exploring our hurt, locate clues that point us in a new direction.

WHY WRITING HELPS

"I guess I'm afraid," you might say, "afraid to allow myself to feel." Don't be. Here is the motive for writing:

The very act of putting pencil to paper is an act of giving shape to amorphous feelings. The act of writing helps name the unnameable: the chaotic feelings we resist, fear, or remain unaware of. Paradoxically, by letting go, by externalizing feelings in words, we gain a greater ability to take charge of our own lives, and begin to see the patterns within the seeming chaos.

Although living includes inevitable crises and disappointments, most of us cope with them without seeking formal therapy. If we're lucky, we discover our own constructive ways to face up to pain, but sometimes they're not enough. It helps immeasurably to have many different tools we can use to help ourselves. Writing is one of the most satisfying: it leaves footprints marking our trail—where we have been, are now, and where we are going. Writing—because it helps us discover our deepest feelings, which often reveal a conflict with what

The body does not lie.

MARTHA GRAHAM

Somewhere in our early education we become addicted to the notion that pain means sickness. We fail to learn that pain is the body's way of informing the mind that we are doing something wrong, not necessarily that something is wrong. . . . We get the message of pain all wrong. Instead of addressing ourselves to the cause, we become pushovers for pills, driving the pain underground and inviting it to return with increased authority.

NORMAN COUSINS

we thought we believed or wanted to believe—is likely to lead to profound changes in how we view our world and our role in it. Such a mind-shift may in turn lead to solutions we might never have otherwise imagined. Sometimes writing illuminates questions we have no answers for, questions we didn't even know we had.

Whatever our crisis, whatever our sorrow, whatever our feeling, to name it is to frame it. A frame of words gives us the safety to claim our feelings as our own, to become receptive to them, to express them. Expression empowers us to transform our feelings; it permits us to connect our stories with the stories of others, to bridge the gulf of our essential isolation from one another.

Writing can be a road map into the invisible geography of your feelings, enabling you to chart their hairpin turns or see unexpected sideroads. Because the web of human feeling creates its own patterns, these patterns are better evoked than explained. To name and frame with words on a page triggers the process of evocation.

The language of the emotions is elusive, fragile, multifaceted, because our emotional being is profoundly involved in the formative, in the logically undefinable. Forms of feeling emerge through the evocative language of images and metaphor. We need open-ended tools to tap this language. Think of the famous lines by e. e. cummings in his poem "since feeling is first."

> since feeling is first
> who pays any attention
> to the syntax of things.

Or those of Theodore Roethke, in "The Waking."

> We think by feeling. What is there to know?
> . . . I learn by going where I have to go.

NAMING AND FRAMING: WORD SKETCHES

One key technique to access feelings is the use of *Word Sketches,* in which you quickly name and frame whatever comes without much preparation or spending much time. A

Sometimes just being alive feels like raw flesh—vulnerable, responsive, irritable, in constant danger. Those are the times when I most need to sense my place among other people, to hear their stories and know they are mine as well. I badly need to be sure someone can hear me: I need to receive his answering cry.

SHELDON KOPP

Word Sketch can take the form of a poem or a short, concentrated piece of prose. It can take any form you like as long as it serves its purpose: to use words to express feelings by naming and framing them.

What do I mean by naming and framing? A frame implies the external form or shape of a thing's identity, like the shape of a leaf or a flower in the natural world. Frames also suggest inner shapes: the internal elements that support and define a structure, like the frame of a house. The verb *to frame* also suggests making, molding, patterning—all that is formative. Its opposite is formlessness, which implies something without shape; something which exists but which cannot be defined, determined, or limited. Indeed, many of our feelings feel formless—and thus frightening—until somehow framed by a safe boundary of language. By giving feelings a name, by putting them into words and connecting these words in certain ways, we actively shape the seemingly formless chaos of our feelings into something we can work with, something distinct, formed, framed, thus, manageable.

Unframed feelings tend to remain a kind of mush, spilling over like the inexhaustible pot of porridge in the Grimm's fairy tale, that ultimately swallows the valley. However, when our feelings are framed, contained, bounded, they become well-lit signposts; they can illuminate aspects of our lives that feel dark. Periodically framing our feelings in words brings them to our conscious attention. Without this ongoing process of periodic reassessment, life is nothing more than an endurance contest. Too many of us live this way. Framing our feelings through Word Sketches allows the emergence of the most ingrained parts of us, parts we don't even know how to acknowledge. It lets us recognize who we are in times of turmoil. It is a formative, *per*forming, *in*forming engagement with our feelings. In this way we cannot become their passive victims.

In our internal world we need a perimeter around our feelings so we can look at them, learn to read them, explore them. In becoming expressive in language, we frame the feelings we are struggling with right now. Each time we do so, we have the opportunity to glimpse the patterns in seeming chaos. A series of glimpses leads us to greater and greater illumination. Naming and framing helps transmute our suffering from mere disconnected pain to a significant process, from destructive ruminating to a constructive act. Through word sketching we are constantly searching for patterns that lead to insight.

There is no freedom if I do not respect my bonds, my bounds, my boundaries.

SAM KEEN

There is enormous satisfaction, even joy, in giving shape to feelings by framing them in language. The pleasure, I think, comes most from being the author and designer of your self. And framing allows us to reframe—reorganize—and see things from a different perspective. Insights, flexibility, emotional shifts come in from the edges, the margins, the spaces of what we have not written. In order to change a life situation that brings us unremitting pain, we must first recognize the recurring patterns. Only then can we redesign our responses to it.

In my own odyssey, I discovered I was not so alone, so different as I had imagined. I discovered we all have metaphoric cracks in our hearts, sad stories to tell, hurts to heal. It is the human story. Only the particulars differ. The goal is not to banish pain, but to develop tools with which to transform it.

LEARNING HOW TO USE THE TOOLS

The activities in this book are evocative, not didactic. Their basic premise is that the impulse to transform pain must come from within, no matter how much we initially resist it, and that our own words on a page are the gentlest, most powerful means to impel us toward new ways of seeing, being, healing. Confucius stated:

> Give me a fish and I will eat today;
> teach me to fish, and I will eat a lifetime.

How do you learn to fish? Here are some of the key elements.

- Letting go, instead of clutching
- Facing, instead of avoiding
- Exploring, instead of hiding

- Doing, instead of vegetating
- Changing, instead of ossifying
- Growing, instead of shriveling

In learning to use the tools presented here, you will gain some lifelong strategies that will serve you well.

- Reconnecting with denied or detoured feelings through the technique of Aware Breathing
- Becoming aware of the stages that are part of any crisis period
- Developing new and unexpected points of view
- Using Word Sculptures to reveal instead of conceal denied feelings
- Using Word Sketches to produce a shift from feelings of helplessness to feelings of personal empowerment
- Moving from fragmentation to wholeness through recognizing the emergence of patterns that recur and connect in your ongoing Feeling Sketchbook

The mind-shift between pain and possibility depends on your willingness to feel, to become vulnerable. Some of us say, "I can't," but "I can't" often means "I won't." We close ourselves off from possibility. The question then is not "Can I?" but "How can I?" The answer is: by focusing on whatever you are feeling here and now, this very moment, and giving it your words on a page. The unwritten wound festers. "Give sorrow words," said Shakespeare.

The next step is to begin. As you experiment, we will return to this issue of why and how writing helps us to discover the possibility in our pain. But first, here are some of the tools you will need to get started.

THE FEELING SKETCHBOOK

To discover and explore pain's messages, you will use a *Feeling Sketchbook*. Only your own personal language has the power to mirror you, has the power to nurture, heal, and help. The impetus must come from within rather than from without. That's why a Feeling Sketchbook is by you and for you. It reflects your feelings today, and becomes a record of your on-going growth.

In your Feeling Sketchbook, you will create a personal, private record of your feelings about such human questions as

- *What ought to be*: Your *shoulds, musts, have to's*—the unrealistic expectations that so often produce pain and sustain the negative feelings leading to unresolvable conflicts;
- *What is*: Learning to begin where you are, opening yourself to the possibility of discovering your own patterns of feeling;
- *What can be*: Your creative, imaginative impulses, inherent in us all, that let you recapture your freedom to grow;
- *What shapes me*: Looking at the role of time—past, present, and future—and how you can invent new futures from an outgrown past;
- *What I do*: How your actions in the here and now affect your long-term feelings;
- *What repeats*: Identifying and exploring the significance of recurring themes in your Feeling Sketchbook; and
- *What is transformed*: Letting go and getting on with your life.

Your Feeling Sketchbook is the place to record the results of the activities suggested throughout this book. The activities elicit the indirect messages of our feelings by such simple acts as

- using Aware Breathing to locate and release the pains hidden within our bodies so we can name them;
- creating your own metaphoric Feeling Flows by simply doodling, and becoming aware of nuances of personal meaning in this nonverbal form of expression;
- word sculpting—creating improvisational patterns of meaning by combining words and visual patterns;
- clustering—a nonlinear gathering process which generates patterns of feeling;

- word sketching—writing rapidly to evoke indirect meanings;
- reclaiming our old hurts and sorrows in an ongoing ritual of writing in order to let them go;
- inverse clustering—another type of nonlinear gathering using a blank circle in order to discover centers of our pain not readily apparent to us;
- reframing our wounds through play and laughter using the twin faces comedy and tragedy; and
- finding new perspectives that permit growth, healing, and lead toward wisdom.

LOCATING YOUR PAIN BY LOCATING BREATH

Opening the breathing is generally the first step to opening the feelings. It creates a condition of stillness, a condition in which we stop running, so that our emotions have a chance to catch up with us.

NATHANIEL BRANDEN

The quickest way to become receptive to denied feelings is to allow yourself to sit quietly in any position you choose, close your eyes, and become aware of your breathing. That's all, just your breathing. Ordinary breathing. Tension, fear, anxiety, all produce shallow breathing—the body's way of keeping feelings at bay. Awareness of deep breathing tends to allow feelings to surface.

Why is Aware Breathing useful, perhaps necessary? Breathing in and out with awareness is life-affirming. Holding our breath or chronic shallow breathing is life-denying. Our denial of feelings intensifies the very pain we are struggling to hold at bay by our unconscious breathing habits. We think we cannot survive our sense of feeling overwhelmed by them, so we try to control, deny. Contrary to common sense, an iron grip is not a plus; a mind that can bend, that can flow into the chaos of feelings, is a mind that can break down denial behavior so entrenched that it is almost impossible to recognize it as destructive.

As you use Aware Breathing, your mind will begin to wander—we can't keep from thinking very long. Instead of resisting, accept the feeling that seems to be sliding in sideways. Name it, then say it silently, repetitively, making it part of your breathing: "sad, sad, sad," "hate, hate, hate," "bicker, bicker, bicker," or "dumb, dumb, dumb"—whatever emerges for you. If you have difficulty naming a feeling, identify a bodily sensation in a specific area, like "knot, knot, knot." This repetition will keep you in a state I call *expectant stillness,* a frame of mind in which the unfolding of specific feelings in the here and now becomes possible. The resonating word, freed from complex syntactical sequences, is a starting point for articulating the inarticulate. Later, we will see that writing extends this potential.

Letting Go

Stop reading for a moment, sit quietly, and try Aware Breathing. Accept the first word or phrase that floats into your awareness and softly repeat it—five, ten, fifty times. If that word doesn't quite reflect the way you are feeling at the moment, allow another to take its place and repeat it as many times as it feels right to do so. In the soft calling up of feelings created by the rise and fall of your breathing, you are gradually moving into a receptive, exploratory mode. You attune yourself to your inner ear.

Exploring the Act

To explore this first act, reflect on

- what words or phrases emerged;
- how many word-shifts you made before one seemed to fit in with your present feeling-state or to focus on a bodily sensation;
- what that recognition felt like—you might even be able to jot down a metaphor or simile, for instance, "It felt as though I was a flower opening," or, "it was like tapping frantically on a shield of plexiglass";
- how often you repeated the word or phrase before you experienced an internal shift; and
- whether the shift produced a lessening of anxiety; a flash of recognition; a sense of lightness; a sense of greater darkness.

Whether a feeling emerged or an awareness of a bodily sensation, this shift is usually best explored metaphorically.

Jot down all the words and phrases that came to you in your Feeling Sketchbook. Date and number your entry, entitling it "Breathing 1." This gives you a starting point. Later on, when you return to them, such entries may provide you further insights. For the moment, however, simply note that the reason for this activity is three-fold:

1. To recognize feelings you may not know are there through receptivity to the life-force of breath;
2. To remind you that breathing is life, that to be consistently unaware of the role of your breathing in your emotional life is restrictive, and that Aware Breathing opens you to its physical power, as expressed in the familiar phrases "breathing freely," or "taking a deep breath";
3. To understand that single words or phrases can express emotionally-charged meanings; that you can use them to catch as many normally inchoate events, feelings, or images in their web as it is possible to hold in language.

WORD SCULPTURES: THE MOVING HAND

Before you move on to writing, you need to understand how to word sculpt. Spending a little time now on Aware Breathing and word sculpting will increase your receptivity and make later progress much more rapid.

Word Sculptures are an evocative way of allowing shapes or forms of feeling to emerge almost unbidden. They are another key to opening the locked doors of your feelings, and building a bridge between denial and receptivity. A Word Sculpture is made by a rapid, kinesthetic movement of your hand. You could say it is a kind of doodle, and doodling is nearly universal.

During my own crisis, I fell into a particular kind of doodling, beginning with a spontaneous pattern drawn in a quick, single line, then sweeping in great swirls up, down, and across the page. (See Figure 1.2.)

Figure 1.2

This flow of lines took no more than a few seconds, but it eased my anxiety, particularly as I began to elaborate on the overall design with lines, circles, criss-crosses, or other shapes in the empty spaces. (See Figure 1.3.)

Initially I thought I was giving my hand something to do; increasingly, I realized there was more to it. In meetings, I discovered that the doodling somehow released me to focus on what was being discussed instead of dwelling without relief on my anxiety symptoms. Soon I also noticed that the emerging patterns helped me feel calmer, quieter. I began to date and file them as a kind of record—of what I wasn't sure. Looking back, I would describe the process this way:

A Word Sculpture is a visual and kinesthetic image. Visual, because its emergent shape is visible on a page; kinesthetic, because you are activating a part of your brain—your sensory-motor cortex—in the present moment to do it. The

An indecipherable thicket of lines, strokes, spirals, maps; the discourse of fire on the wall.

OCTAVIO PAZ

The living of life, any life, involves great and private pain, much of which we share with no one.

BARRY LOPEZ

Figure 1.3

moving pen in the moving hand is activated by the part of the brain which most nearly operates in the timeless *now.* The movement of your hand, making shapes with a drawing instrument, is a powerful kinesthetic way to tap into feelings that are often obscured by self-imposed filters that let us see only what things *ought* to be like.

A Word Sculpture is grounded in a *gesture.* The initial gesture of your hand contains the totality of a feeling in the moment. Allow your pen to move over a page in a single, unbroken line, from the center outward, from the bottom up or the top down, from left to right, on a diagonal, or in whatever way best expresses your feeling in the moment. Receptivity to the totality of a feeling in the here and now creates a design on the blank page long before you attempt to name and frame the feeling in words.

Focus on Aware Breathing, then invite the movement of

the pencil; don't try to control or direct it. To help give your-self permission, think "doodle" rather than any particular shape; this opens you to the indirection necessary for ap-proaching feelings. Our feelings, especially in times of tur-bulence, are so complex, so ambiguous, so conflicted, that they cannot easily be put into words, and still more so if we are out of touch with them. The very act of word sculpting invites calm. The more you play with creating them, the more you in-vite receptivity, which leads to expressivity. You cannot force feelings any more than you can tears.

Word Sculptures become visual metaphors for particular emotions at the moment of gesture. To generate the shape of a feeling or a bodily sensation, breathe quietly and let the shape create itself. Even though what you produce on the page is two-dimensional, there is a three-dimensional quality to it. We tend to imagine feelings as enveloping us or as filling us up; both of these images have a three-dimensional quality. An-other way of saying it is that feelings are not flat but round.

It is this three-dimensional quality of a feeling or the bodily sensation of an unknown feeling—expressed through the movement of your hand—that you want to capture and ex-press through the quick, effortless line-shape you invite onto a page. Like your signature, none of your Word Sculptures will be alike, but over time they will tend to reflect certain qualities of your feeling life in the here and now that will speak to you as you begin to become aware of patterns of meaning.

The initial gesture of spiral sweeps is only the beginning. Later you will embellish without conscious thought. The next time around you will experiment by adding words. Shape *and* words will intersect in ways you hadn't seen before, producing new patterns, new thinking, new possibilities, new clarity. Clarity takes the indirect route. J. Ruth Gendler described it this way in *The Book of Qualities:*

Clarity

My visits to Clarity are soothing now. He never tells me what to think or feel or do but shows me how to find out what I need to know. . . . When I visited him, he presented me with a sketchbook and told me to draw the same thing every day until the drawing started to speak to me.

That's exactly what Word Sculptures are all about. Experiment, play with your creations. They start to speak to you by indirection, allowing the unsayable to surface. Besides, it feels good to create these Word Sculptures; they reflect *your* shapes, your leaps of imagination, your personal connections, ultimately leading to the shape of your feelings in any given moment.

After creating several of these, you may begin to be aware of patterns reflecting your emotional being today, or see how such patterns recur across time. Like the science of chaos— also called nonlinear dynamics, which we will discuss more fully in the next chapter—certain patterns will appear and re-appear. With them comes a strange stability; the process is

Figure 1.4

imbued with tendency, with the possibilities inherent in you as individual. Your Word Sculptures become an emotional signature.

Letting Go

Begin with the initial shape only, just to give yourself the pleasure of the feel of it, the surprise of experimentation, the wonder of your mind/brain's pattern-making propensity. Put pen or pencil to paper in your Feeling Sketchbook—or anywhere—and let the shape create itself. Remember, the initial pattern takes only seconds. As your hand moves over the page, feel the pressure against your fingertips, the movement of your arm, your eye following curve or angle, as you observe the pattern evolving on the page. When you have a feeling of completeness, stop. Simply look at the pattern you have drawn.

Now give yourself permission to doodle, filling in spaces, using lines, circles, criss-crosses, angles, dots, whatever patterns feel right. Continue until the Word Sculpture feels finished, and feels good to eye, hand, gut. If you can't take the time to finish now, come back to it at a later time, perhaps while you are in a meeting, are watching TV, are waiting in a doctor's office.

Exploring the Act

For now, do no more than sign and date your creation, label it 1, and leave it. Signing is significant; it makes it *yours*. Dating it will later enable you to perceive—visually—where you were emotionally at the time of the drawing. Until you are comfortable with the shape-making and elaborating process, do nothing further with these Word Sculptures; be conscious only of the pleasure of creating shapes. As you continue to add to your collection, you might begin to be aware of similarities, differences, or changes among Word Sculptures as they appear in your Feeling Sketchbook.

Seed Words

My experience of moving from pure shapes and their embellishment to words may help you understand the process. One day I was absentmindedly elaborating on yet another curiously satisfying pattern, words spontaneously popped into consciousness. I doodled them in as part of the pattern. Some words went inside the initial shape, others curved around the outside. "A strange adaptation of clustering," I thought.

Connections among the words began to appear. Suddenly, the Word Sculpture with its words seemed to reflect preoccupations of which I had been unaware. There they were, on a page: *Seed Words* growing and intertwining before my eyes to make feeling-shapes visible to me. The word-shape design produced an insight I might not have had otherwise.

Figure 1.5

Let me share what I recall, looking at this strange creation. Did I feel caught? Was I hanging onto a thread? Clearly, I had questions. Where were the answers? Even more clearly, I was afraid. I had to face something and I was afraid. Of facing it? Of feeling? Of what? Questions, yes. Answers, none. The mere framing of such questions was the beginning of receptivity.

Letting Go

Open your Feeling Sketchbook, number and date a blank page. Use Aware Breathing to relax and focus; then make a quick shape. Embellish by adding whatever Seed Words or phrases float into consciousness, allowing shape and words to blend. When no words come, embellish with lines and circles. The Seed Words may be similar to the words that arose during the breathing exercises, or they may be different. As you move further into this process, you are likely to discover feelings you didn't know you had. For now, simply make them when the mood hits you or the opportunity comes. Carry a Feeling Sketchbook and number and date each Word Sculpture.

Over time, a series of Word Sculptures will make you increasingly receptive to your emotional frame of mind. They take little time. They soothe. They will lead you to unexpected patterns of meaning. Give shape to a feeling at some moment; let words flow onto and into it, filling blanks and hollows. Who knows what will surface? Gentle your feelings into shapes to soften pain and, in the process, to open yourself to pain's messages. In doing so you are beginning the process of naming and framing, an essential route to transforming your pain.

WRITING: FRAMING THE FEELING SELF THROUGH WORD SKETCHES

I don't want to close this chapter without providing some examples of how writing has been meaningful to others in times of personal crisis.

Mennet Jacob, now seventy-five and author of *Anatomy of a Loss,* has been writing her way through a series of crises since 1983. In a letter, she wrote that

> too many of us rationalize, pack away feelings which are too painful in the closets of our emotions, only now and then taking a small peek. And when they scare us like paper skeletons on Halloween, we retreat to our own fantasy world. There is no right or wrong in the way we feel. Judgment can be passed only on what we do or say, never on what we feel.

I realized, in the process of helping myself out of the dev-astating moods, that I experience a period of numbness, which settles like new-fallen snow, blanketing my deepest vulnerabilities. It protects me for a while as I think of nothing, stare at nothing. But it is useful, for out of this numbness finally comes a small need, an urge, if you will, to say it—on paper; to use words to help me face the continual excavation of myself. . . . What blew my mind was, after the agony of *doing,* risking, writing, I have found a sense of liberation, options, and freedom it's taken a lifetime to find!

For Barbara Gordon, author of *I'm Dancing as Fast as I Can,* writing become nothing less than a reinvention of her very being.

Day after day, week after week, I sat there sorting things out. Writing. Before a month had passed, writing became my safe place. A way to get in touch with me, to make thoughts and feelings precise, make order out of disorder. Without my knowing when, there was a shift in my identity. I wrote, therefore I was.

For Charlotte Gilman, the nineteenth-century author of "The Yellow Wallpaper," it was release.

I don't know why I should write this.
I don't want to.
I don't feel able.
But I *must* say what I feel and think
in some way—it is such a relief!

Author Gail Sheehy, writing about her adopted Cambodian daughter, notes that "it was through writing that Mohm at last dared, demanded of herself, to see the truth."

Phyllis Davies, author of *Grief: My Climb toward Understanding,* having lost her twelve-year-old son in an airplane crash, found writing unnatural and fearful before learning about clustering from my book *Writing the Natural Way.* Her writing became a tool for unlocking paralyzing grief and moving into healing.

Writing has helped me to enter fully into my sorrow. In doing so, I began to discover that there are gifts hidden in the grief experience. Although there has been great sorrow from Derek's death, there has been great joy in sharing and helping others with their own sorrow. Writing has helped me progress through grief to a release and peace. Most of the time I can now remember Derek without crying inside or out.

Too many people dream about the life others are leading. They may believe that life is "out there." They are perpetually searching for an answer to the mystery of life without realizing they have the key to unlocking that mystery—the key that will liberate their bodies and minds and bring them into the only life that matters—their own. That key is feeling.

ARTHUR JANOV

LOOKING AHEAD

In this chapter we have focused on the very first steps of the process of seeing possibility in pain, those that allow us to recognize and begin to approach our hidden emotional pain.

In the next chapter, we will discuss spirals, chaos, and clustering—powerful metaphors and tools for coming to grips with the nonlogical patterns of our feelings. In chapter 3, we'll learn more about where feelings come from and how we can use the insights of current brain research as personal tools for our self-healing. We will see in chapter 4 how the words that come unbidden into our minds carry their own emotional tones and colors. Together, we will face the darkness of hitting bottom, a necessary way station before we can spiral upward again—chapter 5. In chapter 6, having faced our private darkness, we will learn to navigate the inbetween-time by exploring pain in relation to our consciousness of time. We will relearn in chapter 7 the healing value of laughter and play that reflects the other side of darkness. In chapter 8 we will explore what I call the *both/and* perspective that allows reconciliation of polarities, as for example, in recognizing the "opportunity" inherent in crisis. Finally, in chapter 9, we will once again be able to take up the challenge and vitality of our lives through a new respect for our innate desire to give form to feeling.

The creative impulse is part of being a thinking/feeling creature; it strikes me that the creative impulse is as powerful as the drive to survive. Biologist E. W. Sinnot in *Matter, Mind, and Man,* speculated that "the organizing power of life, manifest in mind as well as body . . . is the truly creative element. Creativity thus becomes the attribute of life." Healing and creativity are two sides of the same coin. Underlying both is the idea of wholeness. The urge to survive and the urge to create are interconnected. We are creative out of necessity and desire. Both can harness the enormous energy of the emotions for constructive purposes.

CHAPTER 2

Spirals, Chaos, and Clustering: Discovering the Hidden Patterns in Feelings

A t certain junctures in our lives, we feel overwhelmed by emotional chaos. We feel our lives shift drastically; we experience unbearable flux; instead of sailing on an even keel, we are pummeled by wave after wave; often we hit a storm so violent it threatens to engulf us.

My emotional withdrawal from myself and others was not deliberate. I believed I *ought* to be independent. I could no longer read the signals, couldn't pin down what triggered the unnerving panic attacks. I looked for reasons outside myself; I went to doctors. All this time, I was expending enormous negative energy to control some dark unknown. And I was afraid.

I was writing a book at the time, in itself a demanding task. My body was in revolt: my nerves felt raw, my insides like jelly. I tried logic: "You can't write because—yes, because the kids are interfering with your concentration." Feeling fragile and helpless, I took what was for me, the superwoman, an extreme step: to leave my children and stay alone for four weeks in a mountain cabin so that I could write in peace and quiet. I envisioned spending twelve to fourteen hours a day on the book. I planned my progress in detail: I multiplied the hours by the days, converted it into pages, deadlines, results. Having taken action, I felt a little more in control.

How little I knew of the power of denial.

I was deposited, manuscript, typewriter, and notes, in the Sierras among tall redwoods. My cabin overlooked a clearing with a small stream winding its way through the wild grasses. It was a two-mile walk to the nearest road, half an hour's drive to the nearest telephone. I had no car.

Reason said that I had what I needed: tranquility, freedom from interruption, the inspiration of nature. Now I could be productive. Nothing, nothing, nothing happened the way I planned it.

Alone, without car, without telephone, without children to blame for my lack of concentration, there was only one interruption which had never crossed my mind: Myself. I had no choice but to face myself: my fears, my feelings, my sanity or insanity, my body and the cold diagnosis of cancer, my denials, my sense of helplessness, my unceasing pain. The assault felt global. Writing was out of the question.

Instead, with my last reserves of energy, I fought for control. I jogged overgrown logging roads, struggled to meditate, ate to fill a need that had little to do with food, lugged chunks of granite to make a border around the cabin—anything and everything to feel useful, to feel real, to deny the necessity of naming my feelings, to escape the wild beating in my chest of something huge that demanded recognition.

I fought the urge to run away—literally; I wanted to run out of my own skin. But where could I run to? I had already run away. It became impossible to ignore my body's signals: I couldn't breathe; the persistent lump stuck in my throat got bigger, like a chunk of apple core that bobbed up each time I tried to swallow; my intestines felt like knotted snakes, roiling twenty-four hours a day, especially during sleepless nights filled with terrors in which I was alone in the darkness.

Such visceral pain was so crippling that control suddenly no longer worked. Tears were not yet a possibility; they had not been part of my repertoire.

In a murky attempt to act, I struggled with other ways to

I became aware that I was losing contact with myself. At each step of the descent a new persona was disclosed within me of whose name I was no longer sure and who no longer obeyed me. And when I had to stop my exploration because the path faded beneath my steps, I found a bottomless abyss at my feet, and out of it comes— arising I know not from where—the current which I dare to call my life.

TEILHARD DE CHARDIN

regain balance. One was visualization. The trouble was that none of the images I had read about worked for me. Imagining a peaceful meadow, I saw columns of ants marching relentlessly up my body which I imagined encased in medieval armor. I imagined a sunlit beach, and instead of feeling tranquility I was plagued by sand working its way into all the wrong places. So it went. As my anxiety escalated, my resistance to the images suggested by others became greater until, unbidden, instead of meadow or beach, I saw myself mentally spiraling downward into a vortex. I was afraid. I swirled around its edges. I felt out of control. Abruptly, I stopped the image.

Figure 2.1   A vortex

The next day the image of the vortex returned uninvited. Again, fear led me to interrupt it. When it appeared a third time, something happened: taking a deep breath, I flowed with the fear instead of fighting it. Focusing on my breathing, I stopped resisting this unasked-for image. Something tight inside me began to loosen and, reluctantly, I spiraled downward. I saw myself moving in smaller and smaller arcs, moving from the rim of the vortex down toward some unknown center.

I had apparently needed to generate my own image of my feeling world. When it came so insistently, flowing with it became essential. Similarly, I felt the need to draw this feeling flow as though it were a map charting unknown territory. "What has hurt you?" I asked myself, and I began to draw a spiral just to be doing something with my hands, not really knowing why or what for.

Figure 2.2   Example of an early visual feeling flow

I continued to draw this expanding spiral until a particular image resonated which showed up as a bump in my feeling map. Each bump would alter the configuration of the flow; each seemed to reflect a strong image or feeling. I sensed that these bumps were points at which image and feeling coalesced. I wasn't sure what these confusing interconnections were pointing to, but I kept on.

Without warning, a particularly large bump led to a flood of unexpected images from my childhood. Pain framed them. My impulse was to shake my head and shake them out of my mind. But I remembered the saying, "Whatever you bury, you bury alive." I stopped drawing. Looking at my strange pattern, so like the whorls of a thumbprint, again I asked myself "What hurt you?" What followed is difficult to explain.

All I can say is that, in my head, the earth shifted. I felt a flood of emotion. Something had broken through to the necessity of tears. With the tears, which had been blocked for years, came one explosive word: "Mutti!"

Gradually, all restlessness ceased, and I came to a still place, a moment of quiet. Absolute. Timeless. For the first time, I sensed that the denial of my feelings reached far back into a childhood permeated by chronic signals of danger over years of war, punctuated by the violent death of a mother from bombs and the repeated destruction of a child's safety zone called home. And, for the first time, I understood that emotional control was not my only option, that other options, unfamiliar to me, were a possibility. Even today, I am amazed at what I continue to discover about the potency of this spiral image which came unasked, unprescribed. Its spiral nature suggests a moving inward, downward, a move toward a still center, a neutral point. Perhaps my receptivity to this image was the starting point of transformation. Even today, during long, exhausting travel or times of struggle, this personal vortical image brings me to a point of stillness, quiet, receptivity, tolerance of the intolerable.

The spiral we travel round life is the means we have to compare ourselves with ourselves, and discover how much we have changed since we were last in the city, met our brother, or celebrated Christmas. Time itself is cyclic, and by the spiral of its returning seasons we review the growth of our own understanding.

JILL PURCE

THE SYMBOLIC SPIRAL

The image of a spiral vortex as it reflects human feeling lies at the heart of this book. The spiral is an ancient symbol; the word comes from the same root as that of the words *spirit, inspire, respiration*—the in and out, the up and down of things. The spiral implies movement, change of a particular sort.

In *The Mystic Spiral,* Jill Purce tells us that the image is a form of multiple dimensions. Learning its dynamics, we recognize that it empowers us to move both down and up. It suggests a quest, a journey, a folding and unfolding consciousness. It is a natural growth form, like the shell; a natural movement for the creative impulse of the universe, as seen in the nebulae. A spiral is particularly significant for our emotions because they too can go up or down, move inward or outward, expand or contract.

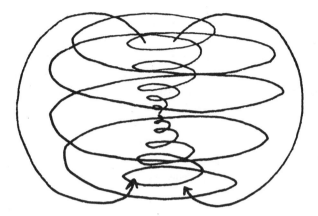

Figure 2.3   A contracting/expanding spiral

As the inward winding labyrinth, the spiral constitutes the human journey to the still center where the secret of life is found. As the vortex, spiraling through its own center, it combines the inward and outward direction of movement.

JILL PURCE

Sidney Jourard said in *Ways of Growth:* "I know I am ready to grow when I experience some dissonance between my beliefs, concepts, and expectations of the world and my perception. I am also ready to grow when I experience boredom, despair, depression, anxiety, or guilt." None of the feelings Jourard mentions are ones we would cheerfully seek out. Yet, when they reflect our present experience, they won't go away unless we move through them. The harder we push them away, the more vigorously they swing back and knock us flat. Moving through them, however painful, represents a living continuum of inner and outer growth, expansion and contraction. That's why the spiral is a powerful metaphor for growth.

In coming to terms with our feelings and channeling them constructively, both directions are necessary; that is, in learning to acknowledge the negatives as well as the positives, we are carried back up by the very same spiral that sucked us down.

The spiral metaphor is also valuable because its extremes are connected and polar. Without the North pole, there would be no South pole; without a negative, we would not know a positive; without the disquieting awareness of stagnation, we could not become aware of the need for growth. The paradox is that we are pulled in both directions.

As many artists and scientists have intuited, the spiral reflects the expanding and contracting orbits of changeable, dynamic systems, from the creative energy of our interrelated ecosystems and the formation of weather systems to human creative energy, human bodies, human minds, and human feelings, and much in between. The spiral of our own expanding awareness is fluid, nothing like a straight line. The shortest distance between two points may be crisp and neat, but it is alien to our feeling life. The mind is *not* a straight thinker. The spiral simultaneously contracts and expands, increases and decreases, always reminding us that life turns, moves, remains unfixed, making us vulnerable to pain but also opening us to possibility.

The image of the spiral helps us tolerate ambiguity, paradox, puzzles, and to take heart from the fact that nothing ever stays the same. Change and chaos are not negatives in the bigger picture of our life spirals. The oscillating rhythms of stability and change are a necessary part of any life. By becoming aware of them as connected, we can learn to let go of destructive, straight-line, either/or patterns in our feeling selves.

A spherical vortex is a double spiral and, like a tornado or a hurricane, it is both *im*plosive and *ex*plosive; somewhere between is the still point. The implosive cycle is a sign of collapse, reflecting such descriptive metaphors as "the dark night of the soul," "the existential crisis," or "disintegration." But implosion can also signal the inception of breakthrough to a new synthesis, such as a life-changing peak experience.

In the private and highly focused moment of creative expression we often experience pain and possibility simultaneously. This synthesis mirrors the explosive cycle: a breaking-through as well as a flying apart—taken together we realize that beginnings are endings, endings are beginnings, which is to say all possibility is present in a given moment. But it is in the still point at the center that the shift originates. Thus, one aim of facing pain is to return to that center, the gateway to possibility.

As you work through this book, recognize that constant oscillation, that flow from the moment's pain to deep within,

To know one thing, you must know the other just as much, else you don't know that one thing.

HENRY MOORE

Whenever we block pain, we also block pleasure. Repression keeps us from knowing how warped our perceptions are, how much more alive we could be to joy and excitement.

ARTHUR JANOV

The resting state originates in movement.

NOVALIS

from the still center back up and outward to a reunion with our lives. Accept it as inevitable. We can no more live without both movements of the spiral vortex than we can breathe without inhaling and exhaling, see without light and darkness, or hear without sound and silence.

REACHING YOUR INNER SPIRALS: FEELING FLOWS

A good way to explore your own inner spirals is the drawing of what I call *Feeling Flows*. Like the thumbprint of Linda Pastan's poem in the Preface, the whorls and bumps of each of our spirals will be different. Not only are they unique to you but also unique to this moment, this place. Your hand can express things your mind has not figured out. A number of bumps may signal a shift to a new shape. No one's Feeling Flow spiral will look quite the same as anyone else's, and no single emotional spiral of your own will repeat the exact shape of another, as you can see from the three samples of Figure 2.4.

Letting Go

Allow your mind to focus on movement; allow it to drift in the spirals of your life. You will discover that, like the Aware Breathing exercise in chapter 1, the drawing of these spiral Feeling Flows releases tension. It is one of the indirect routes to helping you become receptive to your feelings. You cannot be ordered to feel or not to feel. For now, simply be receptive to the movement; it is part of the evocative process which, paradoxically, is the most direct route to your feelings. Your moving hand knows what to do; follow its wisdom.

    The process should only take seconds; no more than a minute or so. It should feel satisfying: both regular and irregular; repeating and changing; expanding and contracting; never the same in the same place. When your hand shifts to express a bump, that is, to break the seemingly fixed spiraling pattern, allow it to do so. Each bump may reflect an emotional life event big enough to change the previous pattern.

    Don't deliberately *try* to think of any life-changing events; just let your hand draw convolutions, involutions,

Because human consciousness must involve both pleasure and pain, to strive for pleasure to the exclusion of pain is, in effect, to strive for the loss of consciousness.

ALAN WATTS

Whether we speak of streaming water or moving air, of the formation of organs or the movements of the human form, of speech or of the movements of the stars, it is all one: the archetypal gesture of the cosmic alphabet, the world of the universe, which uses movement in order to bring forth nature and man.

THEODORE SCHWENK

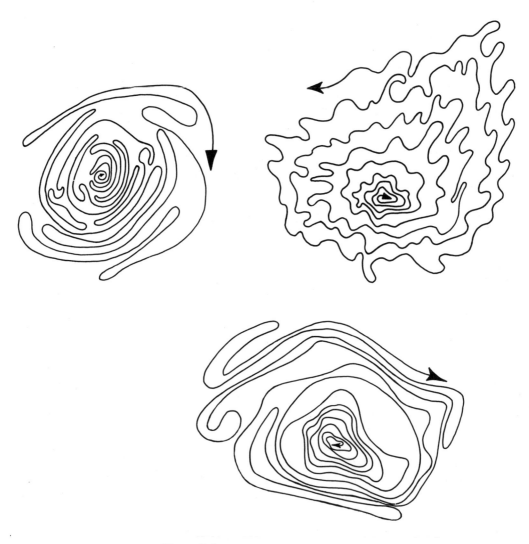

Figure 2.4

bumps, parallels—wherever its flow leads you. It doesn't matter whether you start at the center and work out, or start at an edge and spiral in. The trick lies in the receptivity to the kinesthetic signals of the body, of the tones of feelings, of leaps of thought, of silent rhythms, just as with the Word Sculptures of chapter 1.

Figure 2.5   Word Sculpture

Until then, simply experience the act of drawing these Feeling Flows. Think of them as opening, unfolding, unlayering. Do one now in your Feeling Sketchbook. Number and date it. If it feels right to you, do more, however many intrigue you, on the same or succeeding pages.

Exploring the Act

Notice whether you felt puzzled or whether these little doodles would lead anywhere. Imagine the process to be like a childhood treasure hunt. It is another way of becoming receptive, like Aware Breathing, or Word Sculptures.

Notice whether images or events occurred to you as your hand traced a spiral. If so, jot down in the bumps of your spiral a word or phrase that evokes them. You'll know when a bump is significant. It resonates. If not, don't worry or strain. Most important is that you are connecting to emotional rhythms made visible by the movement of your pen or pencil on the page.

THE METAPHOR OF CHAOS:
A SOURCE FOR HIDDEN MEANING

We have talked much of chaos in our feelings, the sense of being overwhelmed by what we deny. It is time to go beyond simply recognizing that turmoil and understand how and why our inner chaos opens a doorway to personal growth.

Until recently, science was unwilling or unable to acknowledge the function of disorder in the universe. But, as with everything in the world, the assumptions of science change, too. When they do, they inevitably affect the way we perceive ourselves, including our emotional frames of references. A *paradigm shift,* a phrase invented by the noted philosopher of science Thomas Kuhn, is a change in the fundamental assumptions we use to understand the world.

One such paradigm shift in science occurred when Newtonian physics replaced earlier, religiously based systems. Newton's world view still has a powerful influence on our understanding of the world. Many of us still look at our lives as if they were played out in a Newtonian universe: stable and absolute, the same for everyone, as explainable as a clockwork mechanism, and closed. Yet Einstein's relativity and quantum theory—a more recent paradigm shift—have shown us an open-ended universe, one relative to particular points of view, uncertain, and infinite in possibility.

Most recently, within the last few years, a new kind of mathematics has become a promising tool for scientific investigation—and a powerful metaphor to extend our understanding of our emotional lives. It is called *Chaos theory,* a branch of a larger study called nonlinear dynamics.

We need not be concerned with the technicalities of this emerging science in this book. But, in my own terrifying search to reclaim my emotional life, I found that the images of Chaos theory spoke to me in a profound way.

Chaos Science

Chaos science maps the irregular, unpredictable, fluctuating side of nature—the parts not easily explained by classical science.

Ordinarily, when we think of chaos we conjure up darkness, formlessness, utter anarchy. Not so; chaos has its own constantly changing, if not predictable patterns. According to this new science, chaos cannot be defined as formless since it demonstrates powerful patterns in their very irregularity, thus unpredictability, unlike the precision forms of Euclidean geometry. Chaos science is the science of dynamic systems, not static entities, thus enabling us to track the delicate structures and unifying principles underlying such complex realities as the irregularities in crashing waves, dripping faucets, waterfalls, heartbeats, as well as what Judith Hooper and Dick Teresi, authors of *The 3-Pound Universe,* call "the collective song of your neurons."

How did scientists actually show that there are patterns hidden beneath apparent chaos? And how can you and I discover the patterns hidden in our own personal chaos of denied feeling?

Scientists have always been curious about the phenomenon of turbulence, the ways that a smooth flow of water or air breaks up into ragged, unpredictable gusts and currents. There was no mathematical tool that would allow people to predict the chaos of turbulence.

In 1961, M.I.T. meteorologist Edward Lorenz discovered a mathematical model for weather systems which explained why weather was so unpredictable. The reason was an extremely sensitive dependence on initial conditions, more commonly called the Butterfly Effect as characterized by James Gleick in *Chaos: The Making of a Science:* " . . . a butterfly stirring the air today in Peking can transform storm systems next month in New York."

Later, scientists and mathematicians began to use computers to discover more about this powerful butterfly. Generating images of repeated equations on a screen, they discovered families of general patterns like nothing seen before. One was a *strange attractor,* a kind of symbolic orbit that represented

Einstein's space is no closer to reality than Van Gogh's sky. The glory of science is not in a truth more absolute than the truth of Bach or Tolstoy, but in the act of creation itself. The scientist's discoveries impose his own order on chaos, as the composer or painter imposes his—an order that always refers to limited aspects of reality, and is biased by the observer's frame of reference, which differs from period to period, as a Rembrandt nude differs from a nude by Manet.

ARTHUR KOESTLER

. . . the young science of Chaos, wholeness, and change (insists) on the interrelationships of things, an awareness of the essential unpredictableness of nature, and of uncertainties in our science descriptions.

JOHN BRIGGS AND
F. DAVID PEAT

the changing behavior of a dynamic system. The major oddity of this track was that it never crossed itself, never repeated the same pathway, and yet always managed to stay within certain boundaries. Many varieties of chaotic attractors were found, including one (see Figure 2.6) that looks a little like butterfly wings and is named after Lorenz.

In the mind's eye, a fractal is a way of seeing infinity.

— JAMES GLEICK

Fractals . . . baroque spirals, elaborate filigrees, intricate webs spun by non-Euclidian spiders.

JUDITH HOOPER
AND DICK TERESI

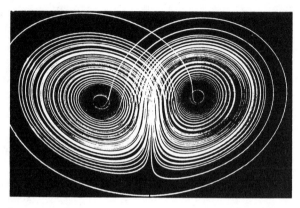

Figure 2.6

Further study of strange attractors led to a major break-through. Mathematically, a chaotic attractor image had to consist of an infinitely long line within a finite space. Such a mathematical object could not even be considered before computers—hand calculations were impossibly tedious—but IBM mathematician Benoit Mandelbrot had begun to develop just the tools needed. From relatively simple equations, his computers produced pictures of breathtaking complexity and beauty, images he called *fractals,* combining the Latin *frangere* 'to break' with *fraction* 'part of a whole.'

These images revealed some amazing insights. A chaotic system, researchers found, never exactly repeats itself in a periodic way. Instead, it forms an intricate, recursive shape—a fractal shape—revealing new complexity and pattern no matter how "deep" one sets the computer to look. Fractal images revealed beautiful, fluid, and complex patterns as shown in Figures 2.7 and 2.8.

Fractal patterns are everywhere in nature. They appear when we attempt to measure a coastline or explain the delicate, irregular pattern of a fern's branches. Fractals are even

Figure 2.8

Figure 2.7

found in our bodies: the branching patterns of our lungs, blood vessels, and nerves, the dynamic electrical patterns of our brain, even the shifting rhythms of our heartbeat. Fractals occupy a unique place between the orderly and the random, a new kind of order, which will be significant to the recursive nonlinear nature of our emotional expressiveness.

Fractals are the mysterious forms which indicate that reality has shapes undreamed of by Euclid and surprises that ridicule the idea of order. The shape of a mountain is not a cone—but a series of fractals.

LANCE MORROW

Fractals and Emotional Wholeness

Although chaos science shows us to be condemned to live with uncertainty, the other side of the coin is that we are also blessedly open to change, to radical shifts in pattern. Chaos science speaks to the range of possibilities these shifts can take, to the adaptive fluidity that can become an integral part of our lives.

The idea of fractals and chaos became a vital aspect of my search for emotional wholeness for several reasons.

- Apparent disorder masked hidden patterns.
- Looking at a fractal part suggested answers about a whole.
- The nature of fractals, like the nature of feelings and the act of writing, is recursive. The word *recursive* (a looping back in ways that may be similar, but not identical) refers to nonlinear processes. Although nonlinear, they do begin to reveal patterns. Recursion is also reflected in the language of Octavio Paz. He asks the question: "Is destruction creation? I do not know, but I do know that creation is not destruction." At each turn my text opens out into one another, at once a spiral of recurrences and reiterations. So it is with feelings.
- The nuance-filled language that evokes emotion seemed more like fractal chaos than like the linear logic of a mathematical theorem.

In sum, the human mind is anything but a straight thinker. The nuances of human emotions, like the stunning images of Chaos theory, seem to reflect the process of becoming rather than any fixed mode of being. Our human experiences, our stories, our feelings are ongoing, interconnected fractals, as artists have long known.

CHAOS AND NUANCE IN EMERGENT PATTERNS OF FEELING

It is precisely the lack of absolutes, the uncertainty in our lives which unhinges us. Yet the paradox is that the very change that frightens us also enables us to harness that change to transform our pain into possibility.

Poets have known qualitatively what science is now quantifying through fractal geometry. The modern poet Wallace Stevens sounds positively prophetic when he states that chaos is "the mass of meaning."

> The law of chaos is the law of ideas,
> Of improvisations, and seasons of belief.
> In Chaos and his song is a consolation.
> It is the music of the mass of meaning.

Science writer John Briggs and physicist F. David Peat echo Stevens. Nuances, they say, are those private, personal subtleties of tone and meaning for which we have no words.

> . . . our wondering, uncertainty, and questioning, are full of nuance. In experiencing nuance we enter the borderline between order and chaos, and in the nuance lies our sense of the wholeness and inseparability of all experience.

Like Wallace Stevens, the poet Brewster Ghiselin, in a 1952 classic entitled *The Creative Process,* anticipated these new discoveries in science.

> Chaos is perhaps the wrong term for that indeterminate fullness and activity of the inner life. For it is organic, dynamic, full of tension and tendency. What is absent from it is determination, fixity . . . But if it were altogether without order of some kind, it would be without life.

When we improvise, we experience spontaneous patterns, meanings that suddenly "leap out at us," seemingly from nowhere. As we will see in chapter 3, our minds seek meaningful patterns; we create basically because patterns of meaning make us *feel* good. In fact, our feelings are one organizing key to meaning. We stumble upon these meanings only by being sensitive to the nuances of feeling that become

The truth is that every piece of work is a realization, fragmentary but complete in itself, of our individuality; and this kind of realization is the sole and painful way we have of getting a particular experience— no wonder, then, that the process is attended by surprises.

THOMAS MANN

*Before we can move into a
new ar-rangement, we
must first go through a
period of de-rangement.*

M.C. RICHARDS

organizers for the chaos of emotions. Systems theorist Paul La Violette and psychiatrist William Gray argue that such nuances are constantly formed and circulated from our emotional and perceptual centers; yet, in much of our daily life, we stop attending to them. We suppress the nuances of our emotional likes or dislikes because they may threaten our customary, simplified categories of thought.

The layers of feeling, cycling through our brains despite our lack of awareness of them, leave the possibility open that some emotionally-charged or chaotic event can lead us to an unexpected epiphany. Framing a nuance of feeling through language transforms our disconnection and emotional confusion. Externalized in words, the continually evolving internal patterns reveal both the familiar and the unknown.

We naturally seek emotional stability, but paradoxically, we rarely achieve it without entering into a state of uncertainty and unpredictability, a state we tend to avoid because it is uncomfortable.

Our nonlinear brains fluctuate in a sea of chaotic nuances, but self-organization creates the possibility of strange attractors—new possibilities of meaning and behavior. It is an ongoing process of forming and reforming ourselves. In so doing, we tap into a living center of possibility, reminding us that the human mind is an open, not a closed, system.

One startling example of this kind of self-organization is described by Hooper and Teresi in *The 3-Pound Universe*. Studying the humble slime mold, scientists discovered that each single-celled creature normally crawls around leading its own little life. But when deprived of food or water, a transformation occurs. Individual slime molds start to cluster into colonies. Then an amazing thing happens. The colonies become *one differentiated animal*. The individual cells suddenly specialize in order to produce a collective organism capable of spreading new slime mold cells into a new environment. Just as a single slime mold cell gives no hint of this possibility for being part of a larger organism, so too single words or phrases may not generate any startling new patterns of meaning. Only when images connect, only when words and phrases cluster together in nonlinear ways, is there a transformation. A loose association of seemingly random thoughts and images suddenly shifts into a pattern of meaning.

CATCHING OUR CHAOS:
THE TOOL OF CLUSTERING

The technique of clustering reflects the dynamically unpredictable processes of the human heart. Clustering reflects the seemingly random, unexpected, surprising shifts that converge and create what James Gleick described as a focus at once "fuzzy *and* detailed, structural *and* unpredictable." Clustering is a self-organizing process made visible on a page. Clustering works even though we cannot explain it. The fact is that in the seeming randomness of a Cluster, patterns do appear; in our apparently undetermined choices we discover self-references; in the irregularities of the clustering process we pick up meaningful recurrences that became strange attractors.

The establishment of a point in chaos lends this point a concentric character of the primordial. The order thus created radiates from it in all directions.

PAUL KLEE

Here is how clustering works. Instead of writing from left to right or top to bottom, clustering begins with a circled nucleus—a Seed Word—in the center of a page. Then, associations follow, spilling out in all directions from the center. These associations come so fast they can only be captured by brief words or phrases. As the Cluster proceeds, the associations begin to resonate and self-organize around nuances of feeling. When a particular nuance becomes strong, there is a shift to a meaningful pattern. This pattern, in turn, triggers the writing of a Word Sketch: a brief, evocative expression of feelings, refining the patterns of significance still further. And so we become our own inner explorers. We begin to take our own emotional pulse. We become aware of something that *is* us, though rarely familiar to our ordinary awareness.

Figure 2.9, a cluster by one of my former workshop participants, is an example of unfolding feeling nuances through clustering, cycling around the strange attractor of the image of a mask, moving to the image of nakedness—whose resonances are expressed in a powerful Word Sketch. The entire clustering and writing took no more than five minutes.

Way in, where I really live, I reject myself. Few see this, for I present confidence, energy, success, even audacity. But when I turn away from my stage, waiting for a new audience to con, I lose the footlights. The inner me wears one costume only: nakedness—from picking my bones clean.

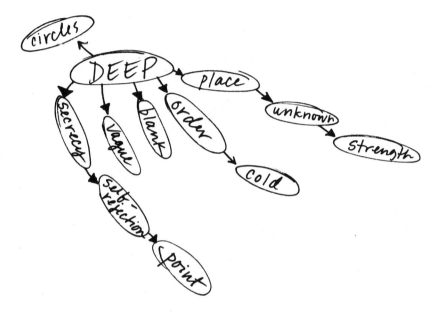

Figure 2.9

As infants, our feelings of distress or pleasure were our only guideposts. When we were small, we trusted them. As we grew up, they often got buried, distorted, or educated out of us. Clustering is a direct pipeline to feelings. Clustering evokes whole memories, feelings, images, complete with associated smells, tastes, sounds, feelings, colors. Once the door to our feeling life is opened through the literally effortless—denial of feelings is enormously effort*ful!*—process of clustering, only then, nudged by curiosity, puzzlement, pain, and desire, are we propelled into writing to create meaning. Recently, a workshop participant said to the group: "Clustering feels like knocking on a bunch of doors and seeing which one opens up."

Look at the immediacy and intensity of a Cluster generated in one minute by a twenty-eight-year-old woman, who was illiterate until she was twenty-five:

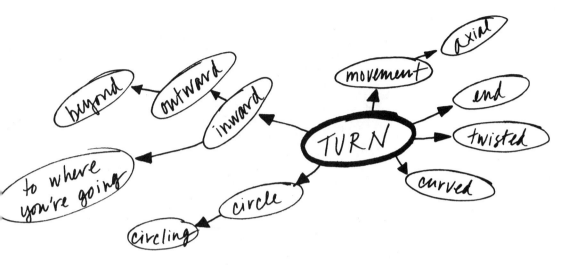

Figure 2.10

What she then wrote took less than seven minutes:

> I feel myself turn to this circling exercise. I love the rhythm, the energy generated within my body, when I'm in this curved process, a circle, movement that has a beginning and end to where I'm going. The journey is inward at this moment of cluster and, as I write, it becomes an outward journey into form. To create is a feeling of glow beyond words to describe and not sound trite.
>
> The twisting and turning of twenty-five years, of uncurling my tension and fear, leads me down a road to enter a different road with a trust in this circle of energy, at its center the human heart.

As she wrote, she wept; to put the feelings into words, to name and frame them, was intensely emotional, liberating, and exhilarating.

A third example: In the Vignette by E. A. that follows, there is a visible struggle between letting go and maintaining control. Her dominant impression of Jawlenski's painting (see Figure 2.11) was "Angles," which she wrote into the circled center (see Figure 2.12). The writing hesitantly unfolds to a vulnerable place as she moves by indirection and metaphor, the only approach to feelings. Suddenly, she pulled up short; control takes over with an abrupt "No more!"

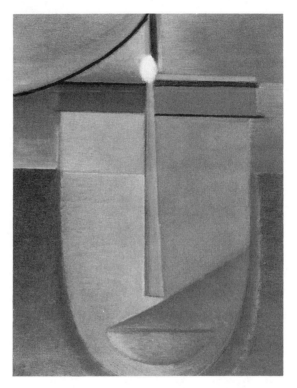

Figure 2.11   Alexei von Jawlenski's, *Head*

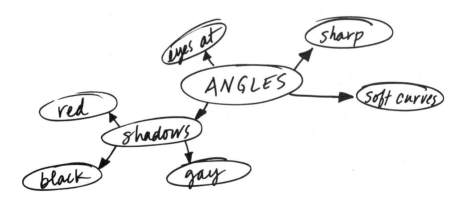

Figure 2.12

My experience of emotion has always been angular, never curved or soft. I have hidden in the shadows of fear, of rejection. Cold, hard—steel, black-and-gray; never deep red, never glowing. A fear of weakness—hide feelings in dark colors, sharp angles; it keeps others at arm's length. The sharp corners, elbows, knees, are hard to get close to. Soft colors meant weakness—mustn't show. No more!

The difference between *over*coming emotional chaos and *dis*covering its emergent patterns is the difference between fighting and flowing. Clustering is essentially a receptive process, nonthreatening because it is indirect. Clustering unveils our mind's images, memories, experiences and it builds a bridge of words and phrases between our nonverbal and verbal worlds.

Traditional approaches to writing concentrate on linearity: obeying rules of syntax, sequence, cause and effect. But it is often difficult to put the complexity of our feelings into full sentences and discursive explanations. If we do try, however, usually our impulse is to edit, judge, critique, and—emotionally—to rationalize.

Evocative writing, however—the writing that clustering generates—juxtaposes, synthesizes, and circles around strange attractors of feeling, blending effortlessly into patterns that surprise. They surprise because they tend to put feelings into focus, giving them form and dimension, allowing us to unwind the tight, one-way contractive spirals of fear, anxiety, or depression which all too often cut off our natural creative impulses. Indeed, a feeling becomes the strange attractor for the nonlinear Clusters that emerge on the paper. From the Cluster, writing flows. Through that flow you become your own guide, wise person, comforter. Surprised into feeling by the nonlinear dynamics of the clustering process, we discover that the writing simply flows into undreamed-of shapes.

Clustering, Word Sculptures, Word Sketches, and Feeling Flows become tools for unraveling emotional confusion. They are bridges between raw feelings and feelings expressed in patterns of our own making. Clustering gives us metaphoric equivalents for our feelings. We could speak of it as a kind of telegraphic speech or an emotional shorthand.

The motives for clustering and its psychological benefits can be summed up as follows:

- discovering patterns in the complexity of emotional turbulence;
- creating a comfort zone in the feeling dimension;
- generating a flow of images, past, present, future;
- allowing us to tap into our vulnerabilities gradually, not radically;
- creating a nonthreatening safety net, inviting growing orbits of self-knowledge;
- honoring what we already know in our bones;
- permitting playfulness as well as tears;
- stimulating curiosity and wonder;
- moving us beyond inertia and resistance into the experience of flow;
- enabling us to perceive patterns of thought and feeling;
- allowing us to experience our own process of discovery; and
- cutting through to a center we rarely see or know.

Clustering allows you to make your mind's chaos visible in patterns on a page; it gives that chaos words, phrases, images, and nuances of feelings. Margi Stevenson in a recent workshop expressed surprise that her writing reflected the mind's nonlinear eye. Her trigger was *The Scene*. (See Figure 2.13.)

Experiment for yourself. Acknowledge your ambivalence; this is not a command, but an opportunity. Begin to set your mind free by clustering, and the writing will flow. Trust the patterns inherent in your chaos of feelings.

Letting Go

On a blank sheet of paper, circle the word MOVE and create a Cluster of any and all associations in any direction. This should take no more than a minute or so. Then stop. Reflect on what is there on the page right now. Let the associations you have put down resonate internally. Flow with them. Wait for that moment of expectant stillness. It only takes a fraction of time to experience a shift from a sense of randomness to a pattern of feelings. Begin writing a brief Word Sketch that expresses those feelings. The clustering and writing should take about five minutes. You will know when to stop. Do it as your gift to yourself, an act of freeing those buried feelings.

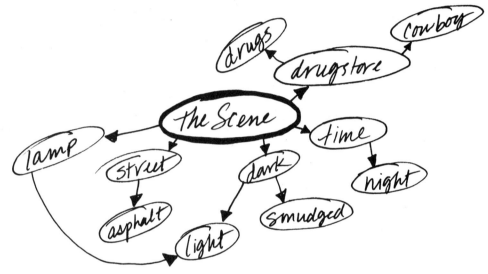

Figure 2.13

The scene
is set
by words
that intermingle:

Street to Lamp
Lamp to Light
Light to Dark
Dark to Night

Poem rewrites
the poem
Words reword
the words.

Cluster.

Exploring the Act

As usual, sign and date your Cluster and Word Sketch. This was a trial run. You've just named and framed something unique to you in this time, this space. Later we will expand on clustering and its process. For now, just know it is a quick process, simple without being simplistic. Its language is so compressed that it cuts through resistance, fear, and blocks.

As you become increasingly receptive through Aware Breathing, Feeling Flows, Word Sculptures, and Clusters, you will gradually become aware of recursive themes or patterns. Pay attention to what comes up again and again; each time you engage in expressive acts, you are touching on patterns of significance only you are capable of interpreting. It is in these tangible acts of writing that healing is rooted.

WRITING FROM A CLUSTER:
FRAMING THE SILENCE OF FEELINGS

Clustering is a two-part process: first, the Cluster itself; second, the framing of what has been clustered into a Vignette. But to describe it in this way creates more of a separation between the parts than really exists. Clustering on a Seed Word offers us the opportunity to be receptive; the Word Sketch allows us to bring something back from that receptive moment— often more than we might have expected.

My twenty-two-year-old daughter, Stephanie, had a childhood radically different from my own. Yet hers too carries its own unique thumbprint of pain. She generated the Cluster in Figure 2.14 in less than a minute, leading to a childhood memory.

> My closet was narrow, dark, close. I used to keep pillows there, making a deep nest for me to recede into. I would hide there when I was hurt, or angry, or sad. Creeping into my closet I would cry, but it was comforting in the softness, pillows and me curled deep in darkness. I could hide from what was hurting me, yet I was never too far away. And always I knew my mom would look for me. I would hear her footsteps approaching, the quiet knock, the door opening. I would hold my

breath, praying she wouldn't find me, angry at her intrusion, hating her for making me hurt—and desperate for her to find me, to pull me out of my dark feelings. Sometimes, confronted with my stubbornness, she would go away, and I would feel my narrow world close in, and I'd run out and reach out. But almost always she'd sit patiently at the entrance, stroking my arm as I receded further into the dark corner, angry and full of love for this person, two sides of me pulling in different directions, watching her sad eyes knowing something, saying nothing, understanding, patiently waiting until I would let her touch me, then taking me in her arms and rocking me, knowing this child full of insecurities, who needs her, even now.

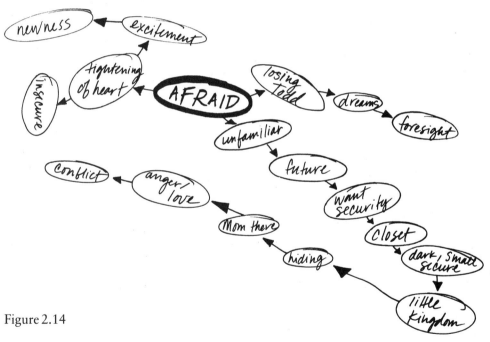

Figure 2.14

On the face of it, this is a childhood memory. As we look deeper, the closet suggests the metaphoric inner world of feelings. Those feelings are in conflict, and express the powerful polarities of love and hate. The writing encompasses an event in the distant past, fluidly telescoped with a sudden awareness in the present: "who needs her, even now." Joanna Field in *A Life of One's Own* wrote:

I realized that the "facts" were not separate things which were there for anyone to pick up, but an ever-changing pattern against a boundless background of the unknown, an immense kaleidoscope changing constantly according to the different ways you looked at it. They were not "given" as in geometry, staying there at the top of the page while all you had to do was to argue about them; they were things which changed completely according to what one said about them, or the way one looked. I (also) saw that my usual attitude toward the world was a contracted one, like the sea anemone when disturbed by a rough touch, like an amoeba shut within protective walls of its own making. I was yet to learn that state of confidence in which my feelers would always be spread whenever I wanted to perceive.

Anyone who lives art knows that psychoanalysis has no monopoly on the power to heal. . . . Art and poetry have always been altering our ways of sensing and feeling—that is to say, altering the human body and the human mind.

NORMAN O. BROWN

The process of naming and framing reminds us that we are by nature creative, capable of self-healing, of relearning to trust that natural inner voice, of re-creating ourselves as often as necessary to keep pace—to make peace—with the changing self.

Letting Go

Begin where you are now. Circle the words FALLING/CALLING on a new page of your Feeling Sketchbook at the top third of the paper, and simply allow whatever words or phrases that come to mind flow onto the paper in whatever direction they want to move. Cluster for a minute or so until you feel a tug, a sense of direction. It is a moment of hooking in to something, finding a pattern in chaos; a delicate, fleeting, often ambiguous moment. It is this moment in which the invisible, inward search for pattern begins to move outward into form—written form. It can be a moment of surprise, a moment of insight, a moment of hindsight or foresight. Whatever it is for you, it is that moment in which the urge to say it on paper intensifies. Flow with it. Write a Word Sketch that expresses it. In doing so, you relearn to be open, vulnerable to your feeling self, expressive in a safe way. The motive for writing is *not* to write what you *should* feel but to help you discover what you *are* feeling. Just do it; let go a little by trusting in the possibilities of chaos. Something will emerge.

Exploring the Act

Number and date your entry in your Feeling Sketchbook. You've framed your second Word Sketch. Most people feel good about framing something in words, even if they are uncertain about what it means. Let's look for a moment at why. Motive is related to emotion, that is, to a desire, a physiological need; it is an incitement to action. Its root is the Latin *motivus* 'to move.' Movement is the antithesis of stasis, thus the beginning of growth, change. Here are a few ways you might try to understand the signals your feelings have sent you.

- Notice what you reached. Was it an event? A person? Something you have been brooding about?
- Notice what you felt when you finished the writing. How strong was it? Did it lean toward anger? Release? A complex mixture of feelings?
- Reread what you've written. Notice whether it feels honest. Confusing. Other. Notice whether the images are fuzzy or clear.

Whatever went down on paper, it is the result of naming and framing; the beginning of freeing up feelings left too long on hold or too long denied. You are beginning to permit your mind to enter a state of expectant stillness. This state is necessary to get at the feelings we often rationalize, deny, avoid, run from, or repress.

EVOKING INSTEAD OF DEMANDING: THE INDIRECT PATH

One reason we may have learned not to trust our natural creative potential is because often it has been educated out of us. Human potential psychologist Abraham Maslow once observed, "If the only tool you have is a hammer, you tend to treat everything as if it were a nail." Well, most human learning is not a nail to be pounded into our thick skulls; to the contrary, much learning is the result of evocative, indirect, metaphoric leaps, a drawing-out, which is the meaning of the Latin root *educare*. The life-long learning touching on our feelings requires "drawing out" tools such as clustering.

Using clustering, you have no need of consistent—even full—sentences. One of British psychologist Joanna Field's entries in *A Life of One's Own* ends like this:

> Hades, shades, dead things, ghosts, was it death I was fighting? blackness, loss of self, . . . dragon, drag-on, drag, plodding on, plod, sod, God, rod, tod, toad, loathly toad.

Whatever appears on the page is right, right for you at that moment. We have seen how the apparent chaos of feeling metaphorically reflects Chaos theory: strange attractors, fractal patterns, sensitivity to initial conditions. Finding the nuances that allow us to name, frame, and understand our feelings can't be done with a hammer. What we seek are delicate, subtle meanings that cling for survival on the edges of the feelings we have too long denied or avoided.

Letting Go

Being true to the evocative rather than direct route, cluster one, some, or all of the following words in your Feeling Sketchbook, as time and inclination permit.

Don't force. You might do one today, two tomorrow, another next week. No pressure. Number and date your entries, beginning each on a new page. Your feelings will emerge and reemerge in your own feeling-designs as you cluster and write. There is no hurry. Allow words, phrases, images, to spill out until something signals for attention. Write it out in a Word Sketch. Name it, frame it. Reread it later. You will be surprised at the rich patterns before your eyes.

 MASK   HEAVY/LIGHT

DANCE/SHUFFLE

SAFE/DANGEROUS   ATTIC/CELLAR

Remember that less is more. Write short rather than long. You're allowing a small but powerful pattern of words to surface, without censoring. You might want to move down the page, placing words in the style of a poem, or you can write a Word Sketch that looks more like a paragraph. Either way, let the feelings cut through short and quick, but if something surfaces that wants to be written in full, flow with it.

Exploring the Act

There is no need to analyze. The naming and framing itself is enough right now. Most important is learning to *trust your process,* to feel comfortable with putting pen to paper, to be curious about what appears, to flow, not force. As poet Peter Meinke writes in his poem "Azaleas."

> We know more than we can say: we live
> in waves of feelings and awareness
> where images unfold and grow
> along the leafwork of our nerves and veins . . .

To which I add, "and our brains!" Waves of feeling are wonderful or terrifying but evanescent, lost like a vapor trail before you can make out a pattern. That's where words—naming and framing—come in. We see the patterns of feeling in words on the page, cleanly. We see the patterns of the images that make us tick.

THE IMPULSE TO POSSIBILITY

Re-creating ourselves through transformative acts is both pleasurable and painful, hard work as well as play.

Yet, if our mental and emotional chaos has patterns, why is it so hard to connect with them? I have already mentioned one reason: losing our original trust in our own creative process by being educated to depend primarily on direct, linear, explanatory writing. Another is somehow seeing our creative expressions as risky. Perhaps we perceive expression, particularly emotional expression, as risky because it makes us vulnerable to others, vulnerable to embarrassment or failure,

As they become known and accepted to ourselves, our feelings, and the honest exploration of them, become sanctuaries and fortresses and spawning grounds for the most radical and daring of ideas, the house of difference so necessary to change. Right now, I could name at least ten ideas I would once have found intolerable or incomprehensible and frightening, except as they came after dreams and poems. This is not idle fantasy, but the true meaning of "It feels right to me." We can train ourselves to respect our feelings and to discipline (transpose) them into a language that catches those feelings so they can be shared. And where that language does not yet exist, it is our poetry which helps to fashion it. Poetry is not only dream or vision, it is the skeleton architecture of our lives.

AUDREY LORDE

and so we resist it. Looking at it another way, we need to re-learn receptivity before we can become expressive again.

It is not easy to be honest with yourself about what you are feeling, especially since we learn to mask, rationalize, and deny our feelings rather than face them. Honest feelings felt make us vulnerable. J. Ruth Gendler personifies honesty in *The Book of Qualities.*

> Honesty is the most vulnerable man I have ever met. I have been afraid of so many things, most especially of the heights and of the darkness. If I had been driving anywhere else, the road would have terrified me. Knowing I was on my way to see him softened the fear. And in his presence the darkness becomes big and deep and comforting. He says if you are totally vulnerable, you cannot be hurt.

Honesty says," if you are totally vulnerable, you cannot be hurt." Most of us, I'm sure, would mistrust this statement. Look at it this way: The more we resist, deny, or run away from a feeling, the harder it is likely to hit us when we finally *do* face it. If we learn to accept all emotions as natural signals, we can also learn that they can be accepted and expressed constructively. Yet, too many of us feel the need to hide our feelings.

Let's look at some of our most common emotions, those we feel particularly bad about having or that make us feel bad: loneliness, anger, fear. Each moves on a continuum of infinite gradations unique to each of us at a particular place, in a particular time, as Stephen Dunn in his poem entitled "Loneliness" observes.

> So many different kinds,
> yet only one vague word.
> And the Eskimos
> with twenty-six words for snow.
>
> such a fine alertness
> to what variously presses down.
> Yesterday I saw lovers
> hugging in the street,

making everyone around them
feel lonely, and the lovers themselves—
wasn't a deferred loneliness
waiting for them?

There must be words

for what our aged mothers, removed
in those unchosen homes, keep inside,
and a separate word for us
who've sent them there, a word

for the secret loneliness of salesmen,
for how I feel touching you
when I'm out of touch.
The contorted, pocked, terribly ugly man

shopping in the twenty-four-hour supermarket
at 3 A.M.—a word for him—
and something, please,
for this nameless ache here

in this nameless spot.
If we paid half as much attention.
to our lives as Eskimos to snow . . .
Still, the little lies,

the never enough.
No doubt there must be Eskimos

in their white sanctums, thinking
just let it fall, accumulate.

*When we close the door
to our feelings, we close
the door to the vital
currents that energize and
activate thought and
action. . . . Without an
awareness of our
emotions, we cannot
associate the effects of
anger, sadness, grief, and
joy—within ourselves or
others—with their causes.*

GARY ZUKAV

*Many of us grow
up believing there is
some terrible flaw at
the center of our being,
a defect we must hide.
Feeling unlovable and
condemned to loneliness
if our true selves become
known, we set up
defenses against sharing
our innermost feelings
with anyone.*

BERNARD SIEGEL

Or take anger. It can come on as a sudden flash or simmer to a slow boil, as Harold Bloomfield shows in *Inner Joy.*

Giving as well as receiving anger seems most often destructive; in fact, getting angry is fundamental to being human. Given enough emotional hurt, the human psyche responds with anger. Adrenaline pours into the bloodstream, creating a surge of energy. Blood pressure increases along with alertness and body temperature. You can't turn this response off; you've got to do something with it. If you fight it and lose control, it comes out in a destructive display. If you block it, it goes underground but continues to smolder like a fire doused with water but not put out. Denying anger is as destructive as expressing it excessively.

An alternative to blocking anger or exploding with it is to acknowledge it, to *allow* it. Utilize the energy of rage to transform it into an expressed form. Listen to Mennet Jacob shout her rage in "Mirrors."

When appropriate out-rage is not expressed, it turns to in-rage.

SAM KEEN

Let me smash them all—
those painful reminders
of what once was,
of what sagged,
of what I hated,
of what I always wished
I could give away—
even cut off!

Let me smash them all,
the ugly reminders
of what they once were:
hideous
   sagging
      the wish from age twelve
        I could cut them off.

I was never proud of them.
Mine weren't the kind
the models showed with pride:
two small uplifted peaks
some lover could climb.

So let me smash them all.
Maybe then I'll begin to see
what is really left behind.

Mennet's anger here is named and framed in explosive language. Less than a month later, she writes about a need to help other women by articulating the unmentionable. Mennet dared to write herself into her grief by expressing her anger and come through. In a letter she wrote me, "I need to explode these feelings and get them down on paper where I can reread my words, where others can read them."

Then there is fear. Although we all know fear, it elicits different reactions in all of us. The fear spiral can move us upward as well as downward. Graduate student Peter Fjeld knows panic and fear as well as I do.

> There is a fear to this world,
> there is an anxiety,
> a quiver in the throat,
> a shaking in the knees,
> a tension of the body into paralysis
> an ignorance of the cause that
> > levels reason into panic.
> Fear of death!
>
> In the spasm of panic
> the seed is sown:
> the prospect of the unknown,
> a defined fear of failure
> running through the body,
> causing me to want to run;
> > the dread of not knowing the power of God;
> > the price of sin
> > > the fear of retribution,
> > > the consequence of life
> > > > ungrounded
>
> I need to know.
> We all need to know.
> This lack of knowledge,
> the fear of suffering
> drives me insane.
> > Lord have mercy . . .

Naming and framing become a safety valve for fears that threaten to overwhelm, a strategy it took me too long to learn. Expressing feelings is a key to tranforming your fears.

Gradually, as you learn to let go of resistance through naming and framing, you will see bits of wisdom, moments of illumination. Listen to former student Mary Ann Parks.

I cannot give
advice, old friends;
I only know
I cannot advise
away your pain.
I am sorry
for the divorces
and the hateful midnight calls,
the broken loves
and triangles,
the distant mothers,
drunken fathers,
the brothers or the sisters
who teased you into pain.

But we all
have our dark secrets,
some present
and painful punishment
for something (perhaps
unremembered) done
a long time ago.
And always
we suffer alone.

My advice, Old friends,
is this—do not be
afraid
to suffer cleanly—
it is our pain

that makes us real.

I began to understand why it was no good arguing against obsessive fears, for the source of them was beyond the reach both of reason and common sense. They flourished in the no man's land of mind where a thing could be both itself and something else at the same time, and the only way to deal with them was to stop all attempts to be reasonable and to give the thoughts free rein . . . my outcast thoughts were in fact seeking expression for themselves, quite apart from any effort of mine, but they could find only an indirect language in which to clothe themselves.

JOANNA FIELD

Letting Go

Cluster the words STUCK/FLOW. Allow any and all associations to pour onto the page. Remember, there is no right or wrong, good or bad, stupid or smart. There is just whatever is. There is only you, here, now. There is your pain, your feelings, images, thoughts, and memories that radiate onto the page. Allow unexpected, surprising patterns to take shape. In the moment of expectant stillness—the moment of something stirring, a sense of direction, a need to explore—simply write a Word Sketch on the same page. An optimum time spent Word Sketching is five to ten minutes. You'll know when you've named what needed framing.

Exploring the Act

Number and date your entry in your Feeling Sketchbook now. Something in your piece will point to where you are today, in this moment. Notice whether your feelings, thoughts, images, words moved more toward the idea of being stuck or of flowing with a feeling or perhaps a little of both.

At this point just remember that whatever was expressed in your Feeling Sketchbook is O.K. There is no right or wrong in any exploratory process. The significant thing is to awaken to what *is* there, not what *should* be there. It is the beginning of reconnecting with your self, of accepting the fact that there are no absolutes. Like the living earth, we are in flux. Paradoxically, you may even experience a sense of flow in writing about a place where you feel stuck or fearful.

Here is the key: The clean white page does not judge. If feelings are wayward, fragile, fluid as water, your words give them shape and form—your form, your frame—and those words become your safety net. Your words permit you to be unbalanced, and to rebalance in previously untried ways. The safety net of your words actually prevents the scattering of feelings; instead, they *gather* feelings into new arrangements—netting these elusive, quicksilver flashes of emotion.

When at last we risk overcoming our resistance—perhaps a better word for it is inertia—we wonder, "Why did it take me so long to make this simple step?"

Letting Go

In your Feeling Sketchbook, numbering and dating your entry, cluster (WALL) and write a Word Sketch using whatever comes.

Feelings dammed up are as destructive as feelings unchecked. The privacy of your Feeling Sketchbook is a safe place to explore. Feelings given voice lead to insights.

- Given voice, they can be directed
- Given voice, they short-circuit the endless agonizing repetitions
- Given voice, they allow us to confront apparent negatives, such as failure and rejection
- Given voice, they pass beyond tyrannical outer and inner judgments, go into and through embarrassment, learned helplessness, lost self-worth
- Given voice, they can transform our pain and inappropriate suffering

An ulcer is an unkissed imagination taking its revenge for having been jilted. It is an undanced dance, an unpainted watercolor, an unwritten poem. It is a sign that a clear spring of joy has not been tapped and must break through, muddily, on its own.

JOHN CIARDI

LOOKING AHEAD

We have explored the role of spirals, the metaphors of Chaos theory, and the value of clustering in helping us move beyond our sense of helpless pain to a new awareness of boundless possibility. We have begun to give a voice to our silent feelings, to resettle our emotional wastelands.

In the next chapter we will look more closely at our brains, the three-pound miracle between our ears that is the source of those fleeting feeling nuances we seek to uncover in our self-healing.

Just as the metaphors of Chaos theory help us to make sense of our own emotional chaos, new developments in understanding the brain can have an ongoing and powerful influence on our awareness of our own awareness. They can point to a direction for healing we need to understand in order to reclaim the self.

The Brain:
The Roots and
Rhythms of Feeling

The frontier of the brain is a vast territory and explorers have only begun to wend their way into the wilderness. Brain models shift in popularity with the frequency of rock stars and it's likely that in a hundred years' time the current maps of the neurophysiological landscape will look as quaint as the sixteenth century charts of the New World. But a map has to start someplace and among the mapmakers is a growing number of scientists attempting to sketch in the big picture with a nonlinear outline.

John Briggs and F. David Peat

Feelings are not magic, although they can seem magical. Feelings are natural to us; they come from within, generated by our brains and glands. According to philosopher Sam Keen in *The Passionate Life*, our feelings "are the heart of our aliveness, the source of our individuality . . . they are our inner resonance of the outer world in which we move."

WHY BRAINS?

This chapter is about the roots of our feelings. We will explore some of what is currently known about the relationship between the brain and feelings. Awareness of how our own organ of awareness functions helps us understand, accept, and work with our emotional nature instead of against it.

We gain insight into our emotions through understanding

63

Awareness of awareness is another dimension. A mind not aware of itself is like a passenger strapped into an airplane seat, wearing blinders, ignorant of the nature of transportation, the dimensions of the craft, its range, the flight plan, and the proximity of other passengers. The mind aware of itself is a pilot.

MARILYN FERGUSON

some of the many overlapping functional divisions of our brains. This allows us to be more able pilots, skillfully guiding the journey of our lives. We can choose. We can know that we are dynamic creatures, that nothing is fixed, not even pain.

Feelings are the barometers of our being. Their roots lie deep in the brain. They are the chaotic attractors that produce shifts in our awareness. Our feelings affect our positive or negative memories of the past, our optimistic or pessimistic vision of the future, our most cherished daily rituals (whether they help or hinder our well-being), how eager or reluctant we are to take action, and our expressiveness in language, to mention only some of the broadest brushstrokes of the mind's delicate design. And recent developments in brain research hold the promise of new breakthroughs in our understanding of the relationship between the brain and feelings, knowledge that can help us understand how we design our selves—and that we carry within us the power to redesign. The moments of crisis and decision—when we become fully aware—are junctures of growth, points of initiation. The end of one turn of the spiral becomes the beginning of another.

Figure 3.1   Michelangelo's *Creation of Adam*

Michelangelo's *Creation of Adam* has always been interpreted as God bestowing life on Adam through the touch of his finger. But a closer look shows Adam with open eyes, already alive. Frank L. Meshberger, M.D. has pointed out that the image that surrounds God, Eve, and the angels (always thought to be a cloak), has been misunderstood for almost five hundred years: it is the image of a human brain. Michelangelo, who dissected cadavers to study human form, seems to have intended a radically different vision of this act of God: it is the gift, not of life, but of intelligence.

Knowing something about our mind's design capabilities is important to our understanding of how and why our emotions are central to every act. The human mind is an open—not a closed—system. We need not be stuck in crisis.

Unlike a computer, our mind can move beyond its programming. Our brain represents a delicate balance of patterns in chaos. In fact, Briggs and Peat assert, chaos is entirely normal for the brain; too much order is devastating for it because living is dynamic, shifting, rather than static, permanent. Again unlike a computer, much of the human mind's activity is nonlinear; what it lacks in logical sequencing and stability it makes up for with its erratic leaps and rich associations.

If we are capable of nonlinear leaps, shifts, and new angles of perspective, then we are capable of redesigning our lives, no matter how severe our pain. In short, we are designed for possibility.

Feelings are signals essential to our well-being. Attempting to close them off or repress them is destructive. If we deny the chaos of our feelings, then we must be ever vigilant about keeping chaos *outside*, a sad expenditure of negative energy. But if we become receptive, we are open to the potential of its hidden patterns.

Understanding something of the open-endedness of our brain functions gives us courage to move into, through, and beyond our pain. Understanding our brains does something more as well. It offers a fruitful set of metaphors to anchor our feelings.

A key premise of this book is that we are not merely spectators of life—as if we were sitting in the audience at a symphony performance—nor merely a participant—a violinist in

The brain has to be largely irregular; if not, you have epilepsy. This shows that irregularity, chaos, leads to complex systems. It's not at all disorder. On the contrary, I would say chaos is what makes life and intelligence possible. The brain has been selected to become so unstable that the smallest effect can lead to the formation of order.

ILYA PRIGOGINE

Because feelings form the underlying structural matrix of thought, they are the key to remembering, to recognizing patterns, and to generating new ideas.

WILLIAM GRAY

the orchestra—nor simply the composer. We are all three: sometimes the creators of our own music; sometimes the player; sometimes the spectator. As composers, we are originators, experimenters, risk-takers. We are feelers of our own feelings, owners of our own mistakes and triumphs, namers, like Adam of all that we discuss in the world, even framers of our own constitutions against considerable odds.

For this reason it is important to understand that our feelings arise less from the events imposed on us from without, than from the way our mind interprets them from within. It is imperative to learn to trust our own emotional signals, to interpret them, and to make constructive use of them. The ways of feeling, all part and parcel of the living self, originate deep in the brain and branch out into the complex puzzle of our self.

GROWING UP: FEELINGS COME FIRST

In human evolution, the feeling brain existed long before the thinking brain. Similarly, in a newborn, emotion develops first. Most recent theories of emotional development indicate that a newborn experiences a generalized emotional sensation of excitement/animation without distinguishing between positive and negative. Soon after, this feeling splits into the bipolar extremes of distress or pleasure. As the child grows and takes in more of the surrounding world, those feelings are honed into increasingly differentiated emotional categories. Gradually the child learns to experience a rainbow of emotional nuances which psychiatrist William Gray calls "feeling tones."

According to research by Rutgers psychologists Jeanette Haviland and Mary Lelwica, the shaping of emotional responses begins in the early weeks of a child's life. In their study, twelve mothers of ten-week-old infants were asked to display happy, sad, or angry facial expressions, each one in turn, four times each for fifteen seconds. Their facial expressions were matched to their verbal statements: "You make me happy," "You make me sad," and so forth. The researchers analyzed videotapes of the mothers and their infants looking

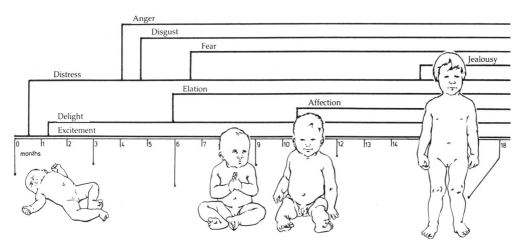

Figure 3.2

for changes in the infants' emotional expression and behavior. Within one second following the mothers' emotional expression, the infants showed consistent patterns of response to the three different emotional states. During the "happy" intervals, infants responded with similar positive expressions each time. The unexpected finding was that, over the time of the four "happy" presentations, the infants' faces became more expressive of interest than of happiness. By contrast, during the "angry" intervals, the infants' anger expressions increased—and expressions of interest dropped.

This experiment underscores three implications:

1. Our emotions are among the earliest signs of our awareness of patterns of meaning;
2. We naturally self-organize to seek out—become interested in—positive feelings;
3. Negative feelings seem to trigger negative responses; hence our awareness of negative feelings and the ability to channel them appropriately is something we must learn.

We need to educate our feelings by expressing them constructively as we mature. It is not only counterproductive, but destructive, to negate or avoid the feelings that form the ground floor of our being.

I thought you could thrash, beat, and pummel an idea into existence. Under such treatment, of course, any decent idea folds up its paws, fixes its eyes on eternity, and dies.

RAY BRADBURY

Something we were withholding made us weak until we found it was ourselves.

ROBERT FROST

We tend to forget that the primary purpose of the brain is the continual making of meaning. Seeing is not merely holding a camera to the world but rather a continuous scanning and searching for meaningful visual patterns. Hearing is not merely recording sounds but a complex process of disentangling sounds we need to hear from useless sounds. Memory is not merely a computerlike data retrieval system but an ongoing reorganizing of personal meaning.

Our feeling life is indirect. We cannot beat and pummel our feelings into, or out of, existence. Under such treatment, feelings retreat into the farthest recesses of our being and continue a life of their own, often finding their own destructive forms of expression. When we withhold ourselves from feelings, the price is high. That is why it is so essential to have some understanding of the physiological role feelings play in the brain.

THE FUNCTIONAL PLANES OF OUR BRAINS

Let's first look at the three major organizational dimensions of our brains.

1. The top/bottom dimension reflects a three-layered brain: the uppermost layer is our neocortical thinking cap; the middle layer is our limbic system, seat of our emotions; and the bottom layer, the R-complex, governs our instinctive survival responses.
2. The left/right dimension reflects two distinct styles of brain functioning, the left focusing on foreground, syntactic, linear information, and the right focusing on background, contextual, spatial information, including the ambiguous characteristics of emotions.
3. The front/back dimension reflects our time-consciousness: future (planning), present (doing and sensing), and past (memory).

Figure 3.3 makes these connections visual. The three sets of connecting fibers, showing the top/bottom, the left/right, and the front/back connections, demonstrate the brain's three major planes.

LEFT/RIGHT   TOP/BOTTOM   FRONT/BACK

   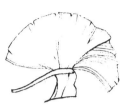   

CORPUS CALLOSUM   PROJECTION FIBERS   ASSOCIATION FIBERS
This thicket of fibers *Forming the* corona *Looping strands link*
joins the hemispheres, radiata, *these fibers* *different sections of*
permitting the two *fan out from the* *the same hemisphere.*
sides of the brain to *brainstem. They relay* *This web subtly mod-*
communicate with *impulses to and from* *ulates the cerebral*
each other. *the cortex.* *cortex.*

Figure 3.3   Three sets of connecting fibers

Naturally, all three of these divisions interact in varied and complex ways that neuroscientists still seek to understand. But for our purposes, we can treat each of these distinct planes as metaphors for our thinking and feeling.

THE TOP/BOTTOM DIMENSION

Figure 3.4 illustrates each level of our brains' top/bottom organization, according to neuroscientist Paul MacLean.

The bottom layers of our brains are often called the Reptilian brain because it is thought to be the part that evolved earliest. It governs our survival instinct, or what philosopher Tobias Grether, in *Homochronos: The Evolution and Development of Consciousness*, calls the four S's: shelter, sustenance, safety, and sex. These translate loosely into our fight or flight mechanisms, our sense of territory, our needs for shelter and food, the security of routine, and the urge for procreation. The R-complex is alert to danger, is cautious, and reacts with lightning speed. It also resists change. Think of an alligator in a Florida swamp.

The limbic system is sandwiched between the Reptilian brain and our cognitive brain. It is the seat of our emotions and is believed to have evolved with the earliest mammals. We could say it is an acceptance/rejection system, signaling "yes"

No matter how much we learn about the brain, we can never learn it all. There will always be something to astound us, to amaze us, to keep us humble, while at the same time stimulating us to greater efforts toward understanding the brain. The human brain is simply the most marvelous organ in the known universe.

MILES HERKENHAM

The routine and ritually driven behavior of reptiles translates in our human expression into obsessive-compulsive acts and a tiresome devotion to sundry habituations. When you find yourself stuck in the rut of an intractable pattern, blame your reptile. But thank this same reptile if you want to maintain some stability in an ever-changing world.

JEAN HOUSTON

Top/Bottom Plane

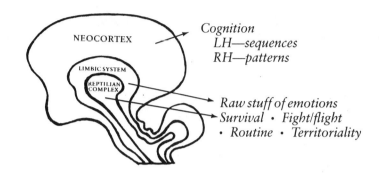

Figure 3.4

The raw stuff of emotion is built into the circuitry of the limbic system.

PAUL MACLEAN

Logic and reason sit on the mental board of directors, but emotions cast the deciding vote.

DAVID SEARLES

to what feels good and "no" to what feels bad. Said another way, it seeks pleasure and avoids, or manages, pain. This area of our brain governs the way we perceive ourselves, others, and our world through a myriad of feelings that develop from infancy on.

The limbic system—the yes/no response—seems to act as the strange attractor for our receptive and expressive acts, the key link to our feelings, our images, our reasoning, our pain, and, yes, our possibilities.

The neocortex—the outermost layer of our brain—is our "thinking cap," so critical to human mental activities. Its left and right hemispheres compose almost five-sixths of the entire brain structure. Because of its relative size and complexity, it may not respond as efficiently to life-threatening or highly charged emotional events; for those, we depend on the smaller, simpler, and therefore faster-reacting brain areas, the R-complex and the limbic system, respectively.

Since our experiences are processed simultaneously by all three levels of the brain, each specializes in what it does best. Sometimes, because each is specialized and because communication between the layers is thought to be imperfect, we get conflicting messages.

Some of the questions that have haunted us throughout history seem to arise out of these conflicting messages. How do we reconcile our deepest polarities, such as our apparently conflicting needs for altruism and self-interest? Why, despite our clear intelligence, do we behave like animals more often than we would like? It bears repeating that feeling plays a central and unifying role in the mind's balancing act. In his book, *Feelings,* psychiatrist Willard Gaylin puts it this way:

> Feeling is—if not all—almost all. It serves utility and sensuality. Feelings are the fine instruments which shape decision-making in an animal cursed and blessed with intelligence.

THE LEFT/RIGHT DIMENSION

The left/right dimension is concerned with functional differences related to the two hemispheres of our brain, connected by a dense band of neural tissue called the *corpus callosum.*

The original research into right and left brain functioning began in 1962 with an operation which cut the bundle of nerve fibers connecting the left and right hemispheres of an epileptic patient with unstoppable seizures. The results of the operation led to the realization that the two hemispheres process the world in radically different ways. Although new findings show that the distinctions between the two brain hemispheres are less absolute than initially thought—the two sides of the brain *do* work in concert, and there *is* a redundancy of function between them—the important differences between the two sides of our brain still hold.

The left hemisphere of the brain (LH), prefers consensual, externalizable knowledge. It classifies and splits. It likes organized sequences, and therefore creates syntax, or ordered language. The right hemisphere (RH), on the other hand, deals best with idiosyncratic, spatial, or internal signals. It is not daunted by the unfamiliar, novel stimuli, paradox, or ambiguity. It creates patterns, synthesizes, and connects. It loves complex images. Roger Sperry's research on geometric forms suggests that arithmetic operations are primarily a LH function whereas the "intuitive processing of geometrical space"

The striving and territorial protectiveness of the reptile, the nurturing and family orientation of the early mammal, the symbolic and linguistic capacities of the neocortex may multiply our damnation or grace our salvation.

JEAN HOUSTON

Neocortical Left/Right Dimension

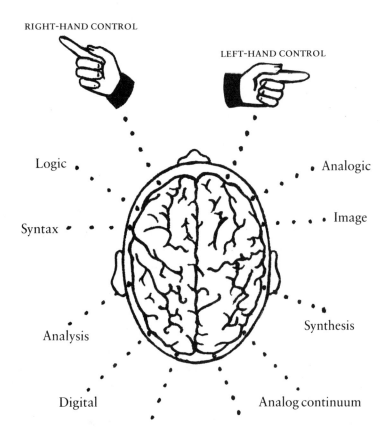

Figure 3.5

tends to be a RH function. Sperry's research showed that topological space which is not easily analyzable into separate features was processed largely by the RH while Euclidean shapes were favored by the LH. He suggests that this is so largely because Euclidean forms have tightly structured detail which can be verbalized easily while more "loosely structured shapes are suited for RH processing" because that side of the brain is attuned to their holistic properties. (Word sculpting may work precisely because it shapes preverbal feelings into loose geometric patterns, which then evoke the naming of words or phrases that illuminate or reflect these patterns.)

We could say the LH responds to rules and order, both important parts of the syntactical aspects of language, while the RH is more sensitive to nuance and feeling, thus better equipped to process the more chaotic internal stimuli from the limbic system that we associate with our feelings. The RH may have limited syntactical ability, but it is good at metaphoric leaps. In short, the two hemispheres are complementary.

Emotions, Left and Right

The conclusion drawn by early researchers, that only the left brain has language, was based on the observation that left hemisphere damage rendered patients aphasic, that is, incapable of language processes such as talking, writing, or reading. However, Eran Zaidel demonstrated that the undamaged right hemisphere has a rich hoard of language; what is largely missing is the power of syntax, the ability to string words together sequentially into subject, predicate, object, and so forth.

The actor Joseph Chaikin is a deeply moving example of left-brain damage. His stroke during surgery in 1984 left him without access to the normal sequences we use to communicate. Instead, as described in Bernard Ohanian's article, "The Lost Words of Joseph Chaikin" (*Hippocrates*, Jan/Feb, 1989), his words must express his inner world by jagged, irregular leaps of mind. In speaking today about the damage to the left side of his brain, he uses a telegraphic, staccato language of facial expression, tone of voice, and gesture to help him communicate: "I died, I dead, i-d-i-o-t. My brain, it's mud, my brain."

He reaches through a jungle of jumbled syntax for ways to describe his state of mind: "I was very very very de, pro, protest, depressioned, depressing, depressed. Protest, depressed it was. I'm hell, hell, hell."

In recalling an earthquake, he uses words that become a metaphoric description of his stroke. "It's tremor, it's trauma. Sleeping. It's dreaming, it's traveling, it's easy. Aphasia, it's chaos."

Chaos creates its own pattern and has its own strange attractors. Chaikin may not have normal patterns of syntactic

Without benefit of scalpel we perform split-brain surgery on ourselves. We isolate heart and mind. Cut off from the fantasy, dreams, intuitions of the right brain, the left is sterile. And the right brain, cut off from integration with its organizing partner, keeps recycling its emotional charge. Feelings are dammed to work private mischief in fatigue, illness, a pervasive sense of something wrong, a kind of cosmic homesickness. This fragmentation costs us our health and our capacity for intimacy.

MARILYN FERGUSON

speech, but they are patterns nevertheless, patterns that produce new ways of seeing, new ways of communicating, unexpected insights. As Ohanian says:

> Communicating with Chaikin can create a state of euphoria,
> the euphoria that comes with speaker and listener hanging on
> every word and searching each other's faces for clues. Chaikin
> himself struggles to articulate something about the emotional
> high of these emerging patterns: "So much feeling between
> words, it's endless. Enough space for endless planets and
> stars."

This is where the intact right hemisphere's connection
with the limbic brain comes in. Although Chaikin scrambles
the normal syntax of language, although he has to take cir-
cuitous routes to discover a word he wants, his relationship
with the emotions seems crystal clear, at least according to the
people who know him best. "I can see better my heart," he has
said. His friends hardly notice his struggle with syntax because they are so absorbed by his emotional presence and richness: "He has finally found ways to express the inexpressible,
finally created a language of his own." In his way, he concurs:
"It's words, everywhere, aphasia, it's worlds."

One of the female participants in a 1983 workshop had
recently sustained left-brain damage in a car accident. She
could only stutter painfully, laboriously explaining that she
was a writer and had been a teacher of writing and that, since
her accident three months earlier she had been unable to put
even a single letter of the alphabet on a page. We clustered.
Since clustering makes limited or no demands on syntactic sequences, it can access words and phrases whose feeling
nuances become strange attractors. Not only did this woman
with the hurt brain create a positively baroque cluster in response to a single letter of the alphabet, *r*, but produced a
word sketch of rich and rhythmic prose, writing for the first
time since her accident.

> High on a ridge where the birds reach, white-boned, like
> wrecks of some standing ruins full of waiting figures, reach in
> supplication against the rigid winter air that ravages them
> fleshless—the railroad runs, iron snapping in the cold air, run-

ning where meadow mice hurry, hiding their furred feet in among the roots, a reprieve. And the railroad hums, like running water, a road made motionless, a right-of-way, rumbling premonitions. No fire here, only a migration of moments, repeating, ridge upon ridge, their birch standing still in bleak resistance.

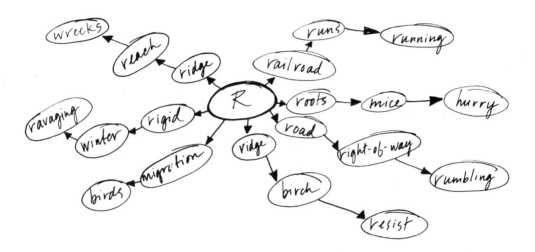

Figure 3.6

It was an emotional moment: her empowerment after months of helplessness. But the experience proved to be more than merely regaining what was lost. Talking with her at the end of the day, this woman—forced to stutter awkwardly by her damaged, left-brain speech—told me: "I think I will be a better writer now; I can see my pictures better." Read her vignette aloud for yourself; she could also hear her rhythms better, the *r*'s at the beginning and in the middle of words, the repetition of *m*'s and *n*'s and *s*'s and *w*'s, creating a pattern of powerful language rhythms.

It was as if, instead of trying harder to write, taxing her already damaged left brain and failing, she was given an alternative route to expression using the nonlinear process of clustering. This was a route to the right brain's rich store of complex images that allowed her to name them with words that simply flowed from her feelings. In so doing, these word-images became available to the left hemisphere via the fibers connecting the two hemispheres, in turn allowing the words to flow in a new and different way, as though the two hemispheres were truly working in concert. Instead of trying to dig the same hole deeper without success—a metaphor creativity expert Edward De Bono uses to describe lateral thinking—she was given a new tool to dig the hole in a different place and to uncover new treasures. And that is the route of the emotions: indirect and evocative.

Failure to connect reason and emotion is wasted motion, according to Sam Keen. Reason alone, he says, creates a sterile world of rule-governed behavior. Emotion alone creates a quagmire into which we sink, losing our footing. Orchestrating the two by learning to express our feelings allows us to channel the best of two worlds into ongoing, constructive emotional growth. Moreover, new research points to what many of us have felt intuitively: that a major factor in heart disease, for example, is the emotions—which can't show up on blood tests or treadmills. Cardiologist Dean Ornish, in his book on reversing heart disease, argues that treating the physical body is only half the story. Addressing the emotions is the other half. Ornish discovered that the group of heart patients he was working with over several years had one thing in common:

> Almost all have a feeling of isolation—isolation from their own feelings, parts of themselves, from other people, and from something spiritual, whatever name you give to that. . . . They felt a sense of being apart rather than part-of. Realizing this isolating force, he gradually worked to get them to share their real stories, to open themselves emotionally—and that became a factor in re-opening the blocked arteries of their hearts.

In order to understand our complex selves, we need to look at one more aspect of our mind's multileveled complexity: the part of us that projects into an unknown, uncertain, often frightening future.

THE FRONT/BACK DIMENSION

For me, one of the most exciting areas of brain research has to do with human time-consciousness. The Russian neurologist, Aleksander Luria, was the first to note a correlation between our sense of time and different parts of our brain along a front/

back continuum. Most of our planning, anticipation, and forecasting may occur in the foremost parts of our neocortex. Most of our sensory and motor information focused on the present moment, is processed toward the middle, while many of the functions of recollection may occur near the back of the neocortex. A 1954 scientific paper by John Campbell, M.D.

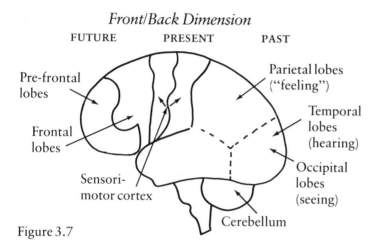

Front/Back Dimension

Figure 3.7

As MacLean has shown in his research, the human forebrain has expanded to its present large size and dominance while still keeping the essential neurological and chemical patterns of our reptilian, paleomammalian, and neomammalian ancestry. We bear the tragicomic burden of being the three-brained ones, and our triunity is not unity at all but an uneasy and easily violated truce.

JEAN HOUSTON

strengthened the idea of a connection between human awareness of the future and the prefrontal lobes. David Loye, M.D., in 1984, published an entire book on human forecasting abilities and how these abilities relate to the brain structures.

The Prefrontal Lobes

Telling evidence for linking the front of the brain with the ability to anticipate the future comes from a largely discredited procedure called a prefrontal lobotomy. This operation was once a preferred method for dealing with severe mental illness. It involves destruction of the front parts of the patient's brain, usually resulting in a loss of planning skills and emotional affect. IQ was generally unimpaired. Similar effects were seen in patients who had suffered accidental brain damage to the same areas.

The future-oriented prefrontal lobes have much to do with volition, empathy, altruism, and choosing. A considerable segment of the limbic system juts into the prefrontal lobes, suggesting that something of the emotional impact of our desires, goals, and images plays a key role in our seeing ahead.

In short, the ways we deal with the anticipated future involve taking responsibility for our lives, creating meaning for the things we do and plan for. Both pleasurable expectation and uncomfortable anxiety require visualizing a not yet existent future. That is the painful power of human time-consciousness. According to psychologist Jean Houston, time-consciousness involves the crucial connection between the prefrontal lobes of the neocortex and the limbic system.

As MacLean has pointed out, we are the highbrowed ones because of the late evolutionary development of the prefrontal lobes. In the crucial link between the prefrontal lobes and the limbic system, we are able to look inward, gain insight into the feelings of others, have compassion, reflect upon where we have been, and finally, orchestrate all of these to become what we might be.

JEAN HOUSTON

It is only possible to live happily ever after on a day to day basis.

MARGARET BONNANO

The Sensori-Motor Cortex

Between the front and back of our brain lies the sensori-motor cortex. When we are engaged in *acts*, such as writing, Word Sculpting, or Aware Breathing, we are involved most immediately in the present moment. We tend to smell, taste, see in the immediate present. We reach for a pen and a pad in the present. We say "I hurt" in the present. All of these activities have been linked to areas found in the sensori-motor cortex, and are related to how we pay attention to things.

An important lesson for this book arises from our awareness of these facts of brain physiology: *Only by attending to our hurts in the present moment can we do something about them*; only then can we take action.

The Back Brain

This is the area of the brain where we find the aptly named temporal lobes, which are involved with hearing and memory. During the 1940s and 1950s, the Canadian neurosurgeon Wilder Penfield discovered that electrical stimulation of areas in the temporal lobe caused patients to experience vivid memories of past events.

Let's look again at the whole of this dimension: front = future; middle = present; back = past. Although an oversimplified view, I think there is enough preliminary evidence to allow us to use it to expand our metaphor for self-healing, particularly with respect to the limbic system's importance.

Note that the limbic system seems to play a central role in each of these areas. The past events we remember best are those having strong emotional overtones, whether positive or negative. Our future prospects make us happy or frighten us. Between these two, our daily life is emotionally colored by what we choose to pay attention to—or avoid. A habitual act tends to blend into a seamless fabric unless something memorable makes us recall it. Feelings that are anticipated. Feelings right now. Feelings of the recalled past.

The Prefrontal Lobes and Our Emotions

Remember, the prefrontal lobes include a significant portion of the limbic system. This crucial linkage of prefrontal lobes and limbic system allows us to feel empathy and have compassion. The prefrontal lobes are, in a sense, the driver that shifts all our gears, playing a major role in orchestrating not only feeling and choosing, but past, present, and future, as well as LH pleasure/pain in creating sequences and RH pleasure/pain at creating synthesized wholes.

Specifically, the prefrontal lobes govern human activities characterized by anticipation and planning. They are the home of intentions, volition of purposes characterized by passion and emotional investment, of the direction of our energy, and of feeling excitement—or fear—of the unknown future. (It is interesting that in Figure 3.1, the *Creation of Adam*, God's forehead is in the prefrontal lobes of the "brain" cloak.) The prefrontal lobes are said to initiate altruism and the ability to feel empathy—perhaps because it is here that our minds can simulate awareness of what another person can or might feel.

The prefrontal lobes seem to be where the motivating force for our acts takes shape, where we take responsibility for our responses to circumstance, whether optimistic or pessimistic, based on how we perceive our future. If the future looks hopeless to us, we will feel helpless; if it looks hopeful, we will feel empowered.

University of Texas neurologist Elliot Ross has pointed out that although the limbic brain is the seat of our emotional reactions, it is the right neocortical hemisphere which interprets, and gives expression to, those reactions. Since the prefrontal lobes seem to be the chief brain system involved in regulating behavior as a whole, neuropsychologist Don Tucker suggests they probably regulate emotional behavior as well. Tucker thinks that the two neocortical hemispheres are preferentially hooked up to the limbic brain. That is, each has its own characteristic emotional repertoire due to its special linkages. Tucker's most important insight is that the left brain is particularly involved in an emotional state of expectation, resulting in both a positive anticipation, or a negative sense of anxious dread. It seems to be the LH which is most attuned to sequence, time, and its attendant temporal images, whereas the RH is more attuned to a telescoping of images regardless of temporality.

Robert Robinson, a neuropsychiatrist, noted in a February 1988 article in *Psychology Today* that the most intense emotional reactions in brain-damaged patients occurred when the prefrontal areas of both lobes were injured. If only the front left prefrontal lobe was damaged—leaving the right side's pipeline to the limbic brain intact—patients responded with depressive reactions because they could *feel* something was terribly wrong. If the front right prefrontal lobe was injured—leaving the left side's connections to the limbic brain intact—the patient responded with undue cheerfulness and a totally inappropriate attitude toward the paralyzed limbs on the left side. This attitude was anything from a total lack of awareness that something was wrong to rationalizing the paralysis. Asked why the left hand hung uselessly, they might say something like, "I bumped it on the door this morning."

For this reason, among others, it is rarely productive to approach personal crises by the direct and logical left brain routes. The LH can invent reasons too readily to offer useful solutions. The most productive direction is evocative, through patterns of feeling processed largely by the RH.

The linking of our mind's thinking and feeling functions to specific brain areas is still in its earliest days. Much remains to be discovered, and it is possible that new knowledge will radically alter how we understand the relationship between brain physiology and our inner lives. For now, we can turn these hints into active, positive metaphors to help us to locate and express the feelings that overwhelm us, to help us transform our pain into a myriad of possibilities—the options available to us as open systems confronted with chaos.

BRAINS, PAIN, AND POSSIBILITY

Knowing something of our brain's awesome complexity helps us to move into our pain, through it, and beyond it. Only the open mind has a chance. The closed mind learns helplessness in assuming a powerless stance. The open mind is able to flow with the ambiguities and paradoxes implied by the multidimensional arrangement of our brains. In understanding the flexibility of open systems, we begin to accept the push and pull in several directions at once by different responses, which come from different areas of our brain. Instead of fighting these directions, we acknowledge them, honor them, move into awareness, and utilize them constructively!

I've used these elements of the brain's structure of function to create a visual metaphor which expresses our different kinds of "sight." Figure 3.8 shows the different dimensions of brain functions as if they represented different forms of this sight, suggesting the various fields of our mental vision.

The Front/Back Dimension: Foresight, Nowsight, Hindsight

Imagine that the front/back plane deals with three kinds of mental vision: foresight (future), with prediction; hindsight (memory), with retrieval; nowsight (present)—right in the center, with our acts or sensory experiences in the present moment.

In my own life, the most subtle workings of this temporal plane were crippled. I was so deeply afraid of the unknown future that I could not project myself into it. I was apparently unable to deal with the hindsight of my early memories because I had mentally denied them, wiped them out. I was accompanied in my nowsight, the ongoing present, by the ever-present pain of unexplored, unresolved conflicts, producing chronic and acute anxiety symptoms which were physically and emotionally paralyzing. In my Feeling Sketchbook I find a muddled entry reflecting a beginning awareness of this sad state.

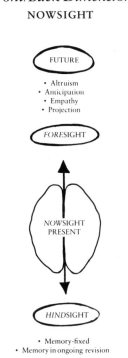

Front/Back Dimension

FORESIGHT   NOWSIGHT   HINDSIGHT

FUTURE

• Altruism
• Anticipation
• Empathy
• Projection

FORESIGHT

NOWSIGHT
PRESENT

HINDSIGHT

• Memory-fixed
• Memory in ongoing revision

PAST

Figure 3.8

I have beaten on the walls of my self-made prison cell while a hooded, shriveled cell mate heaps abuse. I have come to an uneasy truce with my vulnerable underbelly. I have met the enemy, and she is me. My foe is transformed into a faceless friend. She whispers to me on muggy nights. She prods me into uninvited, unsought, searing knowledge that I am more than what I only wish to be.

The Left/Right Dimension: Insight, Nowsight, Outsight

Like the front/back dimension, the left/right dimension also deals with three kinds of sight. RH *in*sight has to do with self-awareness, with intuitive leaps, with reading nonverbal images, and bodily cues. LH *out*sight has to do with our outer world, with consensual knowledge, with approaching the world as it is supposed to be. Nowsight, again central within this left/right dimension, functions to connect RH imaginings with LH sequences, enabling us to act on our images by realizing them in the present moment.

Here, too, I had difficulties. For years I fought for LH control by blocking right brain insight. Very logically, in keeping with my academic training, I read a mountain of books about stress, made lists, resolutions, steps, *anything* to get rid of the symptoms. I was too far out of touch to understand that my struggle to force the symptoms away only made them worse. Not once did it occur to me that, in a very real sense, I was the creator of those symptoms. When they developed from chronic into acute panic attacks, and eventually into symptoms of physical illness, I was finally forced into a hard look at my now. Reading *about,* as though I were learning about the mind structures of some distant, alien race, was no longer enough. I had to make use of what I had been learning in my nowsight. It was no longer an option, but an imperative for survival.

The Top/Bottom Dimension: Throughsight/Nowsight/ Undersight

We have to stretch our terminology a little when we turn to the top/bottom dimension because functions overlap. By *through*sight, I mean a kind of overview that includes all our thinking processes—foresight and planning, hindsight and memory, insight and outsight—our overall cognitive and emotional perspective making up the wholeness that is each of us. It's as if throughsight represented a kind of committee that reviews the actions of a group or team. *Under*sight refers to the bottom-most portions of the team, those focused more or less narrowly on fundamental survival. Between *through* and *under* lies the *now*sight of our limbic system, where the feelings are born which mediate between survival reflexes and our thinking selves by feeding us emotional "yeses" or "nos" for every experience and thought.

When this kind of mediation breaks down, your emotional life can break down with it. I learned this the hard way. Virtually incapacitated, I had to start from the bottom. I can look back now on that process with a hard-won sense of acceptance. My experience in the mountain cabin, which I started to describe in chapter 2, was a personal turning point. Let's use it to better understand what we've been talking about in this chapter. We can now reinterpret that story using the new metaphoric tools of brain organization and the varieties of sight we have explored.

When I sensed my loss of control and became incapacitated with fear, I thought, "I've got to get away!" (R-complex, fight or flight response). I believed I couldn't concentrate on writing my current book because (a frantic search for LH cause and effect logic) my children were interrupting too often. I couldn't acknowledge the deeper feelings. The truth was I felt like a wild thing in a net. So I arranged for four weeks in an isolated mountain cabin. "Peace and quiet for working," I reasoned, or LH rationalized. What I did not yet realize was that when you're really alone, there's nowhere to run. For the first time since earliest and unremembered childhood, I came face-to-face with a me I had never acknowledged.

Fear. Fight or flight. Surges of adrenaline. This is what was happening to me. Mental work was out of the question. Something deep down inside said, "survive." I had no choice but to shift gears from controlled outsight to letting the images of insight flow from the right brain. One image after another tumbled out, circling around the strange attractor *fear*.

I knew enough about the Reptilian brain to focus on my breathing, which was tight and shallow, but brought sporadic moments of respite from terror. I focused on the present moment with an attempt at yoga exercises. I focused on *doing* with Word Sculptures and drawing Feeling Flows. This movement of the hand did some good, but my nervous system continued to blaze.

So, as a final way of facing feelings, I summoned the past by naming and framing, by clustering, searching for early recollections. The denied feelings, the blocked memories, poured onto the page, each naming and framing an act of doing in nowsight. Some of these small five- to ten-minute Word Sketches—revealing patterns I had denied—are presented throughout this book.

Figure 3.9

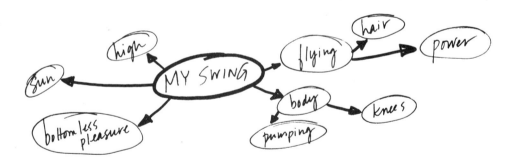

Figure 3.10

Three examples of those Word Sketches of entanglement and disentanglement, of the unexpected emergence of embedded emotional patterns, positive and negative, emerged in the acts of clustering and writing. The first led to my earliest memory of self-awareness. We are living in Rostock, a city in East Germany; I am three or four (Figure 3.9). The memory triggers a feeling, named and framed in a cluster.

Flight

I swing. It's *my* swing. My scary swing.
I love my swing.
Pump. Pump hard, harder, hardest.
Feel air and hair flying.
Feel body arching, bending knees—
power, motion, empowerment.
I'm doing it myself, alone!
Weightless, I fly through air.
    Ecstasy: flight, height, movement.
    Fly, move, high, light.
    Light: ecstasy, movement, flight.

This memory, previously inaccessible to consciousness, produced a feeling high of such magnitude, no words can truly convey it.

The swing Word Sketch led my second-earliest memory which—interestingly—also has to do with flight, but at the other end of the feeling spectrum: a child's terror. It is a memory of a dream, as vivid today as the night I dreamed it at the age of three or four. War must already have been outsight reality, for in insight, it is a dream of war.

Memory. Past. The remembered fear triggered a surge of adrenaline. That day, alone in the cabin, there was no war. It didn't matter; the fear was still real. Except that time I acted: I gave it a name and a frame. Years later, a mature adult, I chanced across a pencil sketch by Otto Dix. It was shockingly familiar, as though I had seen it before. It was an image of the *feeling* of my dream.

First Dream

Planes drone in the dream.
I am three.
My narrow German street feels safe,
the uniform houses lining up like soldiers to protect me.
But a gray plane appears in the gray sky,
    angles sideways to clear jutting rooflines, dives
    to make the impossible dream landing.

The craft is dream-huge.
I am small, stand dream-frozen,
   too close
   too alone
   in the too-narrow street for planes to land.
It glides to the pavement as if made of suede.
I am afraid.
   Its hatch bursts open.
   Tomahawked and feathered—
   moccasined and painted for war,
   hundreds upon dream-hundreds
   spill into my solid street.
I, sensing "war" is a bad word,
   am their first small victim.

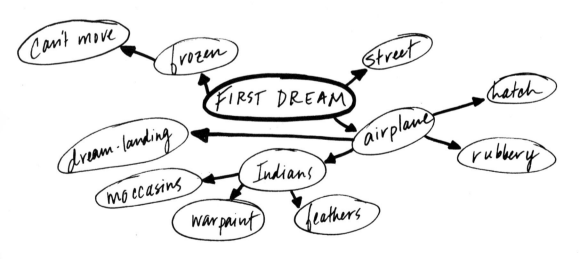

Figure 3.11

Figure 3.12 Otto Dix's *Lens Bombed*

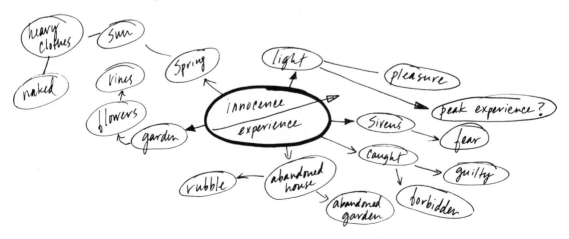

Figure 3.13

Yet another early memory surfaced as I clustered in that solitary cabin, finding my nowsight by recalling my long-denied fear. As I clustered and wrote, I was astonished at the primal mix of ecstasy and fear, negative and positive (see Figure 3.13).

As a point of reference, we had already lost a first home to bombs; our salvaged belongings had been moved hurriedly into one of the few houses left intact after the fire-storm destroyed most of Kassel.

The street is empty of houses:
charred walls jut into improbable blue sky,
fire-storm flames stored in my child's memory.
Easter brings no colored eggs this spring.
I make my own joy, wander into a houseless garden.
    Vines and wildflowers don't know they shouldn't grow
    in this wilderness of broken bricks.
Like me, they point their faces toward the early sun.

Alone, furtive, I obey some primal calling:
shed sturdy winter boots,
    brown woolen leggings, jacket, scratchy sweater
until I stand naked, skinny body touched by pale sun.

My small brain explodes into a halo of light; it flows
through my winter-white body, a sweet warmth.
Someone's abandoned garden,
knowing how to grow when spring arrived,
lights a longing.
White light surrounds me like a song.
But nothing lasts.
The sudden sirens—too familiar—signal danger
The light vanishes. In the sad jungle of rubble,
I fumble into my clumsy clothes,
caught in my forbidden pleasure—
guilty for everything.

Entries like these shocked my feelings back to life. During those interminable days in the mountains I began to face the hammering pain. Long after my return to civilization, I continued the process of facing these feelings. Only later was I able to describe the process.

- Nowsight, awareness of breathing, loosened the reptilian brain contractions of fight or flight;
- Letting go of left brain outsight control allowed past images to emerge in evocative, right brain patterns of Word Sculptures or Feeling Flows;
- Past images, hindsight, brought back feelings from my childhood I had long blocked as too painful to face;
- Accepting those painful and sweet memories in my nowsight was the key to recapturing present emotions, which led to insight; and
- Thus, I faced the future with less fear of foresight.

You can use this process too. We all tend to block out early memories and painful feelings. We all have our own unique thumbprints of pain. In the next section, we will begin to explore the patterns that emerge as we use clustering to give these feelings form.

BRAIN/MIND/MEMORY CLUSTERS

This activity asks you to write briefly and quickly several times. Number and date each Feeling Sketchbook entry. These quickly framed responses will give you a metaphoric sense of each of the dimensions of your brain. Their conflicting messages and claims for attention often confuse us, especially in times of crisis. Disentangling them gives us a chance to experience each dimension one by one.

Letting Go: Bottom to Top

1. THE REPTILIAN BRAIN. Sit comfortably, close your eyes, listen to your breathing. After a minute or two, say the phrase, A SAFE PLACE, as often as you like, simply letting it filter through your awareness. Feel the word on your tongue, in your bones. Naming calms; it is like a mantra. When you feel ready, circle the phrase on a new page in your Feeling Sketch-

book and create a Cluster from it. Do nothing more. Simply be curious to see what will come as you shift from a sense of randomness to a personally meaningful pattern. Now write a Word Sketch expressing what wants to be written.

Exploring the Act

The feeling of safety, of a safe place: as living beings we all need the feeling of safety, at least enough to bear the daily uncertainties of living, the losses, the griefs, the restlessness. However you responded, you will notice

A word is dead when it is said, some say. I say it just begins to live that day.

EMILY DICKINSON

- whether or not you have the sense of a safety zone;
- whether it is internal or external, or some of both;
- if external, where it is, such as your favorite chair, your church, a place at the kitchen table, your garden.

Safe places and safety are associated with daily routines. Routines can be positive, especially in bad times when we may feel a terrible need for structure. Routines can also be negative; for example, our Reptilian brain can lock us into obsessive-compulsive habits we find difficult to break.

2. THE LIMBIC SYSTEM. Repeat the same process described above with the phrase YES/NO. Close your eyes, breathe, say these words like a chant—silently or aloud—as you focus inward on your own emotional landscape. Stay with it for as long as you wish, then cluster YES/NO and write. Name and frame without expectation; flow with what is taking shape in your words. There is no right or wrong, just attention to this significant dimension of your humanity.

3. THE NEOCORTEX, LEFT BRAIN. On a new page, draw a line down the center. On the left side make a list classifying and defining yourself according to your roles in the world's reality, for instance, man, father, engineer, and so on. Don't stop until you can't think of any more classifications. This should take one or two minutes.

4. NEOCORTEX, RIGHT BRAIN. Now, move to the right-hand side of the page and write I AM LIKE. Circle the phrase and use it to create a Cluster. Play a little. I AM LIKE . . . a cat?

An onion with layers and layers of protection for my inner core? A Porsche without a battery? A set of windchimes turning aimlessly? A sandwich with lots of baloney in between? Put down as many images as appear relatively effortlessly. One image will speak to you more insistently than the others. Go with it by framing the image that speaks to you, of you, through you, in a brief Word Sketch.

Exploring the Act

- Note the differences, if any, coming out of these two approaches.
- Note which had the greater emotional pull.
- Note which told you more about yourself.

Neurosurgeon Joseph Bogen suggests that the LH defines the self as a subset of the world. By contrast, the RH evokes the world as a subset of the self. In the first mode, we make generic classifications according to externally verified, consensual reality. In the second mode, we make a metaphoric statement reflecting a more symbolic aspect of our being. Neither is right or wrong; this activity only highlights the different ways through which we perceive and understand our world.

Letting Go: Back to Front

1. THE TEMPORAL LOBES. New page. Number and date your entries. Write the words I WAS and circle them. Focus, eyes closed, breathing in and out gently; say the words *I was* as often as you like. When you feel ready, create a Cluster using *I was* to see what will turn up, then frame in it a brief Vignette. Do not judge. Move right into the next activity.

2. THE SENSORI-MOTOR CORTEX. Write the words I AM and circle them. Breathe, say the word as many times as you like, then, when you feel ready, create a Cluster. When a pattern begins to emerge, write a brief Word Sketch. Don't judge. You should need only two to four minutes. Move on without stopping to the last activity.

3. THE PREFRONTAL LOBES. New page. Write the phrase
(I SHALL BE) in the center of a circle. Eyes closed,
breathe, say *I shall be* as often as feels right, then
create a Cluster. When you have a sense of direction,
write a Word Sketch. Write without judging, simply
letting the naming and framing reflect your images,
your language, your words.

Exploring the Acts

Remember that your entire brain has been involved in the
writing of these Word Sketches. Remember also that we are
exploring, without judgment of what we write or how we write,
the many dimensions of our own awareness: Yes/No; past/
future/present; reflexes/options images/sequences; thinking/
feeling/sensing. All are operative, all are interconnected, yet
whole parts of us can be closed off.

Before rereading any of what you've written, see if you
can remember any overlapping patterns, such as

  · images that are common to all three types of time-
    consciousness;
  · the kind of time-consciousness with the strongest emo-
    tional impact.

Notice which of the three kinds of time-consciousness
felt best, worst, most blocked, most fluid. These acts will come
into play throughout the rest of this book.

Being open to subtle emotional nuances can help us discover our hidden emotional attractors and the patterns in our
personal chaos. Help yourself shift into an exploratory mode
by another quick journey through some of the brain's organizing dimensions. The following writing acts will help you own
the information you have been exposed to in this chapter. Let's
play with a new set of stimuli designed to evoke more of an
emotional charge than the previous ones.

The most difficult part of shifting to an evocative mode is
letting go of a need to have something "make sense." That's
not what this exploration is about. Allow your writing to
be as fragmentary and chaotic as it wants to be. This is the
difference between forcing a pattern and letting unplanned

patterns surface. Think play; think curiosity; think wonder. For a moment or two, close your eyes, do Aware Breathing, and picture the stunning network of billions of neurons in your head, each single neuron having hundreds of neuronal connections, all available to enable you to create patterns of meaning, to change patterns of meaning, to reform old patterns into new awareness. That is the astonishing dynamic pulse of our brain. A six-year-old, creating a drawing of her brain's inner landscape, exclaimed excitedly, "I can feel my neurons dancing!"

Feel your mind's flow through the clustering and writing. Date and number your entries; use a new page for each. No entry need take more than five or ten minutes. See if you can move through all the new, evocative triggers in one sitting without worrying about length.

Letting Go: Bottom to Top

1. REPTILIAN BRAIN. Write the words FIGHT/FLEE and circle them. Breathe in and out, focusing on the air moving in and out of your nostrils, until you feel a calm centering. In keeping with the sense of ritual, say these words, *fight/flee* silently or aloud, as many times as feels comfortable. Now create a Cluster, permitting a flow of images and connections without censoring. As you shift from random associations to a sense of pattern or direction, write a Vignette. Move directly to the next activity.

2. LIMBIC SYSTEM. Write the phrase PULSE OF PAIN on a new page and circle it. Breathe several times until that calm center returns and you are ready to say these words. Then create a Cluster, letting words, phrases, or associations spill onto the page until something demands attention. Give this feeling form by naming and framing a Word Sketch.

3. NEOCORTEX, LEFT BRAIN/RIGHT BRAIN. Draw a line vertically down the middle of a new page. On the left, write WHAT'S WRONG? Numbering, list things you think are wrong—facts or events in your life, anything that disturbs you, whatever you see as reasons for bad feelings. Now, on the right side of the page write the phrase MY BLIND EYE and

circle it. Breathe, eyes closed. Say the phrase for as long as it feels right. Create a Cluster with whatever associations pop up. When something wants to be recognized, do so by writing it out in a Word Sketch. Move on.

4. PREFRONTAL LOBES: FUTURE. Write (WILL/WISH) on a clean page and circle them. Breathe. Say the words repeatedly. When you are ready, create a Cluster. When something signals your consciousness hard enough that it cannot be ignored, flow with it by writing a brief Word Sketch. It can be highly compressed; you don't need to write in full sentences.

5. SENSORI-MOTOR CORTEX: NOW. Write the phrase (FACE TO FACE WITH) and circle it. Breathe quietly, calming, centering on the now. Say the phrase repeatedly. Become receptive without judgment. When you feel ready, cluster until something in you wants to be given words in a Vignette. It can be very brief; a series of fragments; a sentence. Whatever comes, comes. Let it tell you; don't you tell it. Move quickly into the last activity without stopping.

6. TEMPORAL LOBES: PAST. Write the word (TOY) and circle it. Breathe, say the word, cluster, become aware of an image or feeling that impels you to name and frame it. Write a Word Sketch that expresses it.

Exploring the Acts

- In what ways were these last entries different from the previous ones?
- Was there anything in these entries that you haven't thought or felt in years?
- Did anything "ring a bell"? Was there a sense of recognition, of connection with other Clusters or the Word Sketches that followed? Can you give it a name?

One thing will become increasingly clear as you move through these naming acts: You are your own best explorer of your inner chaos. Logic plays a minimal role. Another thing: it is normal to feel some resistance to natural mind processes.

You may be alienated from them, may have learned to ignore them, or have long suppressed them. Trust the gradual unfolding.

WHAT WE HAVE LEARNED: THE RICH POTENTIAL OF YOUR FEELINGS

We are becoming open to some deep truths about ourselves from our exploration of brain organization.

- All living things struggle to survive (reptilian brain).
- All human beings experience emotional confusion and conflicting feelings as well as emotional stability and harmony (limbic system).
- All of us live in a world where our ideas about consensual reality are essential to successfully navigating the world outside us. In this mode, the self is experienced as a subset of the world (neocortical left brain).
- Simultaneously, all of us stand at the center of our own universe. We interpret the world as a subset of the self, metaphorically reflecting our inner being in our patterned images of self in the outer world (neocortical right brain).
- All of us can remember our past in ways that draw out the images which have hurt, soothed, or connected us to our own personal histories (temporal lobes, left and right; time-consciousness of the past).
- All of us experience the present moment. We can act only in the present. This is now, and naming and framing is an act in the now (sensori-motor cortex, left and right; consciousness of the present moment).
- All of us have the built-in ability to project ourselves into an uncertain future tinged with excitement or fear or both. We seek both certainty and risk, stability and the excitement, the mystery of the unknown (prefrontal lobes, left and right time-consciousness of a future).

Finally, the three brain dimensions help us understand something about their looping connectedness.

Through-Sight

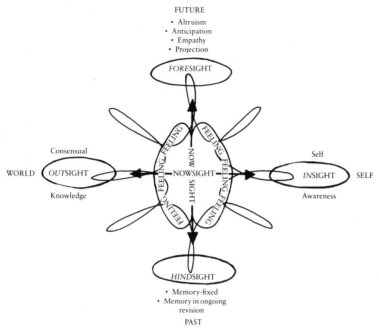

Figure 3.14

- Foresight—envisioning new possibilities instead of feeling stuck;
- Hindsight—revising memory by seeing it from new perspectives;
- Insight—experiencing a realization about some aspect of ourselves;
- Outsight—seeing connections in the world that make sense or illuminate;
- Undersight—putting our deeply ingrained habit patterns, such as habitual routines and territoriality, to constructive use instead of letting them rule us or fighting them; and
- Throughsight—recognizing our capacity to have an overview of the entire process; to redesign our lives by being aware of how our awareness operates; to be able to hear all the voices within us.

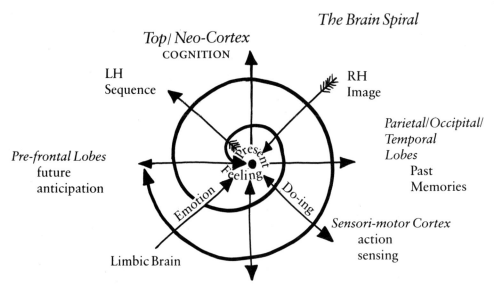

The Brain Spiral

Figure 3.15

There you have the beginnings of the most basic construction of the human mind. Such awareness continues to guide us down the spirals of our personal pain and up once more into the sunlight of possibility.

LOOKING AHEAD

This chapter has been designed to help us understand how our different abilities to make meaning function as a connecting bridge to educating our emotions. Claiming our mind's multiple potentials has been our subject. Even the most basic understanding of these complex processes helps us be more tolerant of ourselves, helping us to be emotionally resilient in the face of adversity.

Our brain's built-in flexibility empowers it to create patterns for its own purposes and on its own terms. Our purpose is to transform pain into an array of possibilities. Let's be aware that feelings are evanescent, dissolving like a vapor-trail before you can make out their pattern. That's where words—naming and framing—come in.

In the next chapter, we will deepen our understanding of the many subtle connections between language and feeling. We will see how the words we choose without thinking, words that merely occur to us when we name and frame images, carry with them hidden patterns of guilt, blame, and self-pity. Yet when we understand the process and accept it without self-judgment, this experience of guilt or blame—negative or self-pitying as it may sound—can be a significant step toward possibility.

Reclaiming Our Losses: The Grammar of the Emotions

We are feeling beings before we are thinking beings, feeling beings before we can express our feelings. Yet, because we all too often become unreceptive to our feelings, and because the connection between feeling, thinking, and language is so ubiquitous, we forget to notice these connections. When we need to reach out, because we are in pain, we no longer know that these tools are available to us. Becoming receptive to, and expressive of, our feelings are two sides of the same coin. If speaking and writing involve the grammar of language, I believe we can also speak of an emotional grammar—a grammar reflecting the silent language of the heart.

Emotional grammar serves as a link between our internal awareness of pattern and its external expression in language. Language is a mental construct, a way to express this sense of pattern. To "story" the feeling-imbued events of our lives is a universal human impulse, transcending all cultural barriers. In fact, psychobiologist Renee Fuller, in *In Search of the IQ Correlation*, suggests that the story—in its widest sense as the innate making of meaningful patterns—is Karl Lashley's "lost engram" of the brain. It reflects the human need to give form to feeling.

In order to reconnect with my internal feelings, I began to

"story" aspects of my life that had significance for me. I did this because of a need to explore denied feelings. Yet we all story constantly for various reasons: to communicate, to feel better, to untangle feelings, to reach out. Our "Guess what happened to me last night!" "Imagine what she did!" "When I was little . . ." help us make mental contact with ourselves or other human beings through language about how we feel, what happened to us, or what we think happened to us.

Words are the most powerful drug used by mankind.

RUDYARD KIPLING

Although language can never fully bridge the gap between feeling (that constant private display of patterns in our limbic system) and linguistic expression, it is a powerful vehicle toward form. Our symbol-making brain creates stories, according to Susanne Langer in *Mind: An Essay on Human Feeling*: our stories, like all forms of artistic expression, are *forms* of feeling. In fact, the basic premise of her book is that all art, including stories, ". . . is the surest affidavit that feeling, despite its absolute privacy, repeats itself in each individual life."

In this chapter, we explore the tenuous and fascinating connection between feeling and language.

GUILT AND BLAME

Language has given us words for some of the universals of human feeling. Let's take guilt and blame as examples. Threatened by something terrible that may overwhelm us, we contract like the narrowing spiral of a whirlpool. Just as we begin to honor our pain, our reasons for avoiding it grow stronger, giving us the illusion of control. We point accusing fingers. We strike out verbally at others. We accuse ourselves.

In naming and framing the language of negatives, we can claim our buried feelings and convert this negative energy into constructive acts. As we allow painful feelings to surface in Clusters and Word Sculptures, it is natural to feel *worse* at first. In this chapter we look at why and how the connection between language and feeling shapes our responses.

For me, this connection became *conscious* early on arriving in a strange country. My father, stripped of his heritage,

*Guilt is the prosecutor
who knows how to make
every victim feel like the
criminal. She follows the
scent of doubt and self-
hatred to its sources. She
will not tell you what you
have done wrong. Her
silence is brutal. Her
disapproval surrounds
you in an envelope of
cold, nameless terror. You
may recognize Guilt's
footsteps before you see
her coming. She limps
like a crippled bird. Even
though her broken ankle
is healing, the wound in
her heart has become
infected.*

J. RUTH GENDLER

his wife, his home, honors, and possessions, is silent. My new
mother is silent too, overwhelmed by five untamed children
not her own. I, too, am silent. I cannot form the words of the
new language. I loathe the old; it triggers memories of sirens,
crumbling walls, the dailyness of hunger and death.

In this new country, surrounded by a new culture, getting
to know a new stepmother, I struggle to utter the sounds of a
language strange to my ears. I want to belong. I want to break
out of my silence. Twelve years old and alone, I roller-skate
over unbroken cement sidewalks. To the rhythmic clicking of
wheels on the squares of cement stretching before me, I chant
silently, "You will. You will. You will." It becomes a song, a
prayer. "You *will* learn these sounds!"

Sometimes the other children taunt me, calling out
"Nazi!" as I go by. I feel guilty and helpless. Language, I
sensed dimly even then, was power. Only *this* language was a
riddle. I was trapped in a space between languages.

Guilt

I learned the voice of guilt early; others may learn the voice of
blame. They are cousins, both expressions of our emotional
"no." Looking outward, we search for someone else to blame.
Looking inward, our bad feelings take the form of self-blame,
of guilt. Relentlessly, we beat at ourselves, and we don't know
how or when to stop.

At first, I did not know how deeply ingrained my early
learned helplessness was, how much of my emotional life was
hidden from me by the guilts I had accepted over the years,
like the hand-me-down clothing. Here I was, well into the
middle of my life, yet my carefully constructed personal world
was falling apart—not unlike the crumbling of my childhood.

To the outside world I projected total control. Inwardly,
my nervous system and my psyche protested. I was in a per-
ilously fragile state when one day my youngest child, Simone,
a rebellious thirteen-year-old, confronted me.

"I'm sick of your sickness!" she shouted from the doorway of my room. "All you do is think of yourself!"

I was stunned into words. This child's explosion of angry
frustration was so stark, so true, that I felt a surge of adrena-

line tightening the tourniquet around my throat. She was thirteen. I was an adult. I had shared little of my emotional life with my children. This was a cry for words.

I knew I had to break my involuntary contract with silence. I took my daughter by the hand and brought her into the room. She lay down on the bed, hostile. Words struggled in my throat. What about my carefully cultivated superwoman shield? My breathing was shallow, my voice thin; haltingly, I broke my silence.

". . . It's true. I do. I do think of myself . . . I don't think it's only because I'm selfish."

Deep breath. Keep breathing to keep from breaking, to keep from choking on the lump in my throat. Risk. Name, frame. I name the unnameable.

". . . Honey, I'm afraid. . . I guess I'm afraid of dying . . . They tell me I have cancer . . . I'm afraid I might die on the operating table . . ."

The words squeeze past the tightness to bridge a dawning knowledge of something unknown, perhaps felt, but too deeply buried to recognize.

". . . I am as old as my Mom was when she died in the bombing . . . Maybe . . . maybe . . . I feel I don't deserve to live longer than she did . . ."

An epiphany, given words. They shock me. Nothing like this has been in my awareness. Simone lies silent in the May sun, listening, heavy gold-brown hair surrounding her head like a halo, tears trailing down temples to disappear in sunbleached strands.

My stumbling words stop after naming more than I ever knew myself, more than a vulnerable, angry thirteen-year-old should have to process. She rises silently, brushing back wet hair. Between us, there is new sound. It resonated enough to find its way into a later Cluster of mine whose resulting Word Sketch reads in part:

> . . . You grew into full-breasted sullenness too soon, determined to unravel—all alone—the center of your being.

> You were grown—you green pea, pea-brain, princess on a pea—demanded I see you for yourself, accused:

Between parent and child there is no monster like silence. It grows faster than children, filling first a heart, then a house, then history. The freedom children seek is the freedom from silence.

ROGER ROSENBLATT

"You don't notice me!"
I didn't,
      absorbed in my own fears and failures . . .
wise one, foolish one, youngest one,
my puzzle, my magic trick, my chameleon,
where are you going, going . . .
When will you be gone?
And how will you come back?

*. . . As silent as my
mother and father were
All day and during dinner
and after
And after the radio
With hardly a murmur all
the way into sleep.*

DAVID WAGONER

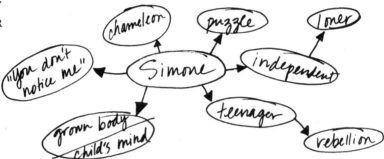

Figure 4.1

Blaming

The other side of guilt is blame. When it is focused outward we
try to make others responsible for our pain: parents who did
not love us enough, sisters who were mean to us, teachers who
were boring, friends who abandoned us, spouses who did not
offer us enough support. Blame is clever at finding logical reasons for our nameless sadness.

Rationalizing, finding logical reasons for our bad feelings
instead of acknowledging them as signals, is largely a province
of the left brain. Because it is built to discover cause and effect
relationships, the left brain is a master at pointing the finger at
culprits, including aspects of ourselves. Rationalizing is a su-
perb strategy for not exploring what those feelings are or to
acknowledge them as ours because the reasons are self-
explanatory.

A Guilt List and a Blame List

One way to open ourselves to possibility is to literally number our guilts and blames as they float into consciousness. By making an ongoing list, we give these inexpressible feelings names and numbers, making them plain on the page, there for us to look at on other days. We begin to see a growing list of guilts, some valid, some imaginary, all destructive if not dealt with. We begin to understand our avoidance strategy of blaming others for our pain. When you feel the impulse to strike out—whether at yourself (guilt) or someone else (blame)—name it by starting two lists: a *Guilt List* and a *Blame List* in your Feeling Sketchbook (see Figure 4.2). Leave several pages blank for each so you can add to them whenever you notice either of those feelings surfacing. Gradually a pattern may become apparent: a pattern of denial, of anger, frustration, helplessness, impotence, rage, self-pity. In effect, what you are doing in making these two lists is acknowledging thought patterns that generate pain. By naming we can start moving away from destructive judgment of self and others. Take a few minutes now, make your two lists, and put down the first things that come to mind in each category.

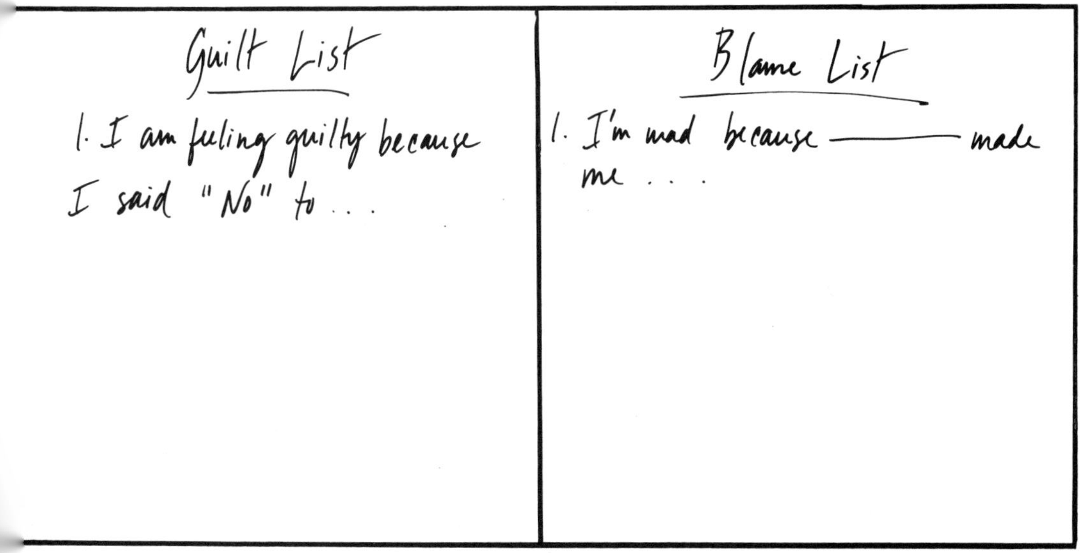

Guilt List

1. I am feeling guilty because I said "No" to . . .

Blame List

1. I'm mad because ——— made me . . .

Figure 4.2

Number Words

Number words play a special kind of role, a kind of ticking off of what's wrong with the world and other people in it, what's wrong with us. Numbers help us to make the fuzziness of frustration surprisingly accessible. The mathematician Warren McCulloch once said that neither the human mind nor numbers can be fully grasped separately from the other. One day someone asked him to articulate the question that inspired his scientific quest. He replied, "What is a human, so made that he can understand number, and what is number, so made that a human can understand it?" One answer is that psychologically, number is an expression of the human need for order.

Number words can name or qualify. Numbering our grievances makes us aware of the rationalizations that protect us. Numbering helps us to count our losses. Counting our losses also makes us aware of the function of number words; they are concepts we use on a daily basis without much thought: a one-parent family, two sides to an issue, a relationship triangle, ten reasons for something, and so on. Numbering is a good way to keep a record of our very human predilection for blame. Working from our numbered lists, we are likely to find unexpected clues to previously unrecognized aspects of our emotional pain.

Word Sculpture: Guilt and Blame

Number and date your entry. Make a quick shape. Let your hand take the lead for a second or two. Now take the given shape and play with words or phrases generated by items in the Blame or Guilt List you have started. Don't rush. As you take time to embellish, become aware of the blamings or guilts reappearing in this configuration. Don't do anything more than this, although you might want to go back to your lists and see which ones did or didn't move into consciousness at the time of word sculpting. Even this will give you an awareness of which feelings are more or less important. My own Word Sculptures of that period show enormous emotional confusion as well as resistance. Figure 4.3 is an early version of a Word Sculpture I had begun on a surface I couldn't tear out.

The judging specter gives fears a familiar face and personifies them—as the parent, the teacher, the political tyrant. It is easy for us to externalize him, to turn him into the Enemy, to look for him outside ourselves in all the persons or factors that may be putting us down, getting in our way. We can spend a lifetime searching him out and blaming everyone and everything around us for the frustrations of our blocked creative voice . . . It is like looking for fire with a lighted match.

STEPHEN
NACHMANOVITCH

Feeling a need to complete it, I made a copy to take with me. Figure 4.4 shows how it finally looked. Note that most of the words that embellish the shape qualified how I felt at the time.

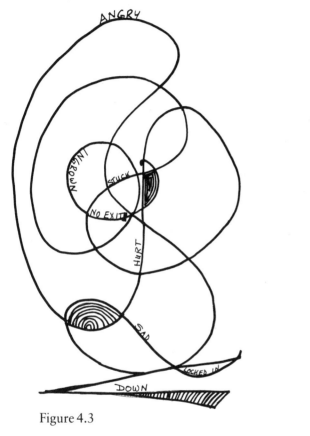

Figure 4.3

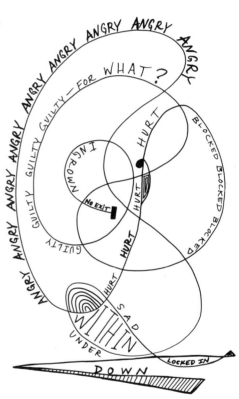

Figure 4.4

Letting Go

Now go one step farther. All you need do is to look at any pattern in your Word Sculpture. Pull out what feels significant. If the whole design speaks to you, name your frustrations, anger, blamings in a word or phrase, place it inside a circle in your Feeling Sketchbook, and create a Cluster using it. If one blaming in particular triggers an emotional response, cluster it—then write a Word Sketch.

Exploring the Act

In this last activity, chances are your mind produced a totally different configuration from the Blame List you made at the beginning of this chapter. Reread what you've written.

- Where the clustering from your Word Sculpture took you.
- Which images or thoughts reflect just one aspect of your pain, your problem, your crisis.
- Whether or not you experienced a shift from blaming to something else.

Look at Figure 4.5 and see what happened to a fourteen-year-old whose naming of her anger led her to a major insight.

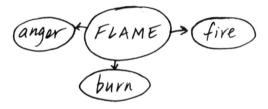

Figure 4.5

Perhaps your writing skirted your pain. Perhaps you hit a bull's eye. The important thing is that the act of naming and framing will guide you increasingly to express the issues that want or need to surface so you can attend to them.

You are letting the recursive, looping patterns of feeling emerge; they are necessary for breakthrough. Trust the patterns; they are your patterns. Trust this process. It is subtle but sure. Breakthrough may not happen all at once, but it will happen. You are becoming your own agent of change playing within the safety net of words. Play with other numbers, as workshop participant Martha Spice did to make a strong statement.

Counting Up
Is that how we know
if we've done right?
if we measure up?
4 hugs a day;
starting at 5 A.M.
5 A's on your report card;
$50 or $100,000 in your pocket;
8 laps around the track.
250 words,
20 pushups
6 good jokes,
2 new clients,
3 cold calls,
900 calories.
That's not quite it.
You are more than what you do.
The way I understand it,
you're just ok
with or without the numbers,
yours or anyone else's.

Blame and guilt are natural, like all our feelings. Turmoil is part of growth. Denial, too, is understandable. Yet, unless it is only a short-term strategy, it leads to emotional stagnation. The longer and harder our attempts at escape, the more difficult our return to a point of dynamic equilibrium.

The key point is this: The very words which serve to name and frame our feelings often make us *more* uncomfortable until we grow accustomed to the process. Instead of returning to the crumbling refuge of denial, instead of frantically searching for temporary relief, we learn to become receptive.

FLOW: THE KEY TO FEELINGS

Imagine you are a naturalist in a new, somewhat frightening wilderness. You could huddle shivering around your campfire, listening to the strange cries of unknown birds and animals.

Or you could observe, explore, and name the various beasts; then you realize you have become so absorbed in this process you've forgotten to be afraid!

Once we stop rationalizing and focus on exploration, we can confront riskier emotional levels safely through the creative acts of naming and framing.

A noted educator, Mihaly Czikszentmihalyi, describes such acts as *flow* experiences. The experience of flow, he believes, characterizes our most enjoyable states of learning. The flow experience is pure involvement in the present moment, in the present feeling. It is like making love; if you are not absorbed in the present moment it doesn't work. If you keep thinking about what *ought* to be happening instead of what *is*, you will not move into the flow state. This is one reason I have asked you not to judge what you write in your Feeling Sketchbook.

Being and becoming, action and awareness, seem to merge in the flow state. This potential merging is built into our genes, although many of us have forgotten how to tap it. Remember when you were a small child, out playing? You were so absorbed in play, so lost in the present that it seemed a week before you were called in for lunch.

Flow can only happen when we momentarily suspend, on the one hand, worry and anxiety, and, on the other, boredom. Worry and anxiety surface when concern about imagined future events or recalled past events become too huge. At the other extreme, boredom leads to restlessness, and restlessness in the extreme, to escape, flight, and denial.

Absorbed in the act of writing, we can reach a sense of unified flow from one moment to the next. In fact, the act of clustering and the writing that follows from it often produces an altered state of consciousness. You become the flow. The flow allows you to move into the feeling, to transform it into words on the page. It may last five minutes; it may last an hour. Exploration of the filigrees of feelings is the way to come to terms with them and gradually transform them.

The paradox is this: the more you try to avoid painful feelings, the more signals you send to your brain that they are important; because they have the power to scare you, your pain becomes worse. Flow is the key to healing the pain, not by avoiding it but by becoming absorbed in the discovery of its

It is not hard to live through a day if you can live through a moment. What creates despair is the imagination, which pretends there is a future and insists on predicting millions of moments, thousands of days, and so drains you that you cannot live the moment at hand.

ANDRE DUBUS

Paranoia, the mind beside itself, becomes metanoia, the mind with itself and so free from itself. Free from clutching at themselves the hands can handle; free from looking after themselves the eyes can see; free from trying to understand itself thought can think. In such feeling, seeing, and thinking, life requires no future to complete itself nor explanation to justify itself. In this moment it is finished.

ALAN WATTS

patterns. This is why Letting Go is the beginning of healing. You cannot run away from pain indefinitely; you can only move into and through it.

In my Feeling Sketchbook I find the cluster in Figure 4.6 and the writing that flowed from it.

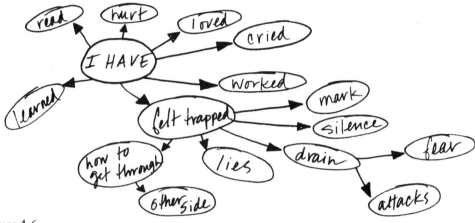

Figure 4.6

I have been trapped by my own
mask of invincibility
where my gut, roiling with unsaid rage
rebelled at the loud silences.
I have learned how mental drain
slides into body pain.
I have lied to the jagged leaps of a hammering heart.
Today past pain remembers me, but kindly.
Sometimes it visits, just to remind me:
The way out is through.
The way out is through.
The way out is through.
How do I learn to be a survivor?

One answer to that question lay in the connections between my words and the painful feelings I was learning to face. In facing, I was able to turn my denial into flow experiences. So can you. My pain became a vehicle for that discovery process. The impetus for this book is not to *tell* you what to do but to enable you to draw on your own resources.

LANGUAGE: THE FEELING AND WORD CONNECTION

The capacity for language is fundamental to the human mind. Neurologist Oliver Sacks, in his book *Seeing Voices*, insists that without it we can't be fully human.

> Intelligence, though present and perhaps abundant, is locked up so long as the lack of language lasts. Nothing is more wonderful, or more to be celebrated, than something that will unlock a person's capacities and allow him to grow and think.

The philosopher Susanne Langer in *Mind: An Essay on Human Feeling*, suggests that the source of language, and its motivation, initially lay in making inward feelings outwardly manifested in sound. Neuropsychologist Colwyn Trevarthen, based on his studies with infants, says in Richard Restak's *The Mind* that the drive to expression in language is heavily emotional.

We can also think of language as a flashlight illuminating the jagged, irregular, swirling patterns of emotional chaos. The poet William Stafford says it best with a metaphor of parachutes in his poem, "Any Time."

> I have woven
> a parachute out of everything broken, my scars
> are my shield; and I jump, daylight or dark,
> into any country, where as I descend I turn
> native and stumble into terribly human speech
> and wince recognition.

The meaning we create through language is inevitably colored by the feelings we have toward the objects in our world. In childhood there is no separation between ourselves and the external world until we become aware of our selfhood. Gradually we see ourselves as the subject, distinct from the objects of our scrutiny. Language develops from internal processes (verbs) into external names (nouns), and only later into the connectives. Langer points out that a baby with only half a dozen words will name processes: "'Daddy gone. Daddy

The development of mind, thought, and language is simply a nexus in which it is impossible to separate one from the others.

MICHAEL
STUDDERT-KENNEDY

come?' Question and answer, assertion and denial, statement and description—these are the basic uses of language." Naming locates feelings and the objects that have generated them. Vygotsky noted that

> inner speech syntactically is fitful, fragmentary, abbreviated, and compressed. In comparison with external speech [there is a] simplification of syntax, a considerably smaller number of words.

Language, both inner and outer, is a potent organizing principle of our emotions. In "The Limbic System in Human Communication," linguist John Lamendella's exhaustive research indicates that language is under the control of two separate systems, "one for normal speech and the other for speech under stress or in situations of strong emotion." Emotional language has its own characteristics; it results from "limbic functions that have found linguistic expression through words that have a special tie-in to the limbic system and provide an emotional release." In fact, bilinguals like me sometimes revert to their mother tongue under strong emotion, possibly because this first language has the deepest links to limbic expression.

Psycholinguist L. Kanner noted that seemingly irrelevant or metaphoric phrases of autistic children "can be traced back to personal experiences that took place in contexts of intense emotionality." An example of this can be found in the film *Rainman*, in which Dustin Hoffman plays an autistic character, Raymond. As Raymond's younger brother, Charly, turns on the tap to run a bath, he is stunned by Raymond's hysterical screams of "Rainman! Rainman!" The metaphoric misnaming of "Rainman" (suggesting water, water triggering fear, fear originating in an early, terrifying memory of a bathtub scalding) becomes a powerful illumination of the invisible process of association-making and its undiminished emotional impact, despite the intervening years.

As children we play with words and concepts as we do with blocks: toppling, reassembling, and rearranging them into patterns of our own that make us feel good.

If play were not pleasurable, kittens would never chase each other's tails and so would lack practice in the motor skills needed for survival. If there were no pleasure in the appreciation of the absurd, if there were no fun in playing with ideas, putting them together in various combinations, and seeing what makes sense or nonsense—in brief, if there were no such thing as humor—children would lack practice in the art of thinking, the most complex and most powerful survival tool of all.

MAX LEVIN

That is what a four-year-old did when she dictated her associations around the word (KITTY,) and from the cluster
proudly dictated her four-year-old view of the way the world
works.

> Well, this kitty-cat is mother and she's laying her eggs and her
> husband is a dog so she won't only have kittens, she'll have pup-
> pies too!

Elizabeth Rose Campbell writes of an early language experience.

> My older sister asked, "What do you want to write next?" She
> was six, I was four. How do you spell swimming pool? I want
> to know, thinking of brilliant sunshine flashing through a large
> deep pit, blue on the bottom, filled with clear water, a sound-
> track of collective laughter and conversation . . . She printed
> slowly and carefully. SWIMMING POOL. I stared at the
> words very hard and watched everything a swimming pool
> had ever been to me shrink to the shape of those black
> crayoned letters on white paper.

The use of language as a connective between an inner
emotional world and the outer world is reflected in the adolescent Stephen Dedalus's observation in James Joyce's *Portrait of
the Artist as a Young Man*. Already highly metalinguistic, he is
sensitive to language as a medium coloring his emotional
frame of mind.

> He drew forth a phrase from his treasure and spoke it softly to
> himself:
>   —A day of dappled seaborne clouds.
>   The phrase and the day and the scene harmonized in a
> chord. Words. Was it their colours? . . . No, it was not their
> colours; [It was more] the contemplation of an inner world of
> individual emotions mirrored perfectly in a lucid supple
> periodic prose.

The reason why words work overtime is, not surprisingly,
that emotions can be felt through words. Words are so much
more than their dictionary definitions; they are constructs, a
fertile record of how we perceive our world, not only outer but

inner. Language reflects the primal processes of emotional needs at a peculiarly human level. In fact, the influence of human language on human life goes far beyond mere communication, mere discourse, on which we place such high value. Words may have their seeds in human consciousness, but their roots lie in the life of feeling.

Words and feelings. How are they connected? Vygotsky implies that the functional elements of language, such as nouns, verbs, adjectives, adverbs, and connectives, reflect—perhaps operate on—emotional direction. Gendler echoes Vygotsky's claim of such emotional coloration.

Language is one of the most complex things that human beings are capable of.

PATRICIA KUHL

> Touch words. I like to be able to touch my ideas . . . I love the mystery in the act of writing, ink and pen and paper, each word calling out to the next one . . . Words as things, tangible as the fibery paper and the liquid ink, almost like small objects, rocks, or gems. Words as stones, as stars, as seed, flowers, tracks, doors, words as mountains, words as skins. Words as colors, the difference between similar words, say imagination and creativity, like the difference between a blue purple and a red purple.

Writers, particularly poets, have known the connection of word and feeling for thousands of years. The poet William Stafford describes the emotional life of words.

> It is as if the ordinary language we use every day has in it a hidden set of signals, a kind of secret code. That code can touch into life a pattern in our feelings. . . .

That hidden set of signals may lie in the intersection between our limbic feelings and our neocortical expression in language. Understanding something of the power of language for emotional expression helps us to take charge of our pain. Richard Restak in *The Mind* agrees that although it is true that language represents our world, "it is a quantum leap beyond mere representation. It makes possible a complete transformation." Linguist William S. Y. Yang suggests that language is not only the best window through which to see the workings of the mind but also plays a major role in shaping the mind: "How we relate to others, how we see things, how we represent reality within ourselves, to ourselves, are all critically influenced by the choices our language makes available to us."

Consider the emotional roots of words in our consciousness of space and time. Given the feeling life of language, it is possible to refer to an *emotional grammar*. Life is matter and motion: Nouns and verbs. Nouns came from the primal need to orient ourselves, our bodies, in the world by naming the things and qualities in it and of it. Verbs put things in motion.

"In the beginning was the word," says the Bible. I recall my childhood puzzlement about this. It seemed to me that it must have been the other way around, that before words, there were flowers, sky, mountains, fish. I named these things to myself—*Blumen, Himmel*—loving their sound, the pictures they evoked in my head, and the feeling of an almost magical empowerment. I recall learning the word *zipper* in German: *Reissverschluss*; suddenly the blue sky was graced with a slash of imaginary zipper which performed an imagined function: I could unzip a blue slice of sky, see beyond that protective canopy, and imagine what was behind it—another whole story. Maybe, I thought, God had the power of naming since the beginning of time, but human beings became human only when they began to point and to name.

As an adolescent I read the story of Helen Keller who, blind and deaf, was able to make a giant leap of awareness with her first naming. Until her teacher Annie Sullivan was able to show her the connection between the word for water and the liquid itself by repeatedly spelling *water* into the palm of her hand, Helen behaved like an animal. The power to name transformed her into a functioning human being.

> I knew then that W-A-T-E-R meant the wonderful cool something that was flowing over my hand. That living word awakened my soul, gave it light, hope, joy, set it free. Everything had a name and each name gave birth to a new thought.

Helen Keller's awakening is one of the clearest examples I know of an epiphany: *re*cognizing—knowing again in a different way.

Similarly, the French philosopher Jean-Paul Sartre, recalls

Language doesn't only convey intentions and information. It also regulates personal relationships . . .

COLWYN TREVARTHEN

his first realization as a child that words have enormous power because they are contained in books. His mother read him a story out of a "box which slit open like oysters . . . which drank ink and smelled of mushrooms." To Sartre, this was Magic. When she told him stories, he loved the rhythms of her voice (think of the patterns in Chaos and the thought that the music of voice, story rhythms of language, and emotional intonation are all intimately interconnected).

> I had ears only for that voice; I took pleasure in her unfinished sentences, in her wavering words, in her sudden assurance, which quickly fled, petering out melodiously, and which, after a silence, came together again.

I, too, recall the unyielding urge to name, scribbling on my little wood-framed blackboard in a place and time devastated by war. "What does it say?" I would ask any adult nearby. Later, when the repeated bombings near the end of World War II made school a memory, I escaped into words and the pictures they produced in my head. I had a big book of Grimm's fairy tales—one of the few possessions salvaged from earlier bombings. These stories let me live big blocks of intolerable time in a world of clear-cut rewards and punishments, briefly obliterating a senseless world that spelled *danger*, in itself an abstraction that was all too real for me.

Feelings. Words. Meaning. Words must have a kind of emotional grammar; words not only name, they evoke the multiple colorations of ineffable feeling nuances. But since words blend so seamlessly into the fabric of our lives, we are usually unaware of the power of this deep emotional/linguistic structure. William Stafford says the "power words" contain a "hidden set of signals, a secret feeling code." A good way to illustrate the emotional impact of "power words" follows with a student's clustering of the modifying word *maybe* (see Figure 4.7). Notice how central a word like *maybe* was to his sense of unpredictability and uncertainty.

What is evoked here is the palpable feeling power of language. We not only use language or make language, we *feel* language. However we choose our words, beneath their surface meaning lies an undertow of feeling. We *feel* their ambiguities,

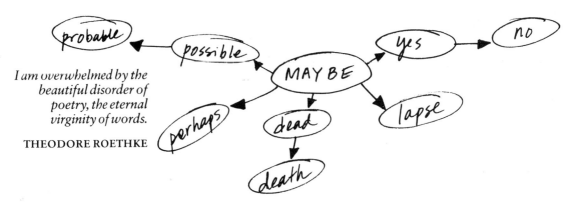

> *I am overwhelmed by the*
> *beautiful disorder of*
> *poetry, the eternal*
> *virginity of words.*
>
> THEODORE ROETHKE

Figure 4.7   Maybe the long lapse between sleep and dreams of sleep and maybe not, not ever, not never, maybe the morning of un-hurried love, maybe, all the long maybe's and still, cold no's and not's and the yes, simple and singular like a fire that may spread beyond the perhaps and the possible and the probable and the inevitable yes and no that moves in and out in a breath passing through the land-scape of dry-as-dust maybe, the undifferentiated scenery, the bland, uneventful, cool as pale blue, calm as noise, dead as death of maybe.

playfulness, insults. Different word forms have "pull"; they influence one another. They act on each other. They act on us in ways we don't yet understand.

Language, infinitely refined beyond the mere howl or whine of an infant, subtly expresses our pain and our pleasure. An emotional grammar has little to do with the dictionary definition of words. The simple adverb *down*, for example, makes us feel—viscerally—a directional movement quite different from *up*. Although the emotions reach beyond language, it is words used evocatively and metaphorically which make patterns of our quagmire of feelings. Through the complex system of sounds we call language, we reach constantly toward expression. Through *ex*pression, we grope our way out of the quicksand of emotional reaction onto solid emotional ground.

There is another side to the language coin, of course, as there always is in dynamic systems. Sometimes our words categorize not the way *we* perceive things but the way our culture orders them. When we look at reality primarily through these social categories, which are often frozen through conventional usage. Language works against us, and we lose confidence in the way we perceive—or struggle to express—our world. The ultimate effect is total *mis*communication, producing a state of routine conformity and helplessness that author Ellen Langer in her book *Mindfulness* labels "mindlessness." Mindlessness is a denial of our perceptions and our expressive needs. Jung told James Joyce, after interviewing his distressed wife, that "you are swimming in waters in which your wife is drowning." Joyce could express his emotional turmoil; she could not. Lack of an emotional grammar sharply curtails our creative adaptability. We become rigid, act by reflex, and forget language can be one of our most powerful improvisational tools, relying instead on greeting-card–style platitudes to express our emotional life.

An awareness of both aspects of language—as fluid, spontaneous, personal expression, and as habitual social convention—is essential to understanding our pain. It can defeat us or urge us to grow. The way I perceived the word *stress* is a good example. Initially, I accepted it as negative. Each time I heard or saw it in print, my adrenaline would surge. I would feel helpless, and my body would react accordingly. Almost too late, I understood that this naming word *stress* can also name a condition that is not necessarily negative, and that my own one-sided negative sense of it played a big role in its power over me. For a long time *stress*—the mere sound, sight of it—seemed to me as villainous a word as *cancer*. I ultimately learned that stress at the other end of the continuum can mean the adrenaline high of a challenge: of skiing down a mountain too steep for comfort, of writing a book no one may read, or of risking loving someone who may never reciprocate.

Let's briefly sum up here how the emotional grammar of words can become a trusted navigator through the vortex of our pain.

- Words have their own deep-rooted connections to our feeling life.
- Our use of words can be uniquely personal, spontaneous, dynamically irregular—or highly constrained by learned social or habitual categories.

I don't feel it is necessary to know exactly what I am. The main interest in life and work is to become someone else that you were not in the beginning. If you knew when you began a book what you would say at the end, do you think you would have the courage to write it? What is true for writing and for a love relationship is true also for life. The game is worthwhile insofar as we don't know what will be the end.

MICHEL FOUCAULT

- Receptivity to the subtle emotional aspects of words is a necessary, though indirect, route to feelings of fluidity, ones that enable us to channel our feelings constructively rather than being at their mercy.
- The grammatical functions of words can have as much—maybe even more—emotional significance than their definitions.
- Simple awareness of the many dimensions of language helps us reach into and move through our pain.

EXPLORING THE EMOTIONAL PULL OF WORDS

Let's use this mysterious, complex human gift of language to name the losses that caused our pain. By noticing how they feel, what they mean, where they fit, and figuring out how to put them in their proper place, we can get on with our lives. In the context of feelings, particularly guilt and blame, let's examine some of our word categories to find out what happens when we become expressive.

Naming Words

Nouns name things. They are names of objects *out there*, separate from us. Nouns, in a sense, are the thumbtacks on our world maps. Nouns point to tangible things: Helen Keller's W-A-T-E-R; brain; or the glass heart. They can also point to intangible concepts, like pain. In naming them, we frame them, making them real to our minds. Words actually seem to create these realities for us, giving them separate identities—clear images in our heads.

When we hurt, a natural response is to blame people or events *out there* for our pain. But there is another way, and that is to respond metaphorically—that is, to use language and its emotional grammar to express our feelings in words that transform the pain into images. In a recent workshop, a group of teachers came up with a rich trove of images for the word *environment,* some of which were "fragility," "beauty," and "death." These metaphoric responses—not part of any dictionary definition of the word—generated a resonance of feeling which surprised the whole group. For example, a word which points to a place, actual or imagined is the word *home*. As we saw in chapter 3, we have a built-in spatial territoriality, intrinsic to the oldest parts of our brain. *Home* can have strong negative or positive feelings. In its literal sense, *home* refers to an enclosed living space. Beyond that, it can suggest a way of life, as did Tara in *Gone with the Wind*; a motherland, as did Ithaca in Homer's *Odyssey*; psychological space, as in the saying "Home is where the heart is" or in journalist Lance Morrow's "Home is the bright cave under the hat." It even evokes our physical self, as in an unusual and powerful passage in *Remembering the Bone House* by Nancy Mairs, whose body is racked by multiple sclerosis.

> One simply is inches of supple skin and foot after foot of gut, slosh of blood, thud of heart, lick of tongue, brain humped and folded into skull. And it is as a body that one inhabits the past and it inhabits one's body . . . The word habit is too worn a word to express this passionate liaison of our bodies . . . with an unforgettable house.

The skull is home. We fly in and out of it on mental errands. The highly developed spirit becomes a citizen of its own mobility, for home has been internalized and travels with the homeowner. Home, thus transformed, is freedom. Everywhere you hang your hat is home. Home is the bright cave under the hat.

LANCE MORROW

Letting Go

Cluster (HOME.) Jot down a first association and others will follow. Number and date the entry in your Feeling Sketchbook, then as soon as a sense of direction unfolds from your cluster, write a Word Sketch that expresses your emotional impulse.

Exploring the Act

You may or may not have been surprised at how the word *home* resonated for you. Wherever this naming and framing took you was good. It indicated where you need or want to be, despite your resistance—which is likely to be a part of the meshwork of feelings at this time. Reread your entry. Look for clues the way a psychic would explore the intuitive, not the way a detective looks for incriminating evidence. Don't force. These Word Sketches are evolving patterns, reflecting larger emotional patterns hidden from reason and logic. If something does not jell now, it will later, as your own visual word-patterns evolve on their own.

This section, like the other sections of this book, does not dictate. Its aim is also to evoke awareness of your own patterns. There are no right answers. "Exploring the Act" is as evocative as Aware Breathing, clustering, writing, or word sculpting.

My own cluster of *home* produced a bewildering tangle of feelings having to do with rootlessness and fear, calling up images of air-raid shelters, fire, broken bricks, hunger. I know there must have been some positive images in my earliest years, yet those come primarily from salvaged photo albums, never from within. In my adult life, *home* has been a major stabilizing force. It seems to be an extension of what I call "the house of my psyche." Very consciously, I have not moved in many years, yet the house which shelters me has undergone many intriguing transformations. When I grow, it grows, takes on new shape, dimension, colors, skylights. I cherish the joy of putting my signature on the wood and glass skin which contains me and those I love. Perhaps because it was not always this way.

Home: A Look Back

Home—
Where is it? What is it? What was it? How do I know?
Home. Swing, sandbox, wading pool, currant bushes.
Home. Sirens, silence, damp cellars—slimy growing
    things;
shivering, waiting for the monotone all-clear to curl back
    into sleep.
grim-faced grown-ups run,
Herd children, wordless, into the night.
Six, I stare
at what the familiar homes.
A bridge of red flames crackles;
A house is not a home.
House, bonfires,
arch of fire.
"London Bridges . . ."
Home? Now, a single, borrowed room, bed-crowded,

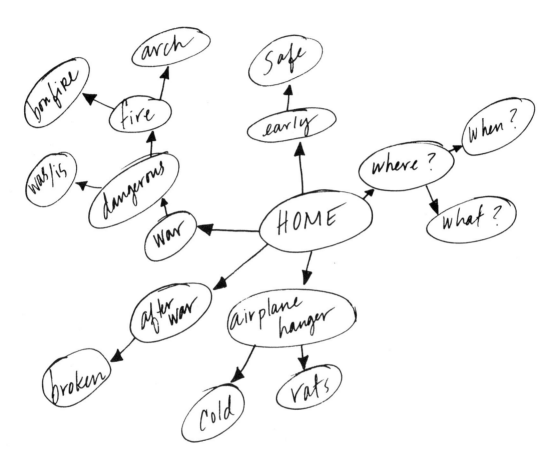

Figure 4.8

a single burner, a mother weeping, waiting for Death
   (like Santa, he arrives on cue).
Home, Motherless? homeless, numb.
Home? Now a structure oddly up-ended, we leap jagged
   cracks—carefully.
Home? Now, a hangar, a garage for planes that do not fly,
houses bewildered children bent on survival. The wind
whistles cold. Rats, cats, fight for food.
Home: Nothing, nothing cozy here. Will one ever—
   never—feel like home again?

The womb is the first home. Thereafter, home is the soil you come from and recognize, what you knew before uprooted. . . . Each home is an unrepeatable configuration; it has personality, its own emanation, its spirit of place. . . . The flesh is home. African nomads without houses decorate their faces and bodies instead.

LANCE MORROW

In the denial dominating much of my adult life, I reasoned that misfortune happens to all, that worse things happen to other people, that emotions are maudlin, that tears are embarrassing or inappropriate. So, I contracted into control. I didn't understand that loss has little to do with reason. Ultimately, these long-buried feelings broke through in my adult crisis. Their fulcrum was *home* in its widest sense: shelter, safety, protection, survival, need, love, womb, tomb. When the dam holding back feeling finally broke, it triggered a flood of acute panic attacks. The final stage was becoming agoraphobic—the fear of moving beyond the confines of an imagined safety zone into the world out there. For a time, the much-loved space I call home became a veritable prison.

Even today, I find significant patterns appearing in what I call my "house dreams." Always different houses; always similar patterns: 1) Living in a Victorian house, I walk up a curved staircase only to discover a door I had never seen. I open it. It reveals an empty room, full of cobwebs and flaking wallpaper. It feels important to clean and claim it. 2) I have bought a new house overlooking the sea. I walk in. It is mostly glass, redwood, and white walls. It is empty. It is my challenge to furnish it. Archetypal dreams? How could they not be? Once I clustered them, their patterns became clear. Look at the German word *Dom*, the Italian *duomo*, the icy dome of an Eskimo igloo, the arch of blue sky, home of God: all images of shelter, safety, security. All are encompassed in the curved center of ultimate protection, the womb. And all of them are variations on the house of my self.

For you, the resonances of the noun *home* may have been altogether different. The word is filtered through experiential sieves unique to each of us. For Nancy Mairs it signaled a strong association with the body.

> The body itself is a dwelling place, as the Anglo-Saxons knew in naming it *banhus* . . . Through writing her body, woman may reclaim the deed to her dwelling.

If you have house dreams, they may reflect various layers of your psyche. Or perhaps you ended up focusing on a mismatch between outside and inside—the connection between outside appearance and inner reality, our masks and our naked selves, the stuff of the psyche few ever see—including ourselves.

Letting Go

In a New York workshop, I read a powerful poem by Sharon Olds to the group.

The Blue Dress

The first November after the divorce
there was a box from my father on my birthday—no
    card, but a
big box from Hink's, the dark
department store with a balcony, you could
stand and press your forehead against it
until you could almost feel the dense
grain of the wood, and stare down
into the rows and rows of camisoles,
petticoats, bras, as if looking down
into the lives of women. The box
was from there, he had braved that place for me
the way he had entered my mother once
to get me out. I opened the box—I had
never had a present from him—
and there was a blue shirtwaist dress
blue as the side of a blue teal
disguised to go in safety on the steel-blue water.
I put it on, a perfect fit,
I liked that it was not too sexy, just a
blue dress for a 14-year-old daughter the way
Clark Kent's suit was just a plain suit for a reporter, but I
felt the weave of that mercerized Indian Head cotton
against the skin of my upper arms and my
wide thin back and especially the skin of my
ribs under those new breasts I had
raised in the night like earthworks in commemoration of
    his name.
A year later, during a fight about
just how awful my father had been,
my mother said he had not picked out the dress,
just told her to get something not too expensive, and then
had not even sent a check for it,
that's the kind of man he was. So I

never wore it again in her sight
but when I went away to boarding school I
wore it all the time there,
loving the feel of it, just
casually mentioning sometimes it was a gift from
    my father,
wanting in those days to appear to have something
whether it was true or a lie, I didn't care, just to
have something.

I read it twice, then wrote the noun *gift* asking participants to cluster and write for eight minutes on whatever image
or memory produced the strongest emotional resonance.
Clustering the word *gift*, one of the participants, Marla
Johnson, expressed a welter of conflicting emotions.

In January my mother took me shopping for a black leather
handbag. I did not want, nor did I need, a black leather handbag. But my mother had decided she wanted to get me one, and
so we went shopping. It was just a month after Christmas, and
she had already bought me many gifts. I guess she didn't feel
she had bought me enough.

"Gift-shmift—who cares," I thought. "Spend time with
me, talk to me, hug me, laugh with me; *that* would be more valuable than ten million black leather handbags." Macy's, Alt-
man's, Lord & Taylor's; I could not find one I liked. I needed
space. I went to the ladies' lounge, sat on an ancient marble department store fixture, and decided, "What I really *need* is
snowboots; last week I froze my feet sloshing around in leaky
leather cowboy boots."

"Buy me snowboots," I told her, flushing, trying to be
nice. "If you want to buy me something I really want, buy
waterproof ones so my feet will be cozy."

"No," she said firmly. "You should have a black leather
handbag. Not too fancy. Not too small. Just big enough to
wear out to the theatre in the evening—with a pocket on the
outside to tuck your playbill into."

I can picture her at the theatre. She has a square *brown*
leather handbag and her playbill fits perfectly into it: un-
scrunched, unrolled, neat, and ultimately lady-like. I hated the
thought of having a handbag that *my* playbill would fit so perfectly into. I hated even more that, like her playbill, she was
trying to put me into a pocket, too.

Time stretched. She bought a black leather handbag for my sister, who had asked for one, and whose birthday was tomorrow. And I went home empty-handed, empty-hearted. Why couldn't I ask for what I really wanted—and why couldn't I accept what she had to give?

Now, do some Aware Breathing, open your Feeling Sketchbook to a new page, number and date. Write the word GIFT and circle it. Open your mind and be curious about what it will trigger. Let associations flow. An image, memory, or feeling will clamor for attention. Then write your way into, around, and through its emotional significance in a Word Sketch.

No noun can capture the pulsing common wealth of cells that make up any one living thing. We exist as verbs, always in process. There are no isolated events or entities in the universe.

SAM KEEN

Exploring the Act

Reread what you've written. What, if anything, reflects your pain, struggle, confusion, or dilemma? What is the underlying feeling? Is it one of yearning? Of anger? Of sadness? Of pleasure? You don't need to answer any of these questions; just know that all of your acts of writing will reveal patterns that sooner or later will speak to you. They are there for you to go back to, to reread, to rethink whenever you are ready.

Being, Doing, and Having Words

Verbs allow us to give a name to our actions: *I do*; to possessing: *I have*; to what we feel we are: *I am.*

- *Doing* is acting in the world. We write, cry, fall, climb. Action verbs enable us to acknowledge that the world is not static but a myriad of interconnected processes, always in motion, dynamic.
- *Having* indicates possession. I *have* an idea, a child, a house. Often we define ourselves through what we have—or don't have.
- *Being* reflects awareness. "I *am*. I exist. I am here, now." Being verbs link our sense of self with a condition or attitude: "I am afraid"; "I am a survivor."

Ruth Gendler wrote a poem which illustrates the power of these verb forms to express feeling.

why do you want to be alone?
I want to be alone to do my work
why do you want to be alone?
because I don't know how to be myself with others
why do you want to be alone?
I want to be alone because I'm afraid of love
why do you write?
I write to find out who I am
why do you write?
I write because for so long there was no one to talk to
why do you write?
I write because I have never not written
why don't you eat breakfast?
I don't eat breakfast because the morning is too short
why don't you eat breakfast?
I don't like to put the milk away in the morning
why don't you eat breakfast?
I only eat breakfast when I have to go somewhere quickly
why are you afraid?
because I was fed fear for breakfast
why are you afraid?
because the people who loved me were afraid
why do you want love?
I want love to protect me from the fears of others
why do you want love?
I want love to protect me from my fear
why do you want love?
because I'm hungry and cold
why do you want love?
because I know it's possible
why do you want love?
because love mirrors love

Doing, having, and being: Conventional grammar makes large distinctions between these three forms of verbs. It took me months of puzzling before I came to what was for me a surprising discovery: The distinctions are illusory. *Doing* always refers to a process, a state of transition. *Having* appears more stable because it shows possession: of material things, of qualities—yet, *having* is also illusion. In an uncertain world we are guaranteed nothing but change. We do not possess anything—we merely hold things or qualities while we are in process ourselves, that process being our life. *Being*, sounding the most permanent of the three, is a reality only of the present moment and subject to change in the next. Being is cousin to becoming. Verbs can only say what we are in the moment, what we have for the moment, what we are doing at the moment. Underlying all verbs is the potential for change in time and space.

These three verb forms reflect varying degrees of desire for permanence, as well as the instability of a dynamic system.

Letting Go: Action Verbs

Here is an action verb. In your Feeling Sketchbook write and circle CLIMB. Stay open to your feelings as you cluster. Something always comes to you. Flow with it and write a Word Sketch. Whatever happens, your increasing receptivity to your own process is central to becoming expressive.

Exploring the Act

As you reread your piece, look for a sense of motion, direction, shifts. Right now you are recording your emerging awareness of patterns. Later, the patterns will become part of larger patterns of meaning.

Letting Go: Having Verbs

To have or not to have. *Have* evokes not only images of material belongings, physical health, relationships, home, pneumonia, child, but also states or qualities of being or life we want to possess: peace, courage, freedom.

Now, in your Feeling Sketchbook, write and circle HAVE/HAVE NOT. See if you can gain clues to your perception of these feelings by clustering. Number and date your entry. As words and phrases come, know that you do not choose them; they are choosing you. Be receptive to when you cut through to something that resonates. Name and frame it in a Word Sketch.

Anyone can see that verbs and adverbs are more interesting than nouns and adjectives. Besides being able to be mistaken and to make mistakes verbs can change to look like themselves or to look like something else. They are on the move and adverbs move with them.

GERTRUDE STEIN

Exploring the Act

Reflect on whether you focused more on material possessions or abstractions, on what you have or what you feel you lack, on getting or spending. Pain has much to do with what we *think* we need and what we think we want to avoid.

Letting Go: Being Verbs

In chapter 3 you clustered (I WAS, I AM, I SHALL BE.) Before you look back at your entries of chapter 3, do a quick re-clustering of these three forms of the being verb and see where you are today, right now. When you are ready to read your entries from chapter 3, notice any changes in content of expression. Notice differences or similarities in feeling.

Letting Go: Expectation Words

There is another category of verb forms—helping verbs—which are used with doing, being, or having verbs. These extend our uniquely human ability to project further and further into a nonexistent future by (1) naming our expectations through such words as *ought*, *should*, *must*; (2) naming our hopes and suppositions: *might*, *may*; (3) expressing our rationalizations: *could*, *would*—implying, of course, that we cannot: "I would if I could but I can't."

In your Feeling Sketchbook experiment with (COULD.) Number and date your entry, and cluster to see where it leads you. Take no more than five to eight minutes. Now, while your mind is still in gear, turn the page, number and date, write and circle (COULD HAVE/COULD BE) and cluster again. Simply follow it where it takes you. Now go right on and make one more entry, (COULD HAVE BEEN/COULD HAVE HAD.)

Exploring the Act

We are in a downward spiral. It is a space and time in which we may strike out, blame, feel guilty, rationalize—all perfectly legitimate human acts—as long as we remember that these acts are short-term, surface ways of dealing with crisis and pain. We will invite the pain back when we realize we need to go deeper into the griefs of our lives. We can only distinguish the surface from the deeper structures of our lives by becoming aware through naming and framing feelings at the hub of our being.

I want to remind you that this is your language, these are your images, this is your exploration. Each brief Word Sketch named and framed adds dimension to your inner world, begins to clarify, opens you, reconnects you to yourself. Each Word Sketch represents a piece of the puzzle that is you: your pain, and your personal route to transformation. Learn to trust the best guide of all—yourself, your own expression. Listen to the sound of your own voice on the page.

Qualifying Words

Adjectives are the "coloring words" says author Shirley Jackson; they tell us more about the things we name. The word *glass*, for example: when we say "the glass half empty" or "the glass half full," *glass* is colored to suggest a negative or a positive image, despite that, literally speaking, the phrases mean the same thing.

Robin Rector Krupp produced her own version of an African poetic form called "Bantu." Note how the qualifying word *dirty* and its repetition changes the meaning and feeling of the entire piece.

> I write dirty words.
> My husband doesn't know.
>
> I write dirty words.
> When will I grow up?
>
> I write dirty words.
> My father would wonder why.
>
> I write dirty words.
> They are heavy in my heart.
>
> I write dirty words.
> We are all naked in our normalness.
>
> I write dirty words.
> My mother said I shouldn't.

I write dirty words.
I get frozen when I don't.

I spit up on the paper,
bad words stuck inside.

Seeing what I wrote
Makes me want to hide. ·

The qualifier, "dirty," characterizing the kinds of words that were "stuck" inside became a kind of emotional strange attractor for questions that were immediate and powerful— and revealing. The instructions had been to write two statements: the first concrete, immediate, speaking of doing, smelling, tasting, touching, hearing, seeing; the second, abstract, speaking generally, philosophically, even vaguely. For example:

I have to do the laundry tonight.
Into every life a little dirt must fall.

Cookies fill the chipped pottery jar.
Childhood is only a brief moment.

Notice how the qualifier "little" changes the naming word "dirt"; how the qualifier "chipped" affects "jar"; how the qualifying "dirty" changed the entire emotional tone of "I wrote dirty words," forms, radically different from "I write words . . ."

The key to the Bantu form is that you do not make a serious effort to connect the two statements logically. This permission to write what pops into your head without worrying about the cohesiveness of the two statements permits a slide into the slippery realm of feelings.

Letting Go

The Bantu form is simple: A concrete statement of doing or sensing, in Robin's case, "I write . . .", followed by a general statement or question. Robin's concrete statement turned out to repeat itself. It was not deliberate, but the emotional impetus of her focus carried her on down the page (all nine were written in less than five minutes). Don't forget: these two state-

By now I had sufficient experience of the workings of my own mind . . . to convince me of the necessity of continually admitting to myself in words those thoughts I was ashamed of . . . I did learn very soon how to know the signs that would tell me when I was evading an unadmitted thought— worry, depression, headache, feelings of rush and over-busyness. . . . Part of my mind seemed quite determined that I should not discover what the trouble was. I put up endless excuses and deceits . . . chief of these tricks of distraction was the making of most reasonable reasons to explain my own actions or desires, and the making of further reasons to explain why it was not necessary to look for any hidden thought, since the reason I was giving was so obviously adequate.

JOANNA FIELD

ments need not go together. Just write as many of these as is comfortable, tuning in to your immediate sensations for the first, to a larger perspective for the second. Later you will discover that the two go together in ways you didn't expect precisely *because* you didn't try to force them to go together.

Exploring the Act

As happened with Robin, you may hit on a strange attractor, in her case, not just any words but "dirty words." In reading her series of Bantus we glimpse a mixture of guilt, shame, perhaps most of all, an explosion of emotional expressiveness.

The Bantu combination is a deceptively simple form you can turn to as often as you wish. It will produce not only new insights but pleasure at the unexpected, which is something we have been talking about all along in this chapter.

Affirmation and Negation Words

This set of words is perhaps the most powerful of all in our emotional grammar. These words are emotionally primal, like *yes* and *no*. If the limbic brain is an acceptance or rejection system, capable of giving an emotional *yes* or *no* to an experience, it then becomes clear that the words *no* and *yes* are primary to what it means to be human. They confirm our power to choose, to affirm or negate, through language. They enable us to confirm our growing autonomy, something we seek to express very early in life.

I recently sat in an airport, watching a young father struggle with his two-year-old's discovery of the sacred no. "Are you Daddy's boy?" the father asked. Each time the child emphatically shouted, "No! Mommy boy!" There was as much distress in the father's increasingly insistent repetition of the question as there was obvious delight in the son's decided "No!"

The small child senses his power primarily in negation. The adult, like Wallace Stevens, perceives the connectedness between negation and affirmation.

> After the final no there comes a yes,
> And on that yes the future of the world depends.

No is the wildest word we consign to language.

EMILY DICKINSON

Letting Go

Now it's your turn to assert yourself through the sacred *yes*, the equally sacred *no*, or both. In chapter 3 you learned that the most fundamental limbic response is *yes* or *no*. In this chapter on emotional grammar, you are learning that *yes* and *no* are expressions of *interdependence*, that is, that *yes* alone can be both constructive and destructive; that *no* can be both destructive and constructive; that, taken together as extremes of a single continuum, you will experience a whole new range of options. *Yes* and *no* are both appropriate at different times. You cannot know one without knowing the other. Write and circle (YES/NO.) Recognize that this clustering is likely to land you in the midst of the most painful issues you are grappling with, the grieving you are doing, the personal crisis that is turning your world upside down. Trust your inner gyroscope by allowing a gradually increasing vulnerability. The safety net of your own words will support you. Don't forget that you are engaging in *your* process, coming from within you; it is not imposed from without. Write a Word Sketch that expresses what you found in your Cluster.

Exploring the Act

Whatever you wrote, it is important in this chapter to recall the other side of the coin: If *yes* is a sign of our most profound affirmation, it can also be a sign of submissive acceptance if we are afraid of contradiction or conflict. Similarly, *no* can signal assertiveness but also the rigidity of fear. Moreover, *yes* can also be qualified by *but*. *Yes* gives the go-ahead sign; *but* is the brick wall, the red light, the flooded bridge, and all too often, the excuse, the rationalization.

As you move through this book by reaching for denied feelings, remember that you are engaged in process. As long as you are in process, you are not bound by impossible absolutes. You are constantly framing feelings and trying on different frames for size. You are exploring the most subtle language of life: the language of feelings.

By honoring your process, you are willing to move to the known edges of your being, to recognize them and to test the expansion of those boundaries.

Words themselves come to us dragging their roots behind them: roots that are as long as the history of language. They satisfy our hunger for a language that crystallizes our intuitions and makes a syntax out of the crisis of our survival.

STANLEY KUNITZ

LOOKING AHEAD

With the next chapter we reach the centerpoint of our spiral through personal crisis. It is a paradoxical place, where we encounter the greatest depth of our pain—and, simultaneously, take the first real steps toward utilizing that pain for growth. It is here that we make the turn from descent to ascent, to realizing the possibilities that can heal us.

The recurrent moments of crisis and decision when understood, are growth junctures, points of initiation which mark a release from one state of being and a growth into the next.

JILL PURCE

A Private Darkness: How Far Down Is Down?

The spiral metaphor is at no time more powerful than when, in our deepest crises, we experience the uttermost depths of a private darkness. I drew wordless spirals. Although we associate a downward spiral with the negative image of an end, it is often the necessary beginning. The only

Figure 5.1

way back up is to first go all the way down. Paradoxically, the downward spiral leads to a still point at the center of the vortex of pain. We resist, not because the pain is unbearable, but because we fear the pain itself. We fear drowning in our own pain. But all transformation flows from that still center. Poet Galway Kinnell ends his poem "The Still Time" by reminding us that

> . . . there is time . . . still time
> for one who can groan
> to sing,
> for one who can sing to be healed.

We have descriptions for this dark time, such as "the dark night of the soul," the "existential crisis," even "disintegration before reintegration." A dark time can encompass days, months, sometimes years. It seems we all must confront at least one such period in our lives. It is a natural if terrifying time. Yet, although we cannot change facts or events, we can learn to face them. As Gendler writes in *The Book of Qualities,* "When you face pain directly, she will give you an ointment so the wounds don't fester."

There is an enormous difference between wounds that fester and wounds that heal cleanly. In learning to face pain, in experiencing pain through honest self-examination instead of hiding, we can let go of it. Becoming receptive allows us to move into active self-healing, a characteristic of the natural life force inherent in all living things.

Ironically, you can't predict how far down your pain may take you. In fact, you usually don't know you've hit bottom until afterward. It takes courage to allow yourself to fall into the very vortex of pain you fear so much, because you won't know how to get back up until, looking up, you can see how you got there. The images you've named and framed have their greatest value here.

What you learn about the dynamic nature of spirals is that you don't have to be locked up in your own story. You may continue to spiral down, to feel worse. But the life-line, the stabilizing influence, is the small act of naming and framing. It is the resting place that allows you to recognize where you are now. Facing your private darkness lets you discover your way out. Instead of merely suffering the pain, you choose to name it. Whether you spend only two minutes a day or ten, those minutes become a small clearing in the wilderness, a breathing space in which mysterious patterns in the chaos of feeling can emerge on their own and be recorded. In a real sense, you are making a willful choice to allow feelings to surface instead of blocking them—and, miraculously, that can be just enough to make a difference.

Poets and writers know the power of language to record, release, and transform these feelings into expression. In "After Great Pain," Emily Dickinson writes

Your father and mother didn't love you as much as you wanted them to. The most unacceptable thing we can imagine has already happened to us. We are abandoned, we will suffer. We will die.

SAM KEEN

I reel back in shock. I retreat into myself in a downward spiral. I fall toward darkness, unable to control my descent. This world is a void. No emotions, no feelings. Only the comforting and disturbing solitude of darkness and a dying. It is wintertime in my soul, a time of hibernation.

STUDENT

. . . We are, each one of us, our own prisoner. We are locked up in our own story.

MAXINE KUMIN

This is the hour of lead
remembered if outlived
as freezing persons recollect the snow—
first chill, then stupor,
then the letting go.

Or Langston Hughes in "End":

There are
No clocks on the wall,
And no time,
No shadows that move
From dawn to dusk
Across the floor.

There is neither light
Nor dark
Outside the door.
There is no door!

The words pound out these sorrowful rhythms of loss: stupor, lost, stuck, lead—but not dead. Naming expresses life's longing for itself.

But you need not be a great poet to use language to express your pain; what matters is that you *use* it. It can express what *you* need to say. Here is an example from a workshop participant.

There is grief in this life.
A forceful undertow
striving to pull me under
seizing the breath from my lungs and
saturating them with dark heavy water.
There is a tidal wave
waiting to overwhelm me
overpowering my spirit and
crushing me with its weight.
There is an ebony night with
no moon
no wind
no North Star to guide me
from this morass.

And another.

> No singer will sing
>   my pain, quiet as a
> monastery, it goes
>   round and round the
>   gardens, kitchens,
>   chapel,
> an everlasting litany
>   of loss
> quiet as lent
> solemn, organized,
> it treads well-worn tracks
>   again,
> never stops to
> fester or heal,
> chimes each hour,
> calls me to worship—
> but never again to sing.

Even the expression of utter despair is an affirmation. Even though you can't see beyond it, can't imagine the light side, can't know that things will change, you are giving voice to the unnameable.

LOOKING BACK: MY OWN DARK TIME

As I've discussed in previous chapters, I finally hit bottom in an isolated mountain cabin in the Sierra, almost ten years ago. I, too, had no idea how far down I would go. What follows is a combination of things I wrote at the time in my Feeling Sketchbook and later namings as I looked back on the experience. Together they helped me recognize it as a turning point in my life. Once I had the courage to go all the way down, I found the strength to come back up my own fearful spiral.

In a Feeling Sketchbook of that time, I came across a Word Sculpture (Figure 5.2) which exploded into a Cluster (Figure 5.3) and Word Sketch. It must have been an attempt to name and frame my terror. Looking back, I realize that it hardly comes close to expressing the level of psychic terror I felt at that time.

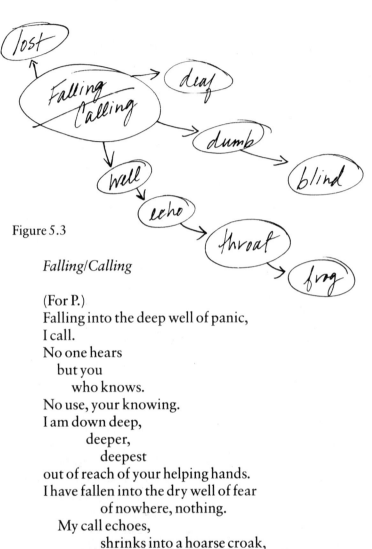

Figure 5.3

Denial is a refusal of painful self-knowledge. When someone or something threatens to breach this refusal, we receive an unconscious shock of the very vulnerability we have denied—a shock that often makes us retreat and more often makes us intensify our denial.

SHELBY STEELE

Falling/Calling

(For P.)
Falling into the deep well of panic,
I call.
No one hears
   but you
      who knows.
No use, your knowing.
I am down deep,
    deeper,
      deepest
out of reach of your helping hands.
I have fallen into the dry well of fear
    of nowhere, nothing.
  My call echoes,
     shrinks into a hoarse croak,
is swallowed by the silence of
     lostness.

LET IT CHOOSE YOU.
IT WILL CHOOSE YOU, IF YOU LET IT

Figure 5.2

    In my effort to find solitude for writing in that mountain cabin, away from the distractions I described in chapter 1, I believed I had come to a safe place; instead, it became my own, personal hell. Ironically, the very safety of the mountain cabin which I had chosen as a means of control triggered the terrifying spiral *out of control*. There was nothing I was more afraid of than myself. And now I was alone.

Those nights alone in the darkness were the worst. My fear worked its own destructive pictures, knotting my intestines. In that peaceful, isolated, silent, night cabin, my terror expressed itself in physical rigidity. I knew I had to stop fighting or lose my life. Again I turned to words, reciting, like a mantra, "This is. I am," over and over and over. The Word Sculpture in Figure 5.6 signaled a breakthrough in tightly compressed, jagged form.

Figure 5.4

Figure 5.5

Figure 5.6

Blue sky.
Spring. Lie.
Death. Die.
Small fists fight tears,
deny damp death
the brutal light of what is.
Swallow tears,
swallow pain,
don't name.
Swallow the right to cry. Die.
Pain is hobbled into
    Lie

Focusing on the everpresent, unnameable fear, I had risked a clear look at the unknown future. There it was: Dying. In my Feeling Sketchbook I find a nutshell sentence from that period that expresses my painful realization.

So. You're afraid of dying, the last loss, loss of control. But just to *accept* dying doesn't mean you actually have to die!

But my realization of the last loss didn't connect with my first loss. Alone in the Sierra darkness, I recalled advice from psychologist Jean Houston, to ask yourself "What has hurt you?" I was not looking for explanations; I was looking for pictures. Images reeled backward through years, jostling each other for attention.

March, 1945—early afternoon, sunshine flooding through an arched window, warming my back. My child-body suddenly tenses at the familiar whine of falling bombs. Shattering glass explodes its slivers against my back. A single, high-pitched scream rings in my ears; only later do I know it comes from my own throat. I am lifted, screaming, over shards of wall into the shocked silence of sunlight. The first stirrings reveal a broken landscape, cows torn in two; later, a white match-box car with a large red cross, parked amid fragments. Child's eyes fear-wide, throat silent, mind numbed. Yes. No. I tell myself, "This is not it."

Another image crowds into consciousness: a sad, small heap of familiar clothes neatly folded next to the ambulance, the brown woolen underwear of German winters on top—she was always cold—in the bone-chilling cold of not-yet spring's setting sun. Nuances of feeling: no home, nowhere to hide, but, no, this is not it either, I tell myself.

Abruptly, the film jogs into fast-forward. May, 1945—brilliant blue sky, a war over. Abruptly, my silent mental film stops at a single frame. In a German churchyard, a skinny seven-year-old stares at a stone engraved with the most important name in her small life. The evidence is incontrovertible. The silence shouts a dawning: dead. Body juices draw together into liquid fire, rise relentlessly. But the late spring sun says, "Look! Life-green spears of crocuses spring from immaculate graves." Something is out of place in this picture. A small, braided head burrows into a sturdy Bavarian apron, small fists crumple the flowered cloth deep into dry eyes as if to blind them, and she swallows, swallows, swallows down something like tears rising in the body—until they are controlled, locked away in a place beyond reaching. This film frame is in full technicolor: blooming spring world, child, grave, chiseled words, hot flood stayed, stopped, frozen. Yes, this is it.

In that solitary cabin, a third of a century later, something big gives way. This adult, with adolescent children of her own, hears her voice cry, "Mutti!" And again, "Mutti!" Hot tears spread like live flames, sear the throat, catch for a split-second, then explode. I cried, and could not stop. I cried, it seemed, almost without stopping, for four weeks. Words began to flood onto the paper brought for a different purpose.

I Remember

"Put on your shoes."
The command is calm;
child's mouth tastes fear.
We walk miles down from
her mountain into the village.
Child-body buzzes danger,
child's mind struggles in a tangled web of meaning;
child's heart knows, doesn't, doesn't want to know.
We arrive. On the hedge, a sign says "Peace."

Peace? Child's thicket of feelings chokes on the word;
child's fear beats its wings like a caged thing.
We stop.
New eyes must see what the child's pictures have hidden.
Wings stop beating. Time stops. Stop!
Mutti! Mother, Mére, there.
Under, beneath, inside,
locked in,
     away.
Stay!
The name engraved on polished stone:
No. Stop. No. Don't go!
Child's mind slams shut. Body speaks:
Heart pumps waves of liquid, looking for an exit,
through legs, trunk, arms, neck—explodes.
Child's eyes burrow into a flowered apron,
throat swallows and swallows and swallows.
Control.
We walk back, wordless, in the lying May sun.

As I write, now, today, twenty-two miles from the epicenter of California's 1989 earthquake I see, for me, the convergence of feeling in that mountain cabin was as radical as that jagged dance of solid earth under feet accustomed to gravity's pull. An old emotional order was giving way to a different way of being in the world. Chaos became the acceptance of absolute potential. It was total, terrifying, ultimately, life-saving.

An experience like this seems so personal, so unique, you can scarcely imagine another human being has ever experienced anything like it. Yet we know this is not so. My life-changing discovery was not at all unique. Novelist William Styron, in *Darkness Visible,* attributes his own breakdown into depression as an adult heavily to "incomplete mourning" for his mother's death when he was thirteen. He calls the denial of the catharsis of grief "an insufferable burden of which rage and guilt and dammed-up sorrow are a part."

Despite my doctor's blunt warnings, "You will die," I had fought surgery almost four years. My unplanned explosion into grief in that mountain cabin was followed closely by

Simone's angry outburst which I described in chapter 4. This opening to my emotional self in turn led to opening emotionally to my children, which in its turn led to my being able to choose surgery. Most important, it was the beginning of letting go of incapacitating fear to face life's uncertainties instead of trying rigidly to control them.

GRIEF AND LIFE'S LOSSES

One of the most devastating sources of our private darkness can come with the loss of a loved one—a parent, mate, close relative, or child. A void gnaws at us. The word *grief* suggests the grave, and may derive from an old French word for 'heavy.'

We tend to be mute in the face of devastating pain and let the grief recycle itself inside us. Naming and framing is a way of recording our emotional stages—clearing the way of marking their completion.

Pregnant with her second baby, Paula D'Arcy wrote her way through her devastation at the death of her husband and two-year-old daughter by composing letters to her lost child. Three months after the accident, she wrote this entry:

> Dear Sarah:
>
> I thought this pain would leave when I remembered I had choices. But choices make it worse than ever. Choices don't help at all because this new person doesn't know *how* to make choices. This new person has no skills at all.
>
> I'm sitting here with this open notebook, facing a page with a line drawn down the middle. Left side: "Pro—Move back to Connecticut." Right side: "Con—Stay here."
>
> I have to write all the thoughts down because I can't hold ideas in my head anymore. You and your father are all I hold in my head. And trying to make this decision is making me crazy. It's too hard. Making up my mind is too hard for me. But I'm not like this. Or I wasn't. How can I not know what I want?
>
> Why do you suppose I am alive? Will I find out? My life just makes no sense. I am flooded by questions without answers. My mind will never be still. Always Roy and Sarah. Roy and Sarah. That's all I know.
>
> When someone talks I can't really listen. Never before

have I been unable or unwilling to lend an ear to another's troubles. But I can't anymore. I'm a madwoman inside. I'm so saturated with hurt and questions there's no room for anyone else. There's hardly room for me. How could this happen to me? When will it stop?

Although the journey through mourning is lonely, letters let us express and share our mourning, let us change mourning into acceptance. We all have mourned, mourn now, will mourn someday. Not one of us is exempt, and it helps to be reminded that nothing stays the same, not even pain. Read this letter written by a widow whose husband was killed in Vietnam to the parents of a young man who died. She reaches out with words:

Dear J. and D.:

It is Memorial Day, a springtime holiday for most, a day that for me lives up to its name since Royce died. It is the right day, then, to reach out to you, to try to help when there is so little anyone can do.

I have spent years reflecting on what might be the ultimate pain. Perhaps I do that to steel myself in case a greater pain than the one I have experienced lurks someplace for me, or perhaps if there is a more ultimate pain than mine, mine will be easier to bear. I now realize with amazement that my definition changes with the seasons of my life: When I was a child in Germany and my mother died in the bombing, I felt the pain of losing one's mother had to be the all-consuming, ultimate sorrow anyone could be asked to bear. It was so fierce that out of love for my sisters and brother I never shared with them how deeply I was suffering because I felt I could not burden them with my pain on top of theirs. My mother, the source of all comfort, all caring, all warmth, all security, the very essence of love—dead.

When Royce died in Vietnam, I knew the pain of losing a mate was the ultimate one. A husband, a mate—what a miracle to have found him among millions to form this union for life, for warmth, for security, the very meaning of love. Then the choice was made for me and out of love for my children I did not share with them *until now,* twenty years later, how devastating this ultimate pain was for me.

Then, as my life went on as of course it had to, I often stood back like a spectator to my life's parade and marveled how *much* joy there was for me everywhere, including in watching my children grow up—how much caring, how much warmth amidst the struggle for security, but above all, how much hope, no, faith I found within myself that tomorrow or the day after there would be a new miracle for me. That faith never never left me, even tough sometimes it was grievously rattled and shaken.

Of late, watching my grown children's life unfold, I began to wonder—fear?—whether the ultimate pain is to know your child is suffering its ultimate pain, and yes, I do believe yours is the ultimate pain: watching your daughter's grief coupled with your own loss, sensing her small boy's confusion, feeling the agony that comes from knowing there is nothing you can do to change anything. The past is past forever, and the future is not yours to shape.

My hope and wish for you is that you have faith that Mary will shape her future into a new and worthwhile life. Take comfort from me: There *will* be a healing. All living things when hurt begin immediately the process of healing. It *has* to be that way, it *is* that way, because no one could live with the nauseating, steady pain all of you feel now. It is Nature's kindness, or God's benevolence to us, this process of healing. I have to admit that I have never made a complete peace with my God for the part He may have had in taking Royce—but I have always felt some strange gratitude for the part He must have had in allowing me to heal. It doesn't mean that the pain goes away altogether, it really never does, but it moves over and in private moments it appears and sits with you like a companion. It still does for me, and I talk to my pain and it becomes the link to the marvelously happy past which will not, must not, cannot be forgotten, but neither will this pain forever block out the joy of life—not if you open your eyes and heart.

I do not remember how long it took, but I do clearly recall the day when I *knew* that life can be, will be, or even *is* beautiful again. We lived directly on the Sacramento River. I had come home from work and was in the bedroom looking through the open door toward the living room and its large sliding glass doors facing the river. The sun was setting on the other side of the river, over there by West Sacramento, and it caused the entire river to light up in a solid stream of glistening, shimmering gold framed by the greenery of the trees on the far bank. It struck me as so incredibly beautiful, I caught my breath, a catch in my throat. And then, with total shock, I asked myself, "How *can* I think *anything* is beautiful, how *can* I feel such joy?" I have never forgotten that shimmering river, and I have never ceased looking for joy. It is there, for you. Please believe me.

With love and concern,

H.

PAIN AND PARALYSIS

When we are in a bad state of mind, it cannot be overruled by logic. The best-intended exhortations to "Pull yourself together!" have little effect.

My own pattern involved panic attacks triggered by acute anxiety, which might be described as a spiral leading to *explosion*. A common alternative is the flat, gray dullness of depression. Chronic depression might be considered a spiral leading to *implosion*—a collapse into nothingness. In either state, we can become paralyzed. Most people aren't aware of their own paralysis although most of us have experienced its symptoms, such as indecisiveness, agitation, inability to proceed, enervation, numbness. An incisive description of this state comes from novelist John Barth's *The End of the Road.*

> So I left the ticket window and took a seat on one of the benches in the middle of the concourse to make up my mind. And it was there that I simply ran out of motives, as a car runs out of gas. There was no reason to go to Lima, Ohio. There was no reason, either, to go back to the Bradford Apartment, or for that matter go anywhere. There was no reason to do anything.

Novelist William Styron describes this condition powerfully in his *Esquire* essay, "Darkness Visible."

> In depression, faith in deliverance is absent. The pain is unrelenting, and what makes the condition intolerable is the foreknowledge that no remedy will come—not in a day, an hour, a month, or a minute . . . One does not abandon, even briefly, one's bed of nails, but lies upon it wherever one goes . . . The gray drizzle of horror induced by depression takes on the quality of physical pain . . . I'd feel the horror, like some poisonous fogbank, roll in upon my mind, forcing me into bed.

Styron says the hallmark of depression is loss.

Perhaps the only choice we have is to choose what to do with our dead: To die when they die. To live crippled. Or to forge, out of pain and memory, new adaptations. Through mourning we acknowledge that pain, feel that pain, live past it. Through mourning we let the dead go and take them in. Through mourning we come to accept the difficult changes that loss must bring—and then we begin to come to the end of mourning.

JUDITH VIORST

There is an inner isolation in me. Friends suspect, but they're never quite sure. I feel like the tree in the forest: when I fall, who will hear the sound? Among cheerful, caring friends I clench my teeth and smile wider, swallowing searing tears of rage threatening my seeming serenity.

ANONYMOUS

I felt loss at every hand. The loss of self-esteem . . . my own sense of self . . . self-reliance. These losses can quickly degenerate into dependence, and from dependence into infantile dread. One dreads the loss of all things, all people close and dear. . . . Meanwhile my losses proliferated . . .

Loss: an abrupt single syllable. The word suggests decrease, damage, dispossession, bewilderment, irresolution, uncertainty, despondency, despair—and possible extinction. In short, loss is suffering. Piero Ferrucci, in *Inevitable Grace*, writes:

Suffering thrusts us into the realm of the inexplicable. When suffering becomes too strong, it imprisons our attention with its impersonal brutality. Its incomprehensibility undermines the psychophysical structure we have come to know as ourselves. In pain, mental or physical, we are faced with the concrete possibility of our own annihilation.

When such numbing pain reaches an unendurable peak, the unthinkable may suddenly become all too powerful, and suicide may present itself as a desirable alternative. Styron again:

. . . sitting in the living room, I experienced a curious inner convulsion that I can describe only as despair beyond despair. It came out of the cold air; I did not think such anguish possible.

He prepares for suicide by wrapping his beloved private notebook in an empty Grapenuts cereal box. His heart is pounding, knowing he has made an irreversible decision. He writes suicide notes, tears them up. Then he happens to hear the sudden soaring passage from Brahms' *Alto Rhapsody*, which

pierced my heart like a dagger, and in a flood of swift recollection I thought of all the joys the house had known . . . the voices and the nimble commotion, the perennial tribe of cats and dogs and birds. . . . All this I realized was more than I could ever abandon.

The issue of suicide is difficult. Suicide looks desirable because it is the ultimate escape from the seemingly unen-

*because
death is so lovely
so self-possessed
we have a tendency
to jump the gun . . .*

*and because
death is so
attractive in the
abstract
a rest
freedom from pain
we should bite our
lips to remember
it doesn't taste good
and it leaves a stain.*

PETER MEINKE

*One thing in my defense,
not that it matters: I
know something Carter
never knew, or Helene, or
maybe you. I know what
"nothing" means, and
keep on playing.*

JOAN DIDION

durable. It is the ultimate escape from our in-built time-consciousness: to stop the present, eradicate the past, and prevent an imagined future. Speaking for myself, for all my panic and fear, I had never had suicidal thoughts—after all, I perceived death as the ultimate loss of control. How could I voluntarily choose it? Instead, my unwitting isolation forced me into the visibility of my own private darkness. But then there was a turning point, a shift from denial to facing my pain; the path of survival rather than destruction. Even as I write, it dawns on me that the path I had been following may, on some deep level, have been an unknowing form of slow suicide—not as different as I might have thought from the long walk into an ocean.

This, though, is the crucial lesson we can learn from those bitter times when thoughts of suicide seem attractive: That we can face and acknowledge the desire for our own death without acting on it, and that to do so connects us to a fundamental life-affirming impulse, thus to a deep wisdom unreachable in a state of emotional denial. Wendell Berry says as much in an untitled poem.

> Willing to die
> you give up
> your will, keep still
> until, moved
> by what moves
> all else,
> you move.

Both Wendell Berry and Styron are speaking of moments of shift having to do with what Kahlil Gibran called "life's longing for itself." The life-force is dynamic; breakthroughs can occur only in conjunction with breakdowns of old orders. Breaking the boundaries of locked-in feelings generates new, open horizons and gives us options for healing. As Nathaniel Branden puts it in *The Psychology of Self-Esteem*:

> When we bury feelings, we also bury ourselves. It means we exist in a state of alienation. We rarely know it, but we are lonely for ourselves.

We are lonely for the aliveness of our own feelings.

HANGING IN THERE

The sense of flatness typical of the downward spiral and hitting bottom cannot be broken through by sheer determination, or will, or exhortation. It takes tiny movements, small acts such as Aware Breathing or word sculpting, which paves the way for the writing that will inevitably come.

If you don't have the energy to write, where do you start? What can you do? Breathe. Breathing is life. An entry reflects the wisdom of the innocent and unseasoned, my then thirteen-year-old, Suzanne.

> Suzanne admonishes me: "Mom, your breath flows in and out; you don't even have to try. It just does it by itself. Just breathe in and out, and you'll *feel* there's nothing to be afraid of. Nothing at all. Just look at the world and breathe; look at the lights in the valley. See? There's nothing bad at all." For a few relieving moments, I breathe easier.

Aware Breathing, as discussed in chapter 1, is a simple, minimal step. We are already breathing, whether we feel good or feel pain. Letting ourselves become aware that we *are* breathing is already a reaffirmation of life. Setting ourselves the task of paying attention to our breathing encourages us to become receptive to other things, to feelings covered with the gray smog of despair. Awareness of breathing is always a first step to open us, wherever we are. Acknowledging that we still breathe, we gradually discover ways to face our deeper pains. Waves provide a metaphor here. Like our breathing, waves have pattern, but it is an irregular one, like all things in nature, including human life and feelings. Much of our fascination with waves comes not from their repetition but from their variability and the surprises within the pattern. To help us become aware of variation in seeming endless pain, we need to become aware of its shifts.

Word Sculpture helps us to extend this same awareness. Word sculpting is a way of becoming still and quiet in the pain. It is a way of listening to its irregular rhythms. It is a way of honoring where you are in the here and now, a way of not fighting before you are ready, a way of being nonjudgmental about yourself. It is a way of simultaneously focusing and

Sometimes pain just is. Today I am simply in pain.
The pain I have has no explanations. My pain is so deep that it never had a cause, and has no need of a cause. What could its cause have been? Where is that thing so important that it stopped being its cause? Its cause is nothing, and nothing could have stopped being its cause. Why has this pain been born all on its own? If they put it into some dark room, it wouldn't give light, and if they put it into some brightly lit room, it wouldn't cast a shadow. Today I am in pain, no matter what happens. Today I am simply in pain.

CESAR VALLEJO

unfocusing. At a time when you may be unable to write there is still time for Word Sculptures.

When pain seems too overwhelming to endure, when suicide seems attractive, you still can draw. Doodle. It is one small step you can make away from extinguishing the only life you have. With so little left to lose, you can chuck your baggage, take off your costumes, remove all your masks, and allow yourself to be naked to yourself.

Remember, we can only begin where we are. The power of Word Sculpture is that you do nothing more than move your pencil over the page and let patterns form themselves. You don't have to try. At the same time, it gives your hand something nonthreatening to do. The drawing moves you forward, even if you are only treading water. Cling to the moving pencil and Word Sculptures will help you tread water when you think you are drowning.

At a time when I remained mute, dissolved in my emotional and bodily turmoil, I turned to Word Sculptures. They helped me hold on to something; they also opened my ears to the cry of denied pain, my inner eyes to my self as it was, not as it ought to be.

The strange patterns that appeared became the strange attractors for words and phrases spontaneously presenting themselves. The words became patterns within patterns. Only later did I understand that this doodling hadn't been mindless at all. In fact, it was simultaneously mindful *and* mindless: mindless because I wasn't making an effort; mindful because a deeper voice in me began to sound again.

Just accept for now that you may continue to spiral down, to feel worse. But the life-line comes in the small act of naming and framing. When even that becomes too difficult, you have fall-back tools that are undemanding and simple: Breathing and Word Sculptures.

Letting Go

Whenever you feel overwhelmed, do a quick Word Sculpture in your Feeling Sketchbook and let the words and phrases adorning it tell you where you are now, at this moment. Date and number your entry, then draw a single line, moving your hand in whatever direction it wants to go. Do this rapidly, taking no more than a second or two to get the over-all pattern onto the page. Now embellish with lines, dots, circles, squares, following the wisdom of the hand. Place what words occur to you wherever they seem to fit best, playing with the design until you are satisfied.

Look at the word-shape you've created. If the pattern and the words of the pattern suggest anything to you as you look at it, see if you can give it a name that expresses it. Write it and circle it as a new entry in your Feeling Sketchbook, then cluster it until a sense of direction, a feeling or an image, presents itself; then write a Word Sketch. Don't censor; simply release what wants to come out.

You have one more naming option available to you: name anything troubling you in the *now* you'd like to let go of for a few minutes, an hour, the next day. No big promises, no New Year's Resolutions, just little things: nutshells. For example, I find the following nutshells in my Feeling Sketchbook:

- I, Gabriele, will put the chest pain on hold until tomorrow morning, when I will look at it with new eyes;
- I, Gabriele, will forego writing chapter 5 today—without guilt—because I *choose* to do other things;
- I, Gabriele, acknowledge the lump in my throat as mine.

Simple statements, little spin-offs from the Word Sculptures. They increased my awareness of the destructive patterns to which I had been oblivious. Having named something burdening you, you can now give yourself permission to let go of it for a while without feeling that you are running away from it. These interludes of letting go, these breathing spaces, can, in time, allow new action, new possibilities, to emerge.

The lesson is this: Hang in there when all seems darkest. Acknowledge your feelings and allow yourself to take breaks. Interrupt the spiral of self-blame, self-doubt, guilt—whatever uses your energy negatively—by going easier on yourself instead of becoming even more demanding.

To go in the dark with a light
is to know the light.
To know the dark, go dark.
Go without sight,
and find that the dark, too,
blooms and sings,
and is traveled by dark feet
and dark wings.

WENDELL BERRY

METAPHORS FOR HITTING BOTTOM: REACHING OUT

Our private darkness has many faces, so many that we can rarely name them except metaphorically. "It feels like . . . , It feels as if . . ." And so, we search for the names that will make our private darkness tangible. Metaphor is likely to be the only way to identify—and therefore express—the experience of hitting bottom. Others have faced this visible darkness, and the names they found can help us to identify our own. Dante's metaphor in the *Divine Comedy* is one of the best-known.

> In the middle of the journey of our life
> I found myself in a dark wood,
> For I had lost the right path.

Some metaphors that may speak to you are: checkmate; blocked by a wall; imprisonment; tangled in barbed wire; locked in a box; behind glass walls; swallowed by a boa constrictor; sand in the oil; a millstone or an albatross around the

*To be helpless means to be
mute,
to sit silent
in cold gray dust,
like a stone, nameless,
voiceless as a prisoner.
To be helpless means to
have
no ears to have a shoelace
tied around the tongue
to touch the grass and not
to feel
the sun
all stretched out there
licking her fur . . . .*

C. CRAWFORD

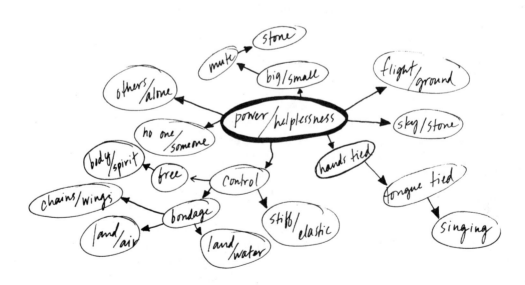

Figure 5.7

neck; bearing a cross; walking into a stiff headwind; feeling impotent; beating against a locked door; feeling invisible—all of these capture a sense of paralysis, an inability to act, a restriction of movement, a block.

For me, the key metaphor became a sense of utter fragility. I felt infinitely breakable. I was the glass vase on a high shelf in an earthquake.

Reaching for a metaphor is a bridge to feelings. If we cannot run from shattering pain, depression, the numbness of loss, we can name it and frame it. Catherine Crawford, then one of my students in a graduate seminar, clustered POWER/ HELPLESSNESS and discovered a meaningful personal metaphor: a "stone's muteness."

During a crisis, a German woman, Eva Riek, named and framed her oppressive feelings in small metaphoric leaps:

Sunday Depression

Since Saturday it squats on the door step.
While Sunday church bells sound, it takes its
   place at the breakfast table
and you know
   the coffee will be cold again,
   the ham salmonella-infested,
   the toast moldy,
   the cheese full of maggots.
Yearning to escape the crushing numbness
of the one-hundred-eighty-minute hours,
your feet wander aimlessly over manure-soaked
   meadows.
There, next to the flowers, trampled and lifeless,
you stumble across birds with broken wings;
in the drought-stricken lake the white-stomached fish
   lie belly-up;
the dying trees in the forest drive you once more into
   your imprisoned freedom.
And there, gathered around your easy chair,
you meet them all:
   the missed opportunities
   the strangled wishes,
   the withered dreams of past Sundays.

In the engulfing infinite dusk,
   your shaking hand spills red wine.
Sounds of evensong.
Translated by G. Rico

Clustering allows you to reach for metaphors that name feelings that feel unnameable. Become still, allow feelings to speak without forcing them, and you will discover your own metaphors that can help you see where you are, and perhaps suggest where you might go.

Letting Go

Number and date your entries in your Feeling Sketchbook, and cluster any or all of the following. Stay open to possible metaphors that fit your frame of mind at this time.

 SHATTERED   WOMB/TOMB

 INSIDE/OUT

 TRAPPED
                    RUNNING BLIND

 ABANDONED   TAILSPIN

 CLING   HUNGER

If these words don't feel right, or others come to you that seem more appropriate, use them; allow any connections to emerge that wish to.

Letting Go

You may feel the need to do more to put you in touch with that private darkness. Depending on your need, in your Feeling Sketchbook cluster KNOTS and see what emerges for you. If it feels right, write a Word Sketch that expresses what has emerged.

On another page, cluster LOCKED IN/LOCKED OUT. Be open. Follow it where it leads you.

On another page, cluster WALL, then write a Word Sketch when you perceive a pattern.

Stay in this frame of mind for as long as there is some small urge to tap that darkness. Each Cluster and Word Sketch will produce something: a tiny insight or a major epiphany—even if you don't see it until you reread your pieces at a later time.

Exploring the Acts

Whatever the images—broken glass, falling out of control, being buried alive, fleeing pursuit—simply recognize which one or ones seemed to strike a chord for you. No need to analyze or force explanations. It is enough to let images surface for now. In time they will take on a dimension and meaning that may not be available yet. Remember, there are no right or wrong answers here. You'll see a pattern, sooner or later, as you continue to name and claim your feelings.

GENERATING YOUR OWN METAPHORS

Perhaps none of the suggestions above really captures your personal feelings at this time of crisis. What happens during great pain? What does great pain feel like? An earthquake? A volcano? A waterfall? The impact of a wrecking ball on the wall of a condemned house? A compost heap? Is it a leaden feeling? Or is it agitated?

Letting Go

What does *your* pain feel like? First, name it by clustering MY PAIN IS LIKE . . When you sense something that fits, frame it by writing a Word Sketch. Number and date your entry.

Illness is a creative opportunity.

DR. KENNETH PELLETIER

Exploring the Act

If any metaphor surprised you, flow with the moment by writing or word sculpting it. It doesn't take much time. Be aware though how some of your metaphors take on a life of their own, speaking to you in ways no explanation or analysis can. You don't want to force significance; it will show its face when you are ready. It will connect to events and feelings in your life you cannot yet anticipate.

Understand that pain will rarely feel the same way twice, rarely fit the same metaphors. That is because we respond to our inner and outer worlds differently at different junctures in our life, at different hours in the day, at different moments in an hour. Explore and capture in metaphors these differences as often as you need or want to.

REACHING OUT BY REACHING WITHIN

When despair is deepest, it helps to reach out. If no one is there, as often happens in our struggles, you do what you needed to do in the first place: you reach out to your self through a dialogue. In a way, a written dialogue is like a dream; you supply the characters and the lines and you play both parts. It is another way of tapping parts of yourself you may not be aware of.

Letting Go

Numbering and dating your entry in your Feeling Sketchbook, cluster ME/OTHER. The "other" in the dialogue could be:

- a person with whom you have an unresolved question, one that will stay unresolved because there is a rift too big to mend;
- a person with whom an actual dialogue is impossible, for instance, a dead father, mother, sister, brother, a distant friend, or former lover;
- a wise person from history you admire, someone who you think might give you some answers, some sense of direction (three that come to mind are Socrates, Christ, or Shakespeare);
- a feeling: fear, anxiety, a doubt, or any other that is very strong in you at the moment;
- an animal or a plant, particularly ones that please you; perhaps an oak or pine tree, a favorite rose bush, a well-loved pet, or a wild animal, like an owl, tiger, or dolphin;
- an imagined stranger or "guide," someone you could turn to when actual people are not available in your time of crisis.

On this last point: If you don't have a guide now, it isn't hard to find one. Take a moment to close your eyes and move into Aware Breathing. As you breathe, simply invite a guide into your mental vision. Sit quietly and pay attention to the pictures in your head. Trust the process. Your guide will take his or her own shape. Someone will walk into your mind's eye who looks friendly, empathetic, willing to talk with you. Give him or her a name. Should the guide look threatening, simply notice what makes you uncomfortable instead of shrinking from it. Use him or her to ask questions in your dialogue.

Once you have an "other," cluster TALK WITH . . . and see where your inner voice takes you. Voice any questions that present themselves. Ask enough questions and they may trigger some tentative answers you had no idea were possible. If anything intrigues or puzzles you, turn the page, number and date a new entry, give it a name and circle it. Write in the form of a dialogue, beginning with the question and then letting the "other" respond.

Exploring the Act

You may want to wait for another day to reread your dialogue. Or you may want immediate feedback. Do whatever feels better to you. But note some of the following: what kind of guide you chose, whether real or imagined; a creature from the natural world; a person. You may already have a sense of how useful or useless this guide was. Don't judge, just notice. You may notice that the issues in the dialogue were already familiar, like a broken record. Or you may see a slightly new angle. Occasionally, there is a complete shock. Right now is not a time for analysis but simply a time for noticing, for allowing the emotional *you* to surface and have its say. You are in the process of becoming aware of what songwriter Paul Simon called the "sounds of silence." Let them speak their language without demanding anything of them. The most important business of this chapter is not to get answers or even to frame logical questions—we have done this all our lives—but to be open to what *is*. Herein lies the key to coming out of your tailspin whole.

If you are drawn to the dialogue form, write several of these. Number and date each entry. Each will provide a small but significant piece of a larger pattern. They may not mean much to you now, but look back at the entries in a few days or weeks. You may find a strange attraction in them—some central issue or looping fractal design of feelings that may be a surprising key to a later configuration.

PAINTING YOUR EMOTIONAL SCENE

Another approach to metaphor that may work for you is to relate your feelings to symbolic spaces. Intense feeling states are reflected in our images of places. Naming these, pinpointing them on our personal world maps, is a way of giving them voice. Read Stanley Kunitz' poem, "The Scene," aloud to yourself and note the slow, heavy feel of the four nouns that set the scene, nouns he repeats in the last line.

The Scene

Night. Street. Lamp. Drugstore.
A world of dim and sleazy light.
You may live twenty-five years more.
Nothing will change. No way out.

You die. You're born again and all
Will be repeated as before:
The cold ripple of a canal.
Night. Street. Lamp. Drugstore.

There is a jaggedness of feeling here, a sense of alienation reflected in Edward Hopper's painting, *Night Hawks* (see Figure 5.8).

© 1991 The Art Institute of Chicago, All Rights Reserved

Figure 5.8   Edward Hopper, American, 1882–1967, *Nighthawks,* oil on canvas, 1942. Friends of American Art Collection, 1942.51.

Letting Go

Cluster the phrase THE SCENE and see if words emerge that correlate with where you are in your feeling world. This Cluster can be a kind of mirror image of your inner feeling state. When you sense an emerging pattern, give it shape in your Feeling Sketchbook by writing a Word Sketch that follows Kunitz' model: eight lines, four nouns at the beginning and again at the end, stopping almost every line at the end, even using fragments ("No way out"). If your cluster contains more feelings or images than can be contained in these eight lines, choose four more nouns and write another, or as many as you like. It is a pattern that does not grow stale. The nouns become like the two slices of bread of a sandwich: they *contain* the ingredients in the middle; they complement the ingredients; ultimately, the whole will be more than the sum of its parts. The form is another way of getting at the indirection of feeling.

Exploring the Act

You may have done only one of these, or a series, depending on how sensitive you are to place. For now, simply look at whether your scene is a real or an imaginary landscape—or both. Look at your nouns and see if a pattern becomes immediately apparent. If you did several, notice whether the focus was similar in each or whether it seemed different. Simply notice. Make no judgment; draw no conclusion.

You are in the process of naming and framing your private darkness, whatever it is. It is an act. By its very nature, acting keeps you from staying paralyzed. In the doing, although it may not feel like it now, there is movement, a shift, however slight. It may be a while before you can pinpoint the shift. Just remember, the life force struggles to assert itself.

INVERSE CLUSTERING

In any private darkness it is difficult to know where to look for help. Submerged in a whirlpool of pain, it is hard to believe that the impetus for moving through it comes from within; it

Lost
Stand still. The trees
ahead and bushes beside
you
Are not lost. Wherever
you are is called Here,
And you must treat it as a
powerful stranger,
Must ask permission to
know it and be known.
The forest breathes.
Listen. It answers,
I have made this place
around you.
If you leave it, you may
come back again, saying
Here.
No two trees are the same
to Raven.
No two branches are the
same to Wren.
If what a tree or a bush
does is lost on you,
You are surely lost. Stand
still. The forest knows
Where you are. You must
let it find you.

DAVID WAGONER

is even harder to believe we can even recognize the key that will unlock our grieving. Again, indirection is essential. The clustering process may help you open to your self. Use another form of clustering to reach out to your own language when you either lack the emotional distance to find a starting word or have too many emotional words rushing through your mind. Inverse Clustering, by leaving the center blank, is a discovery process at a very deep level.

The process is simple: cluster in reverse *in order* to discover your own center. Draw a circle, leave it blank. Cluster whatever floats into consciousness around it. Remember that all chaos has pattern, form, shape. Let your grief, loss, despair, bewilderment, sadness, anger, or whatever it might be shape itself. Let the chaos of images, feelings, memories spill onto the page. Trust the process; something will shift into a pattern meaningful to you.

At some point the emotional nuances producing the Cluster become apparent in a word or phrase. Often the word or phrase is a surprise; sometimes, a variation on a familiar theme. In clustering around a blank circle, we make ourselves particularly sensitive to noticing the non-verbal feedback loops of our feelings.

The aim here is to bring into consciousness a turning point, a tiny shift from a downward spiral to an upward spiral. This small moment offers a key to feelings denied, distorted, or buried, making it possible to enter into the process of active self-healing. It is a moment of expectant stillness leading to new ways of seeing. Make as many entries of Inverse Clustering in your Feeling Sketchbook as you feel the need for.

Letting Go

Focus on Aware Breathing for a minute or two, more if you wish. In your Feeling Sketchbook, date and number a new page, then draw a circle, but leave it blank. Cluster *around* this blank circle—whatever comes to mind, in any direction it takes you. Stay open; don't censor. Trust your mind to discover a nuance which wants to be held in a word or phrase. Keep clustering; something will emerge if you stay out of its way.

Exploring the Act

Reflect on your own thinking and feeling processes for a few moments.

I have forgotten the word I intended to say, and my thought, unembodied, returns to the realm of shadows.

OSIP MANDELSTAM

- Notice how long you clustered randomly.
- Notice when you became aware of a pattern.
- Notice whether the naming was expected or a surprise.
- Notice whether you experienced an illumination of something you were not previously aware of.
- Notice whether you wrote only of darkness or whether you experienced a shift to some glimmer of light.

Just know this: no entry is wasted time. *Every single entry* contributes to an emerging pattern. Your very receptivity to nuances is itself healing. After clustering around that blank center, more often than not, a strange attractor will reveal itself, something normally unsaid, perhaps something you always thought unsayable. Experiment with Inverse Clustering as often as you feel the need. In experimenting with your own awareness, you are giving yourself permission to be confused, to say "It's OK not to know what is right, not to know what to do." With Inverse Clustering you honor the empty space of your private darkness.

In my case, I felt something was eluding me. As my paper filled with images, the center remained blank. I had denied, pretended, swept my feelings under the rug for so long recognition came only when I stopped to explore the wild pattern of words and phrases (see Figure 5.9).

Suddenly I could name the puzzle. The words FRAGILITY/FEAR filled my blank—I had named a host of fearful feelings constricting my breathing, my living, rendering me powerless, clamping such a strangle-hold on my throat that it produced intolerable physical pain.

Gradually—and this is a promise—you will get glimmers of understanding, as I did. Those glimmers will lead you toward finding the personal pattern that lies hidden within infinite possibilities. It is *your* process, not someone else's. Do not superimpose someone's steps on your being, on your pain. Let your own ongoing patterns gently lead you to insight.

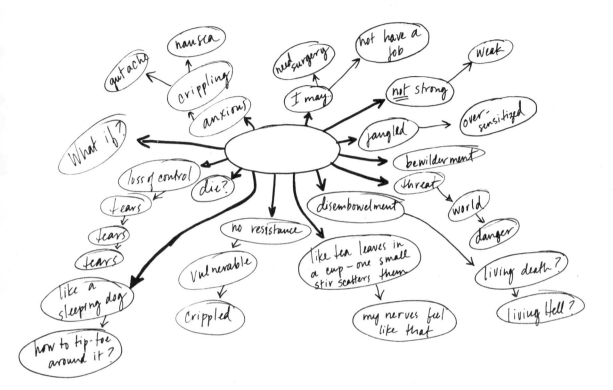

Figure 5.9

Your pain is yours. Own it by naming it. Only then will it let you go. Poet Audrey Lorde, in *The Cancer Journals,* writes

> I want to write of the pain I am feeling right now, of the lukewarm tears that will not stop coming into my eyes—for what? For my lost breast? For the lost me? And which me was that again anyway? For the death I don't know how to postpone? Or how to meet elegantly?

Trust that inner chaos has pattern. Trust the inner gyroscope which will orient these patterns. Trust that these Word Sculptures and Word Sketches will inspire new ways of seeing patterns in pain, ways you never before imagined. In naming and framing our private darkness, we are, in an important sense, befriending it instead of denying it. In return, this silent and fertile darkness will allow new growth. Surrender to it. In the process the pain will lessen, and, consigned to its proper place, will permit us to learn what it has to teach.

ALL THINGS CHANGE

Remember one thing in the dark night of the soul: *all things change*! Nothing in life stays the same—not even our pain.

My youngest daughter, Simone, was on the fifth floor of her university's library when the 1989 earthquake hit. Shelves collapsed, books flew in all directions, and students bolted. Standing quite still in a doorway, she kept repeating in a strong voice: "It WILL stop!" It was a small moment of wisdom. If it is true that all things change, no matter what we do, we can find an opening to possibility. In our bottomless despair, or grief, or fear, we are rarely aware that, as Theodore Roethke writes in "The Poet and His Critics,"

> The moment before Nothingness, before near annihilation, the moment of supreme disgust is the worst. When change comes it is either total loss of consciousness—symbolical or literal death—or a quick break into another state, not necessarily serene, but frequently a bright blaze of consciousness that translates itself into action.

That "bright blaze of consciousness" is enough to initiate change. Audrey Lorde understood the destructive power of denied pain.

> I must let this pain flow through me and pass on. If I resist or try to stop it, it will detonate inside me, shatter me, splatter my pieces against every wall and person I touch.

In crisis, the shift begins when the bright blaze of consciousness makes you aware that pain cannot be pushed away, or pushed off on others with blame. So we can ask in our own way, as Lorde does in hers: "Is this pain and despair that surround me a result of cancer, or has it just been released by cancer?"

Then, as she describes it, comes the small intimation of a major shift in feeling.

> Spring comes, and still I feel despair like a pale cloud waiting to consume me, engulf me like another cancer, swallow me into immobility, metabolize me into cells of itself. I need to remind myself of the joy, the lightness, the laughter so vital to my living and my health. Otherwise, the other will always be waiting to eat me up into despair again. And that means destruction.

William Styron in an *Esquire* article titled "Darkness Visible," testifies to a life force that moves beyond the bottom of the spiral. He discovers that

> depression is not the soul's annihilation; men and women who have recovered—and they are countless—bear witness to what is probably its only saving grace: it is conquerable.

The naming of your pain is a private key. It may not work right away, but it *will* work if you don't rush it. Simply be open to noticing and then record what you notice in your Feeling Sketchbook. The key will not only find the right lock, it will *un*lock a door to new options.

Author Tobias Wolff struggled with his childhood images of his absent father. He coped by banishing the fact of his father's desertion from his mind. When his own first child was born prematurely, he held the infant for the first time.

> Something hard broke in me, and I knew I was more alive than I had been before. But at the same time, I felt a shadow, a coldness at the edges. It made me uneasy, so I ignored it, I didn't understand what it was until it came upon me again that night so sharply I wanted to cry out. It was about my father, ten years dead by then. It was grief and rage, mostly rage, and for days I shook with it when I wasn't shaking with joy for my son, and for the new life I had been given.

Only when he faced the feelings was he released from the destructiveness of his suppressed rage.

One of my students, Mike Valter, in a five-minute vignette, sees the glimmer of something beyond despair in his last two lines.

. . . What we are blind and deaf to within ourselves, we are also blind and deaf to in the outer world, whether it be playfulness, poetic feeling, aesthetic sensitivity, creativity, or the like.

ABRAHAM MASLOW

I speak of a landscape upended by earthquake.
I speak of anger and rage at death,
the desolation of the embrace of an unloving coldness.
The hunger goes beyond the belly,
the thirst goes beyond the throat.
We murder with our mouths—
we heal with our mouths.
There is something beyond cerebral here:
footsteps make hollow echoes
down the corridors of time. There is time
out of mind here. To add insult to injury,
a rain falls.
A small hope rises from the rubble, the
chaos, the pain—the phoenix rising from its ashes?

Inverse Clusters and Word Sketches, as well as Word Sculptures and Aware Breathing, are all tools to help us move into the upward turn of the spiral. We have been using them to discover painful feelings we have denied, but these tools can also serve to relearn a sense of joy.

CONCLUSIONS AND LOOKING AHEAD

In *The Book of Qualities,* J. Ruth Gendler expresses a deeply human paradox.

> Joy drinks pure water. She has sat with the dying and attended many births. She denies nothing. She is in love with life, all of it, the sun and the rain and the rainbow. Although she is spontaneous, she is immensely patient. She does not need to rush. She knows there are obstacles on every path and that every moment is the perfect moment. She is not concerned with success or failure or how to make things permanent.
>
> At times Joy is elusive—she seems to disappear even as we approach her. Yet, she waits for us. Her desire to walk with us is as great as our longing to accompany her.

No matter how deep our suffering, joy has a desire to walk with us. All thumbs look similar, but our unique thumb-print storms need to be given voice. In writing them, we move *through* our pain and come out whole.

The dark night of the soul often takes place in the light of day. Darkness is a subjective experience, not objective. Sometimes, we need only look up from ourselves to see the sun shining all about us.

You have been naming and framing the pain of your private darkness. You may come back to this chapter again. In the spirals of your life, there may be other private darknesses. The difference is that you will have been given powerful tools that make the darkness easier to confront. Your own words, your own patterns, your own shifts in perception have enormous power to frame and to give you a new sense of options when all seems dark and impossible.

Having hit bottom, let's see how, like the princess of my child's fairy story, we can make friends with our glass hearts, despite our fears about its hair-line cracks. The best way I know is to make friends with our pain, to invite it to tell us what it wants to say. Having moved downward into the center of the pain, let's now explore the patterns of the upward swing of the spiral and see how our consciousness of time plays a vital role in our healing.

The real questions are the ones that obtrude upon your consciousness whether you like it or not, the ones that make your mind start vibrating like a jackhammer, the ones that you "come to terms with" only to discover that they are still there. The real questions refuse to be placated. They barge into your life at the times when it seems most important for them to stay away. They are the questions asked most frequently and answered most inadequately, the ones that reveal their true natures slowly, reluctantly, most often against your will.

INGRID BENGIS

Reversing the Spiral: An In-Between Time

With this chapter we move into the upward arc of the emotional spiral. This is an in-between season much like the cold March day when, despite snow and the stark outlines of trees, we get a whiff of the faint smell of spring. It is an interim time, the scarcely perceptible in-between time of blurred boundaries, of letting go of the old as the sense of something different shimmers: the beginning of the shift from hurting to healing. This in-between time helps us become receptive to "noticing" which, in turn, makes change possible.

In exploring the center of the vortex as we did in the preceding chapter, you have come face-to-face with your pain. Wherever you are at this point, you need to understand one thing: you are reading this book because you know pain. You are realizing there are no magic, instantaneous formulas. You are willing to deal constructively with your pain. You sense that change is ultimately up to you. You may have experienced some personal breakthroughs although suffering is still a reality. The important thing in this in-between time is the act of noticing.

Mark Twain, having lost a son, a daughter, his wife, and finally another daughter all within the few months before his own death, describes in *The Autobiography of Mark Twain* that in-between state with the metaphor of a burned house.

> A man's house burns down. The smoking wreckage represents only a ruined home that was dear through years of use and pleasant associations. By and by, as the days and weeks go on, first he misses this, then that, then the other thing. And when

he casts about for it he finds it was in that house. Always it is an *essential*—there was but one of its kind. It cannot be replaced. It was in that house. It is irrevocably lost. He did not realize it was an essential when he had it; he only discovers it now when he finds himself hampered by its absence.

In-between: you are neither wholly what you were and not yet what you can become. The word *between* comes from the German root *dwo*, meaning 'at a middle point of two.' It is an intersection, an interim period, an ambiguous stage, a noticing of feelings instead of fighting them. If the aim of the preceding chapters has been to give you tools to face fear, rage, anger, hostility, suppression, denial, the aim of this chapter is to help make you aware of the role time plays in healing.

This is the time to pace yourself. It is the time between the disintegration of your old order and the reintegration of possibility. It is the time between where you were and where you are headed. As you notice instead of deny or suppress, your body and psyche can begin to move again. The most immediate act of noticing is Aware Breathing, focusing on the moment between inhalation and exhalation.

Letting Go

Begin by breathing. Take a breath, as deep as your lungs will permit, and notice the moment at which you move from inhale to exhale. Move into a normal breathing cycle, but be aware. Now focus your attention on the state between exhaling and inhaling. To me, it is a profound moment; as it lingers in my awareness, it seems to become ambiguous. Just when has the direction of my breath shifted? Do it now, breathing easily, in and out, simply being conscious of the shift in your breathing.

Letting Go

Exploring your breathing is a natural way to begin another exploration. Name and frame your in-between space in a Word Sculpture. Draw a shape. Write IN-BETWEEN somewhere on it. Then embellish with doodles and words and phrases. They may be metaphors—it's like . . . it feels as though . . . it's as

---

Any transitional stage is a profound and very frightening period—fully a time of passage. Presented with a challenge that demands a major and uncertain transition, an individual may see only the fearsome face of loss although the new possibilities may seem rich and worth the risk to outsiders. Not infrequently, people choose the "safe" darkness of physical death over an encounter with the more unknowable figure of transformation that must be met if the journey is to continue.

CHARLES M. JOHNSTON

Three Wisdoms
"Go slow," said the snail.
"Hop! Hop!" said
the hare.
"Pace yourself," said the cheetah, "it's a long run."

M.C. RICHARDS

if. . . . In-between is a time between waiting and longing, between fear and courage, paralysis and motion, in and out, down and up, am and was. In your Feeling Sketchbook cluster (BETWEEN.) See what emerges for you, what expression it takes. Write a Word Sketch.

I go among trees and sit still.
All my stirring becomes quiet around me like circles on water.
My tasks lie in their places where I left them, asleep like cattle.

Then what is afraid of me comes and lives a while in my sight.
What it fears in me leaves me, and the fear of me leaves it.
It sings, and I hear its song.

Then what I am afraid of comes.
I live for a while in its sight.
What I fear in it leaves it, and the fear of it leaves me.
It sings, and I hear its song.

WENDELL BERRY

Exploring the Act

Read what you wrote and notice where these three acts led you. Be aware of surprise, of metaphors that touched a nerve, of possible openings where all was closed.

THE CONTEXT OF TIME

You may not be conscious of it yet, but the process which began with naming and framing the pain gives you a new perspective, thus short-circuiting the attendant feelings of helplessness. We can call this process *contextualizing*. Contextualizing is a braiding together, an interweaving of past, present, and future. Contextualizing pain is different from trying to outrun an unbearable future, an unbearable past, an intolerable now. Contextualizing is, quite simply, the growing awareness of connections in our pattern of pain: Gabriele, afraid of what surgery might bring (future); Gabriele, afraid of the warning sirens of her childhood (past); Gabriele, attempting to control painful symptoms of anxiety (present). So much negative energy spent on attempts to control the uncontrollable! So little positive energy spent of simply noticing and flowing with the feelings. Needless suffering comes from one of two powerful mental habits (1) clinging—knowing or unknowingly—to *past* pain; or (2) anxiety about the *future*, that is, the *expectation* of pain. Contextualizing our suffering invites recognition and perspective.

What we learn from contextualizing our emotions is that, although we cannot banish pain by force, we can transform it. Those are moments of awareness of the present, of nowsight, which move us into a larger, healing context of time and space.

I can remember how I was: not hearing what I was afraid of, walled off, blind to the here, the now. It is amazing to me, as I write now how detached I was then from my feeling life.

I can remember a Saturday afternoon. I am preparing German pancakes for my children and their friends. As often happens, they beg, "Tell us about the bombs!"

Mechanically, I launch into the story of that deceptively serene March afternoon. Mother, sister, brother are upstairs, taking naps. I am braiding the hair of the aproned daughter of the farmer in whose house we were to be safe from bombs. The sunlit kitchen buzzes with flies, the arched window is at my back. Then come the sounds of the bombers.

I tell the story. Six little girls watch my talking mouth, wide-eyed. I tell it as easily as though it had happened to someone else: "We heard the drone of airplanes. We went outside, the two of us, and waaaay up high we saw a "V" formation, like geese. Except they were airplanes. But we were far from cities, safe from bombs. We watched the last bomber leave the formation, like a straggling bird. We went back to the kitchen. I braided her long hair. Suddenly, there was the whining sound of something heavy, falling . . . explosions . . . pieces of glass hitting my back . . . a faraway scream which wouldn't stop coming—coming out of *my* mouth . . ." I tell about the falling wall, my brother and sister buried under four feet of roof and timber and walls, the broken neck of a mother, like a fragile bird's, the ambulance, the coming dark, the March dampness, no bed to sleep in—for the third time in my short life.

The end. My children and their playmates let out a collective breath, shuffle outside to find new entertainment. To them it is not real. To me . . . I turn to the dishes and other thoughts, emotionless.

I do not yet know that to me the story is not real, never has been. Blocked. In all those retellings of that story no whisper of how the child felt at the grave, the difficulty she had swallowing the hardening rock of feeling, how it stuck in her throat. I didn't realize that years spent spasmodically swallowing to rid myself of something stuck in my throat might be connected to my swallowing feelings in that distant graveyard so long ago.

When I first began my naming and framing, the bits of a giant emotional puzzle began to surface, leading over time to fleeting insights, then to awareness of a larger picture that blended past and present. Leafing through my Feeling Sketch-book I discovered an entry about my trip, as an adult, back to the sites of the bombings.

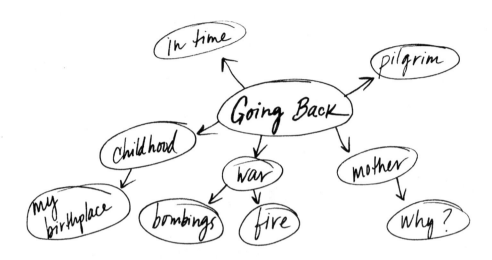

Figure 6.1

> I spiral back in time, a pilgrim, to
> my seventh year, this time to the real places:
> Here, the street of the firestorms, there the house
> of six bombs exploding,
> there the tell-tale grave.
> Last, the place of my birth, still standing, Bauhaus-
>   modern:
> I picture a slim shape under the chestnut tree;
> I feel the urge to know you, mother,
> to breathe your skin, taste your formless sorrows,
> ask the unaskable questions,
> touch unreachable answers:
> Why did you cry soundlessly day after day?
> Did you know you would die?
> How?
>   Why?

When we see our emotional responses in the larger context of time we gain perspective and distance. We become aware that we need not be emotionally locked-in to past pain or future fears. In fact, we can construct and reconstruct both past and future.

British poet, W. H. Auden, in his poem "Progress?" compares human time-consciousness with that of plants and animals, clarifying the intimate relationship between feelings and our inbuilt sense of past, present, and future.

> Sessile, unseeing,
> The Plant is wholly content
> With the Adjacent
>
> Mobilized, sighted,
> The beast can tell the Here from There
> And Now from Not-Yet
>
> Talkative, anxious,
> Man can picture the Absent
> And Non-existent.

In the present, the mind constructs and organizes the past and imagines a future, using many different cognitive strategies that make up temporal intelligence . . . [We become] active participants in the formation of that internal timescape, which plays no small part in the authorship of our own lives.

JEREMY CAMPBELL

Precisely because of our innate ability to project backward and forward, time is not merely a moment-to-moment sequence captured by minute- or second-hands of a clock. That is outer, biological time. There is also a subjective time, deeply attached to the emotions, which we can stretch like a rubber band or compress into a small ball.

Let's explore the context of time and its relationship to our experience of pain.

CHILDHOOD AWARENESS OF TIME

Early images from childhood suggest that most of us know the sensation of timelessness. I used to go outside after breakfast, and after absorbing play that seemed to last three weeks or so, my mother would call me home for lunch.

Vladimir Nabokov in *Speak, Memory* describes the dawning of his time-consciousness.

When the newly disclosed formula of my own age—four—was confronted with the parental formulas, thirty-three and twenty-seven, something happened to me. I felt myself plunged abruptly into a radiant and mobile medium that was none other than the pure element of time. One shared it with creatures that were not oneself but that were joined to one by time's common flow.

Poet James Laughlin in "The Child" frames the significance of the child's sudden awareness of futurity.

The Child
in his little bed in
the dark room clutches

the fluted columns at
the head of the bed his

fists are rigid and he
can't sleep he is think-

ing about how some day
he will not be alive

he will not be a per-
son he will not be him-

self anymore he won't
BE it is a terror to him.

This serious yet playful poem by Jane Piirto Navarre, "Yesterday, Today, Tomorrow," speaks to a child's marvelous time-logic.

Tomorrow, Today, and Yesterday
The three-year-old, wanting to know what day
it is asks everyday what day it is
we tell her tuesday or saturday etcetera
then she asks what day it will be
tomorrow and we go through the naming
of tomorrows in order
chanting the future like a litany

tomorrow is when she wakes up
in the morning and when we tell her
we'll go shopping tomorrow she

remembers yesterday and informs us
that it is tomorrow that today is
yesterday that therefore the time is
always now to do what we plan to do
tomorrow.

As you can see, a central aspect of the uniqueness of being
human has to do with our highly developed sense of time-
consciousness. Animals, on the other hand, live largely in the
world of now. As our time-conscious intensifies, we are subject to the human brain's amazing ability to look back and to
project ahead. It is both a curse and a blessing, as Alan Watts,
in *The Wisdom of Insecurity,* tells us:

> The animal has extremely limited powers of memory and pre-
> diction. For the animal, happiness consists in enjoying life in
> the immediate present—not in the assurance that there is a
> whole future of joys ahead of it. Unquestionably the sensitive
> human brain adds immeasurably to the richness of life. Yet, for
> this we pay dearly, because this increase makes us peculiarly
> vulnerable. One can be less vulnerable by becoming less
> sensitive—more of a stone and less of a man. Sensitivity re-
> quires a high degree of softness and fragility.

*Yet is he neither here
nor there
Because the mind moves
everywhere;
And he is neither now
nor then
Because tomorrow comes
again
Foreshadowed, and the
ragged wing
Of yesterday's
remembering
Cuts sharply the
immediate moon;
Nor is he always: late
and soon
Becoming, never being,
till
Becoming is a being still.*

STANLEY KUNITZ

Contextualizing our past pain and our fear of what might be
through naming and framing is to move beyond them.

TIME-CONSCIOUSNESS AND THE EMOTIONS

As we saw in chapter 3, time-consciousness is built into our
brains, specifically, along the front/back dimension. As we
grow in experience, the brain's time sense becomes more significant. The dawning of time-consciousness allows us to project images of ourselves in a future. This ability to project
brings with it the polar extremes of emotion: the original
compound of excitement and fear that splits, as we mature,
into a veritable rainbow of feeling tones which become guideposts for living. Since the future is by definition uncertain, our
ability to picture the absent and the nonexistent is potentially
productive as well as counterproductive. On the one hand,
our time consciousness produces what philosopher Tobias

Grether identifies as uneasiness, uncertainty, and restlessness. On the other, it is the basis of planning, projecting, motivating. Imagining the future propels us into the willingness to risk change. Most of all, the planning, projecting and motivating side of time-consciousness reminds us that nothing is static, that nothing lasts, not even our pain or fear or depression.

The only thing that makes life possible is permanent, intolerable uncertainty: not knowing what comes next.

URSULA LE GUIN

At the very core of life is the fact that things change. This fact can be variously viewed as both positive *and* negative. Like most of us, I have wished for the known, the changeless, the predictable. Natalie Babbitt, in her novel, *Tuck Everlasting*, makes an eloquent argument for timelessness as a curse: the Tucks have unwittingly drunk from a spring of eternal life and are doomed to moving through the centuries without end. Mr. Tuck says that eternal life has made them like "rocks beside the road":

> Everything's a wheel, turning and turning, never stopping. Always coming in new, always growing and changing, and always moving on. But this rowboat now, it's stuck. If we didn't move it out ourself, it would stay here forever trying to get loose, but stuck. That's what us Tucks are, Winnie. Stuck so's we can't move on. We ain't part of the wheel no more. Dropped off, Winnie. Left behind. And everywhere around us, things is moving and growing and changing. You, for instance. A child now, but someday a woman. And after that, moving on to make room for the new children. And dying's part of the wheel, right there next to being born. You can't pick out the pieces you like and leave the rest. Living's heavy work, but off to one side, the way *we* are, it's useless, too. If I knowed how to climb back on the wheel, I'd do it in a minute. You can't have living without dying. So you can't call it living, what we got. We just *are*, we just *be*, like rocks beside the road.

Change is not only inevitable, it is also a blessing—if often in disguise. The upward spiral is not without its own pain, its own difficulties. To assume that just because a crisis has been met, you can stop moving through, is unrealistic. In *A Grief Observed*, C. S. Lewis records how, after the death of his wife, he felt compelled to write about his loss just to maintain a resemblance of balance. He discovered something about suffering.

Insofar as this [writing] record was a defense against total collapse, a safety valve, it has done some good. But I thought I could describe a *state*; make a map of sorrow. Sorrow, however, turns out to be not a state but a process.

The dominant metaphor for this book, a spiral, has often been invoked by poets. Yeats begins one of his most famous poems, "Turning and turning in the widening gyre." Rilke, the German poet, writes, "I live my life in growing orbits . . ." Words like *gyre, swirl, eddy, circulate, vortex*—are all potential metaphors for the temporal aspects of life's spirals. And those spirals are both biological and subjective, not exclusively one or the other.

Biologist Stephen Jay Gould makes a distinction between images of time as an arrow or as a cycle. Ultimately, Gould reconciles the polarities by acknowledging both aspects of time. "Nature says yes to both"—the arrow of historical uniqueness *and* the cycle of timeless immanence. Our brains say yes to both as well. Our in-between time permits us to look both backward and forward, thus, to contextualize our pain. Our goal in contextualizing is to connect our emotional now both to our feeling past and our feeling future.

The mind cannot measure objective time with the accuracy of a clock, but must construct its own subjective time, which is no more than a model of reality and is often a fiction, a metaphor, a work of the imagination.

JEREMY CAMPBELL

Letting Go

In your Feeling Sketchbook number and date a new entry. Cluster:

WAITING . . . FOR WHAT?

RUNNING . . . FROM WHAT?

Do this without preconceived notions. You are exploring. Then write a Word Sketch using whatever comes. Flow with the direction, the thought, the feeling, the image. You are your own best teller of your stories. You frame your own most necessary questions, discover your own unique insights. You needn't spend much time. In fact, less is more; the less time spent, on each entry the greater the spontaneity, leading to the possibility of insight.

Exploring the Act

Your words on the page may reveal or still conceal. Either way, pay attention to the time dimension of your images.

- Notice how much of your Word Sketch projects into an unknown future or how much it is involved with images of a past asking to be unraveled. Notice whether your Word Sketch reflects uncertainty, uneasiness, restlessness. Notice as well if there was any sense of *now* in your piece. If you felt it, notice whether it came from your absorption in the writing or perhaps in a surrender to a feeling evoked by the past or the future.
- If something in your writing struck a nerve, turn the page and shape a Word Sculpture, numbering and dating it. If not, just put it on hold, and let's continue the exploration of our sense of time.

Recall the diagram of the brain convergence of dimension in chapter 3 (Figure 6.2). Let's expand this figure in terms of our *felt* sense of time, keeping in mind that our inbuilt time-consciousness produces both uneasiness, uncertainty, and restlessness as well as its powerful counterpart, planning, pro-

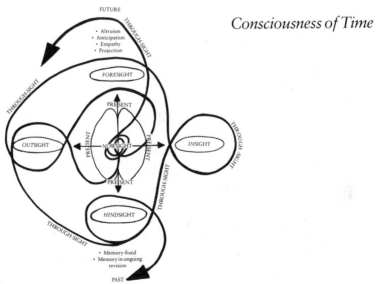

Consciousness of Time

Figure 6.2

jecting, and motivating. The key to contextualizing is to understand that the very sense of time-consciousness that produces terrible feelings—"How can I stand this pain?," "When
will it be over?," "I want to run away from it all"—is also responsible for renewed feelings of possibility, transformation,
vigor, joy. As Figure 6.2 shows, contextualizing has a "looping"
effect, connecting hindsight, foresight, insight and outsight,
all in the *now* acts of feeling and doing. Two of my own Word
Sculptures (Figure 6.3 and Figure 6.4) suggest the pervasive-
ness of our sense of present, past, and future and their connectedness. You may wish to create your own version of a Word
Sculpture before you read on.

Figure 6.3   Figure 6.4

HINDSIGHT: OUR SENSE OF THE PAST

Consciousness of the past is the easiest of the three aspects of
time-consciousness to grasp. We have memories. We call up
past images. We re-experience tastes and smells from our

childhood, recall a song that went along with a heartbreak or a crush. The past is part of our life story; who we have been shapes who we are now and who we are becoming.

The past cannot be altered, but what most of us don't realize is that our memories of the past can be revised, both in meaning and emotional timbre.

> The content of our lives up to the present moment is a fact, and must stand as it is. But we can interpret and reinterpret our past from the standpoint of what we are and of our future possibilities. As a result, the *meaning* of the past is always being altered.

Your self is the totality of what you have lived. We can't just live in the present or we would be mindless. We live with the past.

RUTH STONE

Some die at seventy with an experiential age of seventeen while others are closer to 170, so intimate are they with the happenings of their lives. To gain access to our past, both distant and recent, is to move into a life of incalculable richness and meaning.

JEAN HOUSTON

This is the power of contextualizing memory. Hindsight is not just a matter of calling up a fixed fact as memory. The flexible brain/mind can transform that memory in light of present understanding. In that light, memory can be fluid and flexible instead of fixed and imprisoning. Which of these roles memory takes will depend on whether a memory is replayed like a stuck record or whether it is revised in the present moment to become the source of insight.

When memory is revised and given new shape it can mark the beginning of our upward spiral. When we let go of the blame we inflict upon ourselves at the urging of an old feeling, we are free to move in new directions. The facts of our past may be fixed, but even so simple a revision as the full emotional acceptance that those facts are *in the past* can be enough to transform our present behavior.

The poet Sharon Olds has mined her past, coming to terms with it by integrating it into her creative process. Rather than bemoaning the past, in her poem "I Go Back to May, 1937" she transforms her feelings about it into a powerful creative act.

I Go Back to May, 1937

I see them standing at the formal gates of their colleges,
I see my father strolling out
under the ochre sandstone arch, the
red tiles glinting like bent
plates of blood behind his head, I

see my mother with a few light books at her hip
standing at the pillar made of tiny bricks with the
wrought-iron gate still open behind her, its
sword-tips black in the May air,
they are about to graduate, they are about to get married,
they are kids, they are dumb, all they know is they are
innocent, they would never hurt anybody.
I want to go up to them and say Stop,
don't do it—she's the wrong woman,
he's the wrong man, you are going to do things
you cannot imagine you would ever do,
you are going to do bad things to children,
you are going to suffer in ways you never heard of,
you are going to want to die. I want to go
up to them there in the late May sunlight and say it,
her hungry pretty blank face turning to me,
her pitiful beautiful untouched body,
his arrogant handsome blind face turning to me,
his pitiful beautiful untouched body,
but I don't do it. I want to live. I
take them up like the male and female
paper dolls and bang them together
at the hips like chips of flint as if to
strike sparks from them, I say
Do what you are going to do, and I will tell about it.

The poet's language moves from description of two people as she imagined them to be before she was even conceived,
through pity, through anger, finally, to defiance: "I want to
live!" And then comes the move beyond defiance to an artistic
manifesto: "And I will tell about it."

One approach to the reframing of your past is to use an
old photograph as the trigger for a Cluster. Go to a photo al-
bum or drawer or wallet and let your feelings focus on a picture that speaks to you. As you open yourself to the associations that the picture inspires, let your feelings go back in
time. Address the picture, the people in the picture, the event,
the feeling that accompanies it or any combination of these.
Create a Cluster that expresses those feelings, and, if you feel
the impulse, a Word Sketch.

Not all memories carry a negative charge; in fact, some of our past memories are seen as if through gauze, a picnic devoid of thorns or ants or anger. Author Ray Bradbury, in *Dandelion Wine*, elicits a child's enchanted view of a 4th of July night.

> A final memory. Fire balloons . . . In 1925 Illinois, we still had them, and one of the last memories I have of my grandfather is the last hour of a Fourth of July night forty-eight years ago when Grandpa and I walked out on the lawn and lit a small fire and filled the pear-shaped red-white-and-blue-striped paper balloon with hot air, and held the flickering bright-angel presence in our hands a final moment in front of a porch lined with uncles and aunts and cousins and mothers and fathers and then, very softly, let the thing that was life and light and mystery go out of our fingers up on the summer air and away over the beginning-to-sleep houses, among the stars, as fragile, as wondrous, as lovely as life itself.

Yale surgeon Richard Selzer in *Confessions of a Knife* calls the mining of our pasts a pleasure. He demonstrates how we do—and why we must—make metaphoric leaps between then and now, between self and other.

> Forty years ago my father was a general practitioner in Troy, New York. I never watched him standing at an operating table making an incision. But I did see him every Sunday kneeling in his garden which he treated as though it were a ward full of patients. All day he spent there, pruning, excavating weeds, or splinting a slender stalk and marveling aloud at the exuberant swelling that bloomed at its tip. Now I am the age that he was. Then we are the same age! And now I can see what I must have seen years ago but had forgotten—his hairless white wrists submerged among the carnations. I do not see his fingers, hidden in the foliage, busy down below, repairing the works. But I remember the air carved by bees, and the slow respiration of the trees.
>
> Sometimes, even now, in my operating room, as I incise, clamp, ligate, and suture, I know a deeper kinship with my father. Something arcs across the decades like a rainbow. Why, just today a red flower bloomed at the end of my scalpel: a

poppy, I think. It seemed a miracle. I pinched off the bloom and tied down the stem with thread. My father was right. Surgery is gardening.

Our temporal intelligence is a source of both pleasure and pain. Memory can hurt; it can heal. Named and framed, it can be transformed, arcing across time to connect the you of the past with the evolving you of today.

Letting Go

In your Feeling Sketchbook, date and number a page and cluster ARCING ACROSS TIME. Allow feelings, images, fragments of taste, touch, smell, and sound to surface. Follow the one that tugs at you most insistently. Name an incident, a feeling, a memory. Frame it. Write its story in a Word Sketch using the nowsight of your mind. Like Selzer, try to use both present and past tense, connecting nowsight to hindsight.

Exploring the Act

You may reread your Word Sketch immediately but if the memory was strongly negative, you may want to come back to it in a quieter moment. When you do read it look for signals to help you reframe it.

- Notice whether it sounds like a stuck record—a repeat, repeat, repeat. Are there clues in your sketch about why that memory has retained its power over the years?
- Notice any appreciable hindsight, any shift, however slight, to a different angle of vision. If so, note what that new angle tells you about who you are now, compared with who you were then. Write down in a nutshell, a single statement, your insight about that shift. Write it at the bottom of your Word Sketch in another color and date it. If you have no insight, at the bottom of the page, write, "No insight yet, but I'm open." These nutshell statements will serve you well as you look back over where you've been.

If your nutshell statement feels like a stuck record, don't despair. Trust the power of the surprising shifts of living things. It will happen.

If your nutshell statement indicated no insight, recluster this same memory once, twice—as many more times as you feel you want to. Do this on different days. We *do* revise memories in light of new feelings, new angles. Trust the process. The slight shift to an odd, new, unfamiliar angle *does* happen, *will* happen. For example, you might suddenly see the remembered scene through your mother's eyes, or your brother's, or a stranger's, or a pet's, or your own as an adult instead of a child moving you from a stuck place into a different light. That change of perspective could be enough to give you a whole new insight into an event of long ago.

You need not work with the same memory if it doesn't feel right. Instead, you can recluster ARCING ACROSS TIME and be open to other memories vying for attention. Remember, it is more difficult for us to be receptive to our feelings if we have blocked our pasts too insistently. Our time of being in-between is a time for opening locked doors. Depending on your momentum, cluster LOOKING BACK as often as something in you prods you to oil the lock or try an unused—or unfamiliar—key. Be flexible. Memories that hurt can be transformed into rainbows of healing. In all you name and frame, less is more. As you look back on your written record of this in-between time the short Word Sketches will usually surprise you more than long, rambling ones. If you limit your Word Sketches to five-minute entries here and there, one of them is bound to contain a surprise.

NOWSIGHT: THE FLASH OF NEW CONNECTIONS

Moments when we permit ourselves to be in-between are moments of nowsight. We can only begin where we are. Nowsight is suspension between past and future, that moment of immediacy which often leads to insight. Nowsight is the silken flow of oil poured in a silent arc, so smooth it looks motionless. If we are always running to escape where we are now or how we feel now, it is difficult to allow time for moving into insight.

A workshop participant, Dave McKay, clustered (TOY,) opening himself to nowsight. This five-minute focus on the noun, toy, brought up an image from the past.

> Somehow the thing was alive, a little miracle, flying. The urge to aim at the feathery fluff took over. The shiny wooden stock and blue trigger and little copper ball shocked a bird—a small one. Its thud on the packed dirt echoed inside the enamel silo across the barnyard. Funny film over a dead bird's eye proves it was never alive. My brain's just a sparrow, too.

Nowsight contradicts the child's rationalization that "funny film over a dead bird's eye proves it was never alive." Hindsight acknowledges an equivalent smallness: "My brain's just a sparrow, too." Nowsight—the act of writing in the present—leads to insight, self-forgiveness, putting to rest a troubling event.

[Now] is both our most immediate and our most intangible experience of reality. Now has no length, yet it is the only point in time at which what happens, happens, and what changes, changes.

PAUL WATZLAWICK

FORESIGHT: OUR REACH INTO THE FUTURE

Since the future is unknown, it holds both threat and promise. Threat, because we have no guarantees that life's movement wil reflect our desires. Promise, because when we accept change as inevitable, we also realize we need not be trapped. The very process of naming and framing lets us claim our own emotional shifts as *ours*—and move on. In claiming our negatives, we tame them, permitting their transformation into new projections. In using our temporal intelligence constructively, we understand that our natural resistance to growth is born of our inbuilt uneasiness, uncertainty, and restlessness.

Growing and changing pushes us from the known into an unknown future. Most of us would rather be miserable in the known than risk the unknown. But life, by definition, is dynamic. It does not stand still. Alan Watts again:

> The future is quite meaningless unless, sooner or later, it is going to become the present. Thus, to plan for a future which is not going to become present is hardly more absurd than to plan for a future which, when it comes, will find me "absent," looking fixedly over its shoulder instead of into its face. So many

people of wealth understand much more about making and saving money than about using it and enjoying it. They fail to live because they are always preparing to live.

Here is the paradox: Always preparing to live for a future that is not here yet is just as destructive as always living in and through the past. Living only in the present and failing to plan creates problems as serious as planning too much and failing to live. Unlike most animals, we have evolved a brain which permits us to live between these extremes. It is like a gear shift mechanism: sometimes it is appropriate to be in neutral, sometimes in reverse, sometimes in forward. At a time when I was intensely future-oriented, Sandra Hochman's poem "Postscript" struck me hard.

Postscript

I gave my life to learning how to live.
Now that I have organized it all, now that
I have finally found out how to keep my clothes
in order, when to wash and when to sew, how
to control my glands and sexual impulses,
how to raise a family, which friends to get
rid of and which to be loyal to, who
is phony and who is true, how to get rid of
ambition and how to be thrifty, now that I have
finally learned how to be closer to the nude
and secret silence, my life
is just about over.

Overindulgence in spontaneous urgings reminds us that we can only eat so much, drink so much, make merry so much. We discover that we do, after all, define ourselves by our projects, our projections, whatever they may be. Projects (from the Latin *ject* 'throw forth') propel us mentally into our unknown future. They inspire our willingness to persist for the sake of a particular goal we feel strongly about.

Our projects, big or small, long-term or short-term, inevitably contain the seeds of the future. As a teenager, I was struck by Martin Luther's statement: "If I knew the world

---

We actually construe the world and ourselves in the light of the projects we live for. It is our commitment to these which "structure" our world. The world and my experience of myself change with the change in projects. If you help me give up old projects which are no longer satisfying or fulfilling and encourage me to dare new ones, you are helping me grow.

SIDNEY JOURARD

would end tomorrow, I would plant an appletree today." I thought then, "How stupid!" Yet, his words clung to the fringes of my memory. Today, in light of Chaos science, they make perfect sense. Consciousness of time is a built-in survival mechanism, a means by which we remain flexible, ready for change. Change is the only constant in a dynamic universe, or a complex life. People who deny, or are afraid of, the inbuilt consciousness which urges them to plan for, hope for, strive for, futures of their own creation tend to get sick and die sooner. And, those who cling too hard, stay too rigidly on a single track, cannot adapt to necessary change. Flexibility is the essence of emotional intelligence. Transpersonal psychologist Ken Wilber's telling statement in *No Boundary* is a reminder that flexibility is essential to emotional growth and survival.

> The more I hold onto pleasure, the more I necessarily fear pain. The more I pursue goodness, the more I am obsessed with evil. The more I seek success, the more I must dread failure. The harder I cling to life, the more terrifying death becomes. The more I value anything, the more obsessed I become with its loss.

The key is to shift constructively between foresight, hindsight, and nowsight. We need a balance between flexibility and stability to make the best of an uncertain existence.

We can learn much about our sense of the future by reading about people with brain damage that deprives them of this uniquely human quality. Aleksander Luria, the great Soviet brain researcher, discovered that soldiers with frontal lobe brain injuries

- were captives of past, stereotyped behavior, whose thoughts and actions were guided only by prelearned, automatic action sequences; they were unable to show flexibility by reordering old actions to meet new situations;
- showed a loss of caring, a loss of emotional responsiveness and empathy for others, including "team spirit" and altruism; and
- had lost the ability to create plans or to choose actions to carry out those plans; they were more subject to distractions in the moment.

In sum, people with this sort of brain damage seem unable to distinguish between a past and a future. They live at the mercy of moment-to-moment emotional states instead of acting in the present by synthesizing their experience of the past and their expectations of the future.

Our awareness of the future is inseparable from the search for meaning and purpose in our lives. We project images which allow us to envision our possibilities; these images become a larger framework through which we identify ourselves and our place in the world, the universe.

> *Only if consciousness moves beyond the moment, out toward the possibility of writing a page, a chapter, a whole book, does my situation acquire meaning, because then the future, what is not, is brought in and placed alongside the present, what is. We can understand what is only through what it can be.*
>
> JEREMY CAMPBELL

FORESIGHT AND WORRY

Our worries live in the future as well; they feed on our uncertainties, uneasiness and restlessness. J. Ruth Gendler in *A Book of Qualities* makes the quality of worry very real.

> Worry
>   Worry has written the definitive work on nervous habits. She etches lines on people's foreheads when they are not paying attention. She makes lists of everything that could go wrong while she is waiting for the train. She is sure she left the stove on, and the house is going to explode in her absence. When she makes love, her mind is on the failure rates and health hazards of various methods of birth control. The drug companies want Worry to test their new tranquilizers but they don't understand what she knows too well: there is no drug that can ease her pain. She is terrified of the unknown.

We already know that the future is an unknown quantity. Sometimes worry can be constructive, since it may warn us of a need to act. But many of us worry just to feel alive, and that is not only unproductive, it is destructive. As Gendler reminds us, worry can become a nervous habit. The problem is that chronic worriers don't know where to draw the lines between necessary concern and energy-sapping anxiety.

Physiological psychologist Barbara Brown in *Supermind* makes a useful distinction between normal, reasonable worry and pathological worry. She defines worry as "a problem-solving activity fraught with uncertainty." When legitimate problem-solving becomes unproductive or frustrated, worry triggers overt anxiety and emotional reactions. Brown delineates several mental steps that lead from normal worry to distress. Note how many involve the uncertainty, uneasiness, and restlessness of time-consciousness.

1. EXPECTATIONS. Wherever there is a gap between what we *expect* (future) and what *is* (now), the problem begins.

2. WORRY. Worry appears when the difference between our expectations and our perceptions is magnified. Our minds begin to ask "why" and provide reasons.

3. UNCERTAINTY. The inability to account for gaps between what we expect and what really happens is seen as a threat to our well-being. Threat triggers down-shifting from the neocortical brain to the Reptilian brain to protect ourselves against danger. The problem is that the physiological defenses against physical assault, including the adrenaline surge that readies the body for fighting or flight, are inappropriate defenses against assaults to emotional well-being.

4. IMAGES OF WORRY. If worry persists, the mind begins to construct threatening images, generating adrenaline surges of fear. If the images constructed provide no new information (nowsight), understanding (insight), or perspective (throughsight), worry degenerates into unproductive rumination.

5. RUMINATION. Brown describes rumination as the "insidious, persistent preoccupation of the mind with pondering, speculating, and projecting images back and forth in time. It is a rehashing and regurgitation of a perceived or real problem but without success." Think of the way a cow must rechew and redigest its food. For a cow, this physiological process is necessary. For our psychic process, once rumination starts, our attention becomes fixed on the distress signals themselves rather than on constructive acts to solve the problem. At this stage, worry has become a circular process: we are worrying about our self-created images of worry, not the original failure

of our expectation. Yet, despite this vicious cycle, the human mind still has a inbuilt potential of flexibility. Some sudden shift in nowsight or insight can break our fixed barriers, letting us see ways out—ways to throughsight.

6. SELF-DECEPTION. In this extreme stage we see and hear only what we want to see and hear, focusing only on images that will fit the projections of our ruminations. At that point we have precluded change. We have lost our choices.

Writing our way through personal crisis prevents us from getting to that last stage. Its very flow helps us regain the power of choosing built into the human mind.

Having risked the move through your private darkness, you have begun making breakthroughs. Yet, in the in-between state, you are still vulnerable to allowing worry to become rumination.

Since rumination is ultimately ossifying and since you cannot order yourself not to ruminate, the indirection is essential. Aware Breathing, Word Sculptures, or Clusters are tools of indirection. Word Sketches let you discover patterns to help you see the way through. You may already be using other strategies such as ongoing physical exercise or meditation. The stage of being in-between is for getting unstuck, moving into action; moving from the destructive toward the constructive.

The good news is that, just as your time-conscious mind can manufacture stress by looking back in rumination or looking forward in fear, it has a simultaneous healing potential for looking back or forward to reconstruct or reveal.

Letting Go

Quickly cluster the word IF several times, on the same page. One of those clusters will trigger a more intense emotional response than the others. Go with the one that tugs at you most insistently and name it and frame it in a Word Sketch. Give it words. Your words.

Exploring the Act

- Notice what thoughts, feelings, or issues loomed largest among your Clusters. Notice also that *if* is a word which presupposes a future time, a projection of images carrying threat or promise.
- Notice which issues are familiar, even boring. Issues you worry about continuously without acting on them are most likely to be ones where worry is counter-productive.
- Notice whether there seems to be a temporal pattern of your worries—whether they are mostly past "should have dones" or future-oriented "what would I do if?"

What is fascinating is to watch your own pattern of awareness unfold, whatever it may be. Your inner voice is much more capable of revealing patterns of meanings than your outer voice, which has learned to rationalize.

As you continue your noticing, write down a nutshell statement at the bottom of the page of any entry which yields an insight. Do so in a different color so that, at a later time you can compare the entry—which is often indirect—with the nutshell statement, which is usually a more direct statement of your perception. This is a new step in your understanding of the patterns you are producing. Nutshells will integrate your indirect and direct perceptions.

The harder we look at our aches and ailments, the more we will be startled by the painful truths they are trying to convey about our dangerously disembodied way of life . . . Illness is an indication of blocked emotion. Jung called cancer a disease of despair, arthritis a disease of rage and anger. Skin problems indicate conflicts that are very close to consciousness. If the problem is profoundly deep and a long way from consciousness, it will manifest in the bowel. If we are to be aware of what we're feeling, the body will exaggerate it.

MARION WOODMAN

RECONNECTING FEELINGS AND THE BODY

In this uneasy in-between state, we are likely to tap into heretofore denied feelings. Unresolved hurts of our pasts, imagined fears of the future finally register in our bodies as pain: in our guts, our neck muscles, our wrists, our throbbing temples, our lower backs, wherever we are most vulnerable. The body sends messages. We may have difficulty reading them. Certainly I couldn't—didn't know how to—read my body's insistent signals of protest. Insight came through the indirection of metaphor.

In looking back over Sketchbook entries written here and there in workshops, I came across two different body metaphors, written at two different times, expressing what I was not conscious of at the time but must have known at a bodily level. The first comes from my period of denial. The writing activity had involved reaching for a metaphor for our bodies.

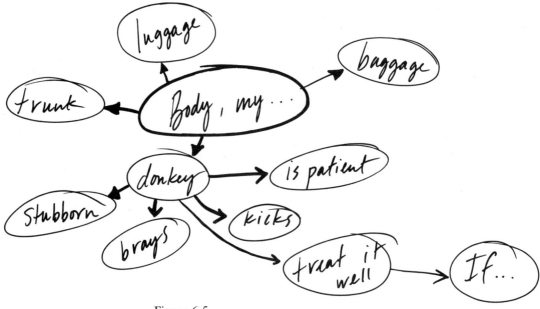

Figure 6.5

Body, my donkey,
you haul my excess baggage of nerves
patiently, patiently.
You sit in gray airplanes,
stand obediently on stage all day, all day,
letting me bray.
now and then you balk:
kick me in the gut, throat,
between shoulder blades,
just to let me know I've pushed too far.
Be patient, please, a little longer.
I can still learn
In time.
If I have time.

Even though I wrote it, I did not see the warning in the "My body, my donkey" until much later. An entry about two years later in a different time, a different emotional space reveals a new metaphor, radically different in tone, indicative of a between-time following serious surgery and before moving into emotional healing.

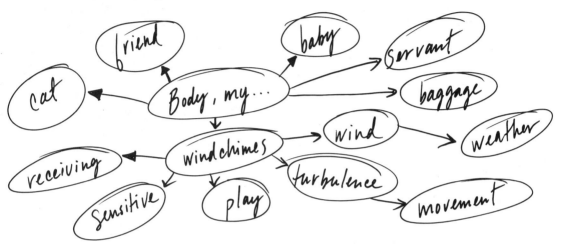

Figure 6.6

Body, my windchimes,
tuned to the air of change,
now catching harmonies,
now cacophonies,
urgent, strident to the soul's ear.
Your adrenaline surging silently
still turns into a Niagara Falls in a held breath
at the paper tiger prowling at the door.
I am learning to hear your clumsy music,
buffeted by wind and rain.
Together we will weather well.

Letting Go

In your Feeling Sketchbook, numbering and dating your entry, cluster BODY, MY . . . Let any number of metaphors spill onto the page. One will call out to you. Name and frame it quickly in a Word Sketch, letting the feel of the metaphor guide your writing.

Exploring the Act

- Notice what kinds of metaphoric reachings occurred in your Cluster. All of them speak to you, some more clearly. Notice which one had the strongest message.
- Note your level of resistance to the metaphor—whether your writing simply poured out or whether you kept trying to push the metaphor away.
- With a different colored pen or pencil, make a nutshell statement at the bottom of the page about the body metaphor you named and framed that seems honest and right for now. Later you can come back and reassess it. Later you may find that a different space a different time, produces a more fitting metaphor.

Our synthesizing time-consciousness is constantly making connections between past, present, and future, constantly defining our now, constantly speaking to us metaphorically, whether we hear it or not.

It takes time for body and psyche to regroup, time to heal, time to adjust—time, just time. To expect otherwise is to thwart the healing. To accept where you are in the aftermath of a private darkness is to give the unconditional support your time-bound psyche and space-bound body intuitively know they need.

Letting Go

Take a few moments for Aware Breathing. Close your eyes and say quietly, "aftershock . . . aftershock . . . aftershock . . ." Let the sound and rhythm of the word guide you.

Now, numbering and dating your entry, create a Word Sculpture. With one sweep of the sketching hand, produce an initial visual shape of PERSONAL AFTERSHOCK. As you embellish the shape, allow words and phrases to merge with it until associated words float into consciousness. Give them a place in your Word Sculpture.

Turn to a new page in your Feeling Sketchbook. Cluster the words PERSONAL AFTERSHOCK and see where it takes

---

We usually come for help only when we are desperate and finally have to listen to our illness. Until then, the body is seemingly living its own independent life and we feel victimized by its symptoms.

MARION WOODMAN

When the body is finally listened to, it becomes eloquent. It's like changing a fiddle into a Stradivarius.

MARION WOODMAN

you. You can use words from the previous Word Sculpture, or you can just start fresh. The object is not to dredge up something you *ought* to be feeling, thinking, or imagining, but rather to discover where you are, what counts at this moment, what you notice. Move on to a Word Sketch, letting whatever impulse feels strongest take you in the direction it seems to want to go.

Exploring the Acts

- Notice whether there was overlap between what emerged in the Word Sculpture and the Cluster and Word Sketch.
- Picture possible patterns between this exploration and any of those you did in chapter 5. Note whether you can link your deepest darkness with the aftershocks of being in-between. Note any perceptible differences between the darkness and the aftershocks.
- Notice your time sense in this exploration. Observe whether your aftershocks are more related to the past, the present, or the future. At the bottom of the page write one nutshell statement that presents a possible insight.

Pain, an inward index of health, is tied to the time sense in our consciousness. And time, as we have learned in this century, is a chimera. Through relativity we know that one man's past is another's present—and the future of yet another. Health and [dis-ease] are not to be acquired so much as they are to be felt.

LARRY DOSSEY

Isn't it strange that life is lived forward but understood backward, if understood at all? It takes all our glimpses of past, present, and future to produce insight, and even more distance to be able to see the larger picture. Our writing acts help to guide us toward integration of our many selves.

As time-conscious beings, we merge time present, time past, and time future to give our experience of life fresh meaning and to reorganize our sense of self.

Our time-consciousness is the product of both nature and nurture. We live in two time-streams at once: objective linear time as told by clocks, and a more subjective, metaphoric time, delineated by our feelings, creating a delicate dynamic balance that allows us to put our pain in various contexts until we can face it clearly, learn what it has to teach us, and move on. Only by facing feelings can we *become* our potential.

In the next chapter, we will move out of this in-between state and put our new skills to one of their best uses: learning the lessons of laughter.

CHAPTER 7

The Other Side of Darkness: The Comedy in Chaos

When we have faced feelings we've run from, dealt with our anger and blaming, hit bottom and come through, discovered how much of our pain is rooted in the past or the future, we rediscover gifts we had forgotten; one is our sense of humor. Humor attunes us to the music of life. A smile dissolves most language barriers, and laughter even more so. But although smiling and laughing are inborn, a sense of humor must be cultivated.

Laughter is the other side of darkness. Laughter is the sound of freedom. Our returning sense of humor tells us we have entered the spiral of healing. My often unfathomable German father would say, "Humor ist wenn man trotzdem lacht (Humor is laughing in spite of it all)." As I look back on my years in his presence, however, I don't recall that he practiced what he preached. Like my father—and like me for a long time—many of us grit our teeth and try to tough our way stoically through personal crisis.

In prehistoric times humankind had only two choices in crisis situations: fight or flight. Today, our evolved sense of humor offers us a third: fight, flee—or laugh!

The comic is an inherent potential of our human mind, and—like all polarities—remains in constant dialogue with its complement, the tragic. We are capable of surviving via the low road of utter seriousness and control; but there is available to us a high road of playfulness and risk. Perhaps a sense of humor is a bridge between the two, as those who are intimate with this mysterious, uniquely human gift will tell you.

We can welcome joy into our lives and rediscover its place in our emotional kaleidoscopes. Permitting us to move past our in-between time, genuine laughter signals emotional flexibility. Our minds can see laughter in sorrow and sadness in laughter. Eventually we come to know that humor is not incompatible with suffering.

Hearing ourselves laugh in the midst of personal crisis sometimes shocks us because we have been so out of touch with the full range of our feelings. My oldest daughter Stephanie said to me recently, "You know, Mom, I can remember when you didn't ever laugh and, if you did, it was a fake laugh." I've come a long way since then; so can you.

Humor and chaos are closely connected. Laughter is a common reaction to the unexpected, the unpredictable. Just as the irregularity of chaos has been shown to exhibit higher-order patterns of meaning—the strange attractors discussed in chapter 2—the perception of humor in pain indicates a higher level of awareness. Just as humor and creativity have much in common, the combination of humor and pain help you break out of expectations and work with what *is* instead of the paralysis of what *ought* to be.

As we search for solid emotional footing during personal crisis, our thinking can become increasingly erratic. In this state, an insignificant insight, mind-leap, or an unusual association can produce an effect out of proportion to its everyday importance. As this strange attractor becomes amplified, it can lead to a discontinuity, a break in our patterns of feeling or thought. When this happens, physicist David Bohm tells us, "your mind must move to a new level." You are suddenly forced to perceive differently.

Humor often results from such nonlinear reactions—from the tension between the expected and unexpected. The contrast between the false comfort of fixed meanings and the shock of new insight can generate laughter which, in turn, may lead to new ways of seeing. Children have little trouble making mind-leaps, as in this anecdote from *Reader's Digest,* contributed by Michael L. Crawford, of an eight-year-old sitting before a bowl of blueberries which looked suspiciously like her number one dislike—peas. Her mother tried reason.

If you can find humor in anything, you can survive it.

BILL COSBY

He who laughs, lasts.

MARY T. POOLE

What is a sense of humor? Surely not the ability to understand a joke. It comes rather from a residing feeling of one's own absurdity. It is the ability to understand a joke—and that joke is oneself.

CLIFTON FADIMAN

Life is a tragedy seen in close-up, but comedy is a long-shot.

CHARLIE CHAPLIN

"Tricia, it's true blueberries are small and round like peas, but they're a fruit. They're sweet. They're delicious. And they're *blue*." Tricia looked hard: "They *still* look like peas to me—like peas holding their breath."

Adults need reminders to recall the sudden pleasure of humor. My seventy-five-year-old correspondent, Mennet Jacob, recently wrote to me on this subject.

> It's a challenge . . . to keep a keen, well-lighted sense of humor, which can be off the wall if I give it half a chance. I hope others catch the fever, the humor, pass it on, let it light up severity and laugh at themselves as I am laughing at myself and how funny I *can* be. A rare discovery! Humor puts me in a pragmatic perspective, lets me see the reality of priority.

"If I give it half a chance." How often do we give humor any chance? "A rare discovery." Why must something so healthy and life-affirming be so rare? "Pragmatic." What an insight on Mennet's part! How things *are* and how they *should* be—the difference exactly, as well as the connection, between comedy and tragedy. "The reality of priority." We all face the necessity of setting priorities in the real world.

It is ironic that the greater the drive to survive, the greater the force toward both tears *and* laughter. The emotional expressiveness of laughter is as much a tool of survival as the emotional receptivity to tears. Humor is a vital sign of being alive. It affects us both physiologically and psychologically.

HUMOR AND HEALING: OUR BODY'S RESPONSE

Symbolically as well as physically, laughter is the very opposite of holding your breath. Physically, we involuntarily contract and expand our chest when we laugh. Our arms move. Our heart-beat speeds up. Blood flows more rapidly. We feel so much livelier that, for the moment, we are free. Curiously, laughing involves functions which have little to do with the biology of survival. Reptiles don't joke. Some have called laughter the luxury reflex because all it seems to do is relieve tension. Like a sneeze or an orgasm, however, a genuine laugh feels wonderful. It certainly relieves tension, but it does more.

Humor is a sort of permissible rebellion against things as they are.

HOWARD NEMEROV

Life is too short for men to take it seriously.

GEORGE BERNARD SHAW

The secret source of humor is not joy but sorrow; there is no humor in heaven.

MARK TWAIN

It reflects the human brain's capacity for flexibility. In a sense, it reflects the nonlinear geometry of chaos in that it constantly adjusts for rigidity and inflexibility by helping us adapt to unexpected, unfamiliar stimuli.

The physiological effects of humor have become the focus of considerable research, perhaps stimulated in part by Norman Cousins' well-known reports about his own use of laughter as therapy. William Fry of the Stanford Medical School says that "laughing one hundred to two hundred times a day is equal to [the exercise of] about ten minutes of rowing." Moreover, his research shows that hearty laughter causes "internal jogging" (a Cousins phrase), because it speeds up heart rate, raises blood pressure, and increases oxygen consumption. Hearty laughter causes our facial muscles, stomach, diaphragm, and shoulders to get a vigorous workout.

But equally important, in the aftermath of laughter, we experience physiological relaxation. Breathing and heart rate slow; muscles relax, and blood pressure drops; we feel calmer. People who regularly rely on humor to cope, can more easily let go of anger, fear, anxiety, hostility, and a host of other negative feelings that often accompany crisis.

The poet Conrad Aiken once wrote a series of silly limericks for reasons not at all clear to him: "They were the immediate result of a coronary," he explained. "Inexplicably, I at once had a seizure of limericks, beginning the day after the attack. It was, I suppose, the attempt of the unconscious to keep me amused, and it worked very well." Here are two of his silly examples.

> Said a curve: I'm becoming hysterical.
> It is hell to be merely numerical.
>   I bend and I bend,
>   But where will I end
> In a world that is hopelessly spherical.

> The limerick's, admitted, a verse form;
> A terse form, a curse form, a hearse form;
>   As pale and as frail
>   As the shell of a snail,
> It's a whale of a tale in perverse form.

Humor is tragedy revisited.

PHYLLIS DILLER

Humor is emotional chaos remembered in tranquility.

JAMES THURBER

The hardest years in life are those between ten and seventy.

HELEN HAYES

There are three things that are real—God, human folly, and laughter. The first two are beyond comprehension. So we must do what we can with the third.

JOHN F. KENNEDY

*Total absence of humor
renders life impossible.*

COLETTE

*Our receptivity is our
readiness to possibility.
To receive is to take part
in reality as living change.
To be receptive is to risk;
yet, how fully alive we are
is precisely a function of
how deeply we can trust
in, and engage, that risk.*

CHARLES M. JOHNSTON

Scientists are learning much about our moods and health. Laughter is a complex facial, muscular, respiratory, and oral process, a *physical* expression of a variety of sometimes conflicting *emotions.* As infants we cried before we smiled; we smiled before we laughed, but we did all three before we talked. It's as though we are capable of reacting in different ways simultaneously, as though we were two beings. One observation is that humor is the result of release of uncomfortable feelings because the uncomfortable emotions are not only faced, but transformed into pleasure through discharge.

Look at the language we use. We "come to our senses," as though there were another being inside us preventing us from being sensible. We are "beside ourselves" with laughter or fury. Part of this duality may be some awareness of left and right brain autonomy, two distinct ways of seeing the world, despite their overlap in function. The two neocortical hemispheres are not always in accord, nor can they be, since they each process information in radically different ways. But words, processed differently by each hemisphere, have a life of their own. The psychological roots of humor may depend on a kind of both/and awareness of language and of its feeling power.

Psychiatrist Jerome Rothenberg, in *The Emerging Goddess,* named this double awareness "Janusian thinking," after the Roman god Janus, guardian of doorways, who looked in two directions at once (see Figure 7.1). Philosopher Arthur Koestler called it "bisociation," meaning the ability to see how something is associated with two different contexts at the same time. The incongruity of the two contexts, he thought, was what gave rise to our reaction of humor.

HUMOR: BEING RECEPTIVE AND EXPRESSIVE

Laughter is unique to the human species, and we all laughed naturally as infants without needing to be taught just as we also cried. All we need is receptivity; expression will come on its own. Laughter and tears are intimate partners. At some moments we laugh until we cry; at others we cry until we laugh. Sometimes it is hard to distinguish between them. One seems to make a seamless shift into the other. We laugh at the most absurd *and* at the most earnest moments.

Figure 7.1

Laughter interrupts the panic cycle of an illness.

NORMAN COUSINS

Warning: Laughter may be hazardous to your illness.

NURSES FOR LAUGHTER

Once we accept the chaotic flux of the world we can learn to laugh at rigidity, at the absurd one-sidedness of all that is deadly serious. When we are so inflexible we can see only one side of the coin, we are not only deadly serious, but we have lost perspective.

I recently came across a cheerfully corny and irreverent book, *Driving Your Own Karma* by Steve Bhaerman. Had I found it during my crisis, I might not have hit bottom so hard. Its very irreverence might have shed a sliver of light on my own grim seriousness—intensified by every deadly serious book on stress I was reading at the time. It provides a healthy jolt of pragmatism, makes fun of illusions about control and the desperate need for certainty, and nudges the reader into letting go, if only for a moment. For example, the section on "The Magic of Incompletion" asks a reasonably serious question and comes up with refreshingly ridiculous answers, followed by advice we could do without—which nevertheless have a strange ring of truth since they ask us to break our obsession with our own problems and adopt a humorous distance.

Have you ever stopped to think how empty our lives would be if everything were complete?

- There'd be no reason to get up except to wind the clock and feed the cat.
- There'd be no leftovers.
- There'd be no more pleasant surprises, like finding a $20 bill in the pocket of a pair of pants, $20 you didn't even know you had.
- Pass defenders in football would have to find another line of work.
- And you could just forget soap operas.

If everything were already complete, Robert Frost would have no promises to keep and he could just crawl off and sleep in the snow and nobody would even notice. So I say to you, never finish anything. That's confusion, you tell me. And I tell you, if the road to hell is paved with good intentions, the road to heaven is paved with confusion.

The book goes on to suggest "Incompletion Training." For someone like myself, who believed her worth depended on being superwoman, this tongue-in-cheek "Training" just might have opened my eyes long enough to recognize that I had been setting myself up for a serious crash because I thought I should have been able to achieve the impossible.

You can enter a humorous perspective by focusing on what you forbid yourself or what seems to be forbidden to you. Humor shocks us into a different perspective because it violates what is supposed to be inviolable: the rational order of things. Enter the irrepressible mind-leaps of childlike playfulness. We can all benefit from an occasional dose of silliness. It leads to surprise, improvisation, novelty, and it gives us a new lease on life.

Regaining my own sense of humor was particularly difficult. Even today, I search my memory for laughter from a childhood of wailing sirens, black-out shades, and hours on hard benches in clammy cellars with shadowy strangers, all of us yearning for the strident monotone of the all-clear signal. I cluster HUMOR and words and phrases flow onto the page that have nothing to do with humor, like "bewilderment," "fear of fire," "shrapnel toys," "unrelenting hunger," and "war." Funny? Little strikes me as funny about those days. I keep clustering, trusting by now the unpredictable patterns of the mind; chaos. Suddenly, out of nowhere, comes a strange attractor in the word "hungry," which leads to "barley," and, like a dust storm, the scene swirls into my memory, taking on a jagged shape.

> 1946: mother dead; a jagged second-floor crack to leap over in half-destroyed living quarters; a hundred-pound gift-sack of barley (uh-oh! beware of Greeks . . .); hungry children; soup—obviously cooked by *someone,* but someone not part of the memory. The memory generates images of the meaning of hunger, hungering, hungry. Barley soup in mismatched bowls. *So* hungry. Child's eyes stare at the speckled liquid. Child's stomach goes on strike. Next to each barley corn floats a brown bug. There are thousands of them. They have pincers.

[Healing brings] the patient from a state of not being able to play into a state of being able to play . . . It is only in playing that the child or adult is able to be creative, and it is only in being creative that the individual discovers the self.

DONALD WINNICOTT

Not funny, not funny at all. I stop writing, breathe, let the images wash over me: how my older sisters and I carefully separate barley from bugs; how my small brother, oblivious, shoveled it in; how for me, it wasn't so much the bugs as those outsized, crablike pincers; how our father, acutely conscious of his role as a model, stoically swallowed spoon after spoon of the mottled mix; how, in the absorbed silence of eating for survival, of separating the survival need of food from its pleasure, he glanced up and saw the painstaking resistance of his children. "Eat!" he roared, "It's protein!" And we ate. Rather, we swallowed whole the carefully separated black piles and white piles, careful, so careful not to bite down.

Writing about it for the first time, the ugliness of the memory disappears. There is some absurdity in pitting aesthetics against hunger, of the futile attempts to separate the literally inseparable bugs from barley, of thinking we could defy an autocratic German father bent on the survival of his family. We are barley eaters. We are survivors.

Not funny then. Today, I smile. It is a story—and others like it—that bonds us siblings psychically, binds us in the commonality of survival. Healing. Wholemaking.

Strange how the mind works: as I write, the barley and bug story triggers another memory of unintentional humor—this one in the midst of a blinding snowstorm of fear.

The surgeon has been talking steadily, quietly. Only one sentence registers.

"We will probably have to cut out your large intestine."
Silence swirls around us.

"But . . . but—" I blurt, "But I'm *attached* to my colon!"

Laughter comes as a reprieve; we laugh so as not to cry.

EUGENE IONESCO

The protest echoes so absurdly in that doctor's square and sterile cubicle, that I laugh aloud, the sound alien to my ears; it has been a long time. My inscrutable Chinese surgeon stays inscrutable. But my spontaneous laughter is an unexpected affirmation, a flash of light in my darkness, a tiny release of intolerable tension. I shall not forget it—ever.

HUMOR AND RECEPTIVITY

The moment of incipient laughter is a one of emergence. It is the moment of recognition that our pain and sorrow have their own veiled purposes. This movement beyond crippling fear reflects an incipient awareness of our center. It is a healing awareness, the acceptance of not knowing what that center is, yet smiling at the feel of an unfamiliar receptivity. Rainer Maria Rilke writes about this center.

> Were it possible to see further than our knowledge reaches, perhaps we could endure our sorrows with greater confidence than our joys. For they are the moments when something new enters us, something unknown to us; our feelings grow mute in shy perplexity, everything in us withdraws, a stillness comes, and the new, which no one knows, stands in the midst of it and is silent.

There is a kind of active quiescence that paves the way for receptivity to a subtle sense of the absurd. It is just this kind of stillness that allows the speaker of Peter Meinke's poem to reassess his "plans for suicide."

The Heart's Location

all my plans for suicide are ridiculous
I can never remember the heart's location
too cheap to smash the car
too queasy to slash a wrist
once jumped off a bridge

almost scared myself to death
then spent two foggy weeks
waiting for new glasses
of course I really want to live
continuing my lifelong search
for the world's greatest unknown cheap restaurant
and a poem full of ordinary words
about simple things
in the inconsolable rhythms of the heart.

Rilke's "the new, which no one knows," and Meinke's
continuation of "the lifelong search" underscore our acceptance of futurity as well as the humor that can smile at uncertainty by expressing it, ultimately even satirizing it.

Victoria Register, whom I first met as a participant in one
of my workshops, regained perspective over her own extended
midlife crisis—precipitated by a divorce she did not choose—
with an ever-expanding sense of humor. She sent the following
poem, prefaced with this note: "Growing up in Jonesboro,
Georgia, I overdosed on *Gone with the Wind* early. I wrote this
on my forty-fourth birthday! My ex had Gable's ears."

Scarlett's 44 today
and Rhett's gone
not back to Savannah
but to the blonde
next door.

And Tara's
been converted into
condos
to house carpetbagging
computer programmers
who come en masse
down the Jonesboro Road.

And nobody
barbecues
anymore.
It's all pasta salad
with house dressing
and chives.

God it's changed
since
the war.

Victoria's birthday manifesto demonstrates that she not only mourned her pain but looked hard at her old illusions of what love *ought* to be. In becoming receptive, she discovered a wry sense of humor in herself which emphasizes the comic in a situation that at an earlier point, had paralyzed her with pain.

That sense of humor, which helps to ground the self, emerged in the Word Sketch of a workshop participant after we had all clustered "Body, my . . ." Donalee Frounfelter was so surprised at, and pleased with her metaphor on that day that she volunteered to read the piece aloud, to the delight of the entire group.

> My body is a car. Now, I'm not talking about a VW or a Yugo. No way! We're talking about a big old '64 Chevy: safe, secure, smooth, curvy, big enough to handle the shocks, controlled enough to take the corners. People can look in to see some of my parts, but not all I have to offer. What really makes me run is tucked away, secure beneath the hood. I'm cheery-looking and barely rusted. I've got all the essentials—and I've got my spare tire. This car has plenty of miles on it. But, honey, the radio still plays and the clock still ticks!

When I finally reached her by phone, several years after that workshop to ask if I could use her Word Sketch, she agreed, adding, "You know, I've lost 150 pounds since I wrote that."

My own illusions of control turned into a life-threatening illness, but I fought life-saving surgery for almost four years. I sensed intuitively that my chronically high levels of fight or flight adrenaline would not let my body survive even anesthesia. My doctors, sympathetic but determined, told me flatly "You will die; untended colon cancer has a predictable trajectory." My maelstrom of anxiety escalated to what I can only label "night terrors," a phrase I borrow from novelist Walker Percy.

In the months following my false alarm, my small jokes helped neutralize my embarrassment. Writing about it, I freed myself from my terror—and my shame. Laughter was still only a small tickle, the tentative tackling of my panic attacks with ludicrous exaggeration.

HUMOR AND LUDICROUS TRANSFORMATION

The ludicrous puts painful events in context by suspending logic in favor of the mind-leaps of association. If our seriousness is like Euclidean geometry, the ludicrous is like the flexible math of chaos. The ludicrous you offers a vacation from the serious you. In the ludicrous context you're not looking for answers or making judgments; you're simply open to the odd angle that gives pleasure, however brief. All it takes is a bit of receptivity.

Letting Go

Look through your "blaming" entries of chapter 4 and read over some of your Word Sketches. Choose one in which you felt especially aggrieved. Re-create that entry from a ludicrous point of view by reclustering that episode. Now write a new Word Sketch and try to bring out the absurd in the situation. Don't *try* to be funny, just let the event filter through the light of the ludicrous. My own attempt was not funny, but it helped me to acknowledge my situation's absurdity and, at the same time, its reality. Your aim is a glimpse of human folly—your own or someone else's—and the possibility of reclaiming your sense of humor in the deadly serious.

Exploring the Act

- Notice whether you became aware of an absurdity in this re-creation. Think of other people's absurdities that are not so very different from this one.
- See how much of a shift was possible by rereading the original and the re-creation, one after another. In what way is the anger, frustration, or grief tempered, changed, or softened? Note any shift to changes in perspective—whether it has grown larger, remains the same, actually has shrunk smaller; whether or not you were able to produce in yourself a wry smile, a small chuckle, or even a guffaw.

If not much has appeared yet, take heart. Laughter is a gift we sometimes forget to use. If we have forgotten how, it will take a bit of patience to relearn what once came naturally.

Custom and civilization urge upon us the conventional, the usual, the regular, the customary, the decorous, the logical. Laughter is a celebration of the unconventional, the unusual, the irregular, the indecorous, the illogical, and non-sensical.

ROBERT ORNSTEIN AND DAVID SOBEL

If you can't say something good about someone, sit right here by me.

ALICE ROOSEVELT LONGWORTH

A bachelor never quite gets over the idea that he is a thing of beauty and a boy forever.

HELEN ROWLAND

As we saw in chapter 6, we cannot change the past; we can only revise our understanding of it. Adopt that simple strategy, and what Howard Nemerov speaks of as the "permissible rebellion against things as they are" will come without effort on your part. It takes only openness, a relaxing of stiffness, a softening of rigidity, a massaging of the mental muscles that have held our pain or anger or bitterness knotted too tightly to be easily able to unwind into releasing laughter.

Among those whom I like or admire, I can find no common denominator; among those I love, I can: all of them make me laugh.

W. H. AUDEN

A smile, even in retrospect, fosters healing and quickens our pace in the upward spiral. But we can do other things in the present to help us get new points of view.

LAUGHTER AND RAGE

Laughter offers us a way to

- let go of rigidity, which is a defense against an excessive fear of the unknown;
- let go of despair, which is excessive hopelessness; and
- let go of the defensive stance which indicates an excessive fear of vulnerability.

The more deadly our seriousness, the deader our lives become. A sense of the absurd balances out seriousness. Eskimos know this. In settling grievances, the angered parties must engage in a community ritual. They must recite absurd poems, sing silly songs, and publicly insult one another to the accompaniment of drums. It is a safe form of letting go, of externalizing anger—a release infinitely preferable to shooting at one another. This ritualization of rage through humor probably helps them to see not only the other person's point of view but also how trivial their hurt may be in a larger context.

You don't need a community ritual to engage in this kind of healthy release of rage through comic insults. You can turn comedy and satire against your pain by playing the curmudgeon. A curmudgeon is anyone who hates hypocrisy and pretense and isn't afraid to point out uncomfortable facts in a witty way. You can indulge yourself in the acid wit of the curmudgeon and vent your anger against the objects of your pain, allowing rage to be transformed to laughter.

Letting Go

Allow yourself to be a real curmudgeon. We already know that venting anger releases tension. Yet there are ways and then there are ways of venting anger. Common swear words are easy, but they are not elegant or terribly witty. Besides, some of us are not comfortable with swear words. Use humor instead. Release your rage by writing it—and, in the process, play, recover your perspective, and maybe even garner the bonus of a good belly laugh!

We are growing serious and, let me tell you, that's the very next step to being dull.

J. ADDISON

Poet Theodore Roethke showed his curmudgeon's side in an essay entitled "A Tirade Turning" for which he not only used a pseudonym, but which was published posthumously. His attack on writers, which goes on for two pages, shows a delicious release of rage in words:

> I think of my more tedious contemporaries:
> Roaring asses, hysterics, sweet-myself beatniks, earless wonders happy with effects a child of two could improve on: verbal delinquents, sniggering, mildly obscene souser-wowsers, this one writing as if only he had a penis, that one bleeding, but always in waltz-time; another intoning, over and over, in metres the experts have made hideous; the doleful, almost-good, overtrained technicians—what a mincing explicitness, what a profusion of adjectives, what a creaking of adverbs!

As he gets wound up, his attention focuses on critics:

> —And those life-hating hacks, the critics without sensibility, masters of a castrated prose, readers of one book by any given author (or excerpts thereof), aware of one kind of effect, lazy dishonest arrogant generalisers, tasteless anthologists, their lists of merit, their values changing with every whim and wind of academic fashion; wimble-wamble essayists; philosophers without premise, bony bluestocking commentators, full of bogus learning; horse-faced novelists, mere slop-jars of sensibility.

H. L. Mencken, a notorious curmudgeon, tackles the bad writing of Warren G. Harding, in the *Baltimore Evening Sun*, 1921. Notice Mencken's obvious enjoyment with wordplay.

He writes the worst English I have ever encountered. It reminds me of a string of wet sponges; it reminds me of tattered washing on the line; it reminds me of stale bean soup, of college yells, of dogs barking idiotically through endless nights. It is so bad that a sort of grandeur creeps into it. It drags itself out of the dark abysm of pish, and crawls insanely up to the topmost pinnacle of posh. It is rumble and bumble. It is flap and doodle. It is balder and dash.

Ritualize your anger like the Eskimos by writing some insults about someone. Begin seriously, but in the end, you may find that you begin to sound so absurd, or so unlike yourself, your words so exaggerated and dreadful, that you will experience the freedom of laughing at the very thing you're attacking.

Cluster the words (MAY YOU/MAY YOUR . .)! Ritualized insults work best if you focus on one aspect of a person's personality or work or hobbies. Close your eyes and picture a real or imagined adversary. Picture him or her in a favorite setting; for instance, on a sail boat or in a garden, on a golf course or baseball field, cooking at home, or involved in their profession. As soon as an association in the Cluster clicks, focus your insults, getting more and more absurd as you go and write a brief Word Sketch that gives them free rein.

Exploring the Act

- Notice whether your choice of a topic for insults or bad wishes tells you anything you hadn't realized about your feelings, or the person who is the focus of your anger.
- Observe whether you found it easier or harder to allow your insults to become absurd or outrageous.
- How did you feel about letting your unexpressed anger out on the page? For many of us this act is vaguely threatening or fearful. Yet confronting a negative wish and exaggerating it not only helps you move beyond guilt and shame but makes you feel lighter, and genuinely playful. Most important, acknowledging our very human wish and making it ridiculously terrible, usually generates an impulse of forgiveness, laughter, or reconciliation.

No matter what your response, merely engaging in this exploration is a release. If it doesn't feel funny at first, no matter. You've let go of some feelings of hostility, rage, or anger, by framing them in words and producing a moment of nowsight. For now, the act itself is the key to a wider frame than you have had in the past.

COSMIC HUMOR

May your life be filled with lawyers.

TRADITIONAL MEXICAN CURSE

Another way to laugh is to look at the larger perspective. Humor flourishes when you enlarge the frame of reference from the personal to the cosmic. The cosmic perspective transforms private misery into comedy. It lets us laugh at those small frustrations that tend to overwhelm us if we remain trapped in too narrow a viewpoint. With the emotional and physical release of laughter, the big patterns become accessible, and we recognize that those patterns can free us from that entrapment. Genuine laughter disarms us. It sets the stage for more open explorations. It gives us the confidence to explore more freely what we may have perceived only as very serious and very dangerous business.

Whole cultures once knew what we sometimes forget as individuals. American Indians, for example, encouraged the release of inhibitions during festivals by welcoming laughter at what was normally sacrosanct. Shakespeare's tragedies all have their indispensable fools. A bit of irreverence helps. Not taking yourself too seriously helps. Risking a little foolishness helps. Letting go helps. Life is no laughing matter—yet all life is ultimately laughable.

No matter how serious our topic, the language we use to talk about it is booby-trapped with pratfalls and practical jokes. Even the dreadful, self-absorbed seriousness of self-help books can be satired deliciously, and can remind us that sometimes the most effective means to move through and beyond our problems is to achieve a little distance—the kind of distance comedy blessedly bestows.

Psychiatrist Paul Watzlawick has written a tongue-in-cheek book entitled *The Situation is Hopeless but Not Serious,* in which he satirizes the sometimes appealing idea that we are mere victims, not actors, in our lives.

What was inflicted upon me by God, the world, fate, nature, chromosomes and hormones, society, parents, relatives, the police, teachers, doctors, bosses, and especially by my friends is so grievous that the mere insinuation that I could perhaps do something about it adds insult to injury.

When the situation is desperate, it's too late to be serious. Be playful.

EDWARD ABBEY

In a similar vein, some imaginative spoofs of typical self-help course offerings make light of our genuine needs by twisting them into absurd variations.

Course #101: Overcoming Peace of Mind.
Course #104: Guilt without Sex.
Course #108: Dealing with Post-Self-Realization Depression.
Course #111: Creative Suffering.
Course #113: Whining Your Way to Alienation.

Stress has a bad reputation in modern life. Stress makes us feel bad, makes us ill, makes us lose our cool. Journalist Kathleen Fury in the *San Jose Mercury News* takes a long look at what she calls "Stressmania" and discovers the light side of a dark and heavy subject.

Stressmania

Sure you have stress. Maybe once you thought you had a headache because you skipped breakfast. Now you know it's stress. And stress, as we are all learning, makes you sick. The only trouble is, you can't call the office at 9:15 and say "I can't come in today. I have stress." You can't put down "stress" on the diagnosis blank of your insurance form. When friends say "Hi, how are you?" you can't say "Under stress, thanks. How about you?"

What use is a disease you can't use? Maybe they're overdoing it a little. Maybe the major cause of stress has become: Reading about it.

If you have overdosed on Stress Reading, I am here with a few simple steps to help you unwind from the stress of thinking too much about stress.

Rounding up a suitable group of stressees is easy: They are the ones who chant their mantras out loud in the cafeteria, or wear crystals around their necks, or keep Valium out on their desks.

Week One: We're going to go cold turkey here. Everybody will sign a pledge not to read anything with the word "Stress" in the title. We'll pair off, so everyone has a Stress Buddy she can call if she feels tempted to take a little peek at that article called "How Stress Causes Dental Cavities."

Week Two: The subject is spouses and how stressful it is to live with them. Some of the topics will be: Why he refuses to get to the airport on time. Why she insists on going to the airport three hours before the flight. Why he won't have sex more often. Why she wants sex all the time. Why she doesn't buy a decent reading lamp for the den. Why he is the only man on the block without a Weed Eater.

Week Three: The children. Stressees will learn the following: Your children are not short grown-ups. They will not do what you want them to. This is life. Get used to it.

Week Four: This is our grand finale, a marathon session. The subject is Your Job . . . etc. etc. When our marathon is over, every member will receive a headband embroidered with the motto: STRESS: ANOTHER WORD FOR LIFE.

Any form of "enlightenment" that removes comedy and laughter from life is likely to be counterfeit because life *is* innately funny. A cosmic perspective reminds us that our problems have their absurd aspects along with their pain.

HUMOR AND CLICHÉS

The more we suffer, the greater our pain or distress, the more difficult it becomes for most of us to know what to say. In fact, the more we care, the more we rely on tried and true expressions designed to make the sufferer feel better. The result is—clichés. One way to regain laughter is to become conscious of cliché—a trite, outworn expression we cling to because it is easy, ready, safe. It is an initially sound response that has become ossified. Since we are looking for the unexpected, the unpredictable, let's see what the lighter side of the cliché offers in the way of little surprises, lifts, and changes in attitude. Erma Bombeck deossified one of them with the title of her book, *If Life Is a Bowl of Cherries, What Am I Doing in the Pits?* Others are all around us: If at first you don't succeed, try, try again. If at first you don't succeed . . . quit! or If at first you don't succeed . . . you are running about average.

Letting Go

Cluster (CLICHÉ) to come up with some of your most disliked platitudes. Now play with them. If none come to mind, play with some of the following:

Proverbs are always platitudes until you have personally experienced the truth of them.

ALDOUS HUXLEY

Platitude: a statement that denies by implication what it explicitly affirms.

EDWARD ABBEY

> *You win some, you lose some.*
> *This too shall pass.*
> *It could be worse.*
> *Nothing is perfect.*
> *Look for the light at the end of the tunnel.*
> *Life is hard.*
> *Don't cry over spilt milk.*
> *What's eating you?*
> *You bit off more than you can chew.*
> *Pull yourself together!*

The mixed cliché is a wonderful source of humor. *Visualize* these mixed clichés for a smile.

> *Let dead dogs sleep.*
> *That's a very hard blow to swallow.*
> *You can lead a horse to water, but you can't*
> *   make him float.*
> *You are out of your rocker!*
> *The promotion was a real plum in his hat.*
> *She's out to butter her own nest.*
> *A virgin forest is a place where the hand of man*
> *   has never set foot.*
> *When we get to that bridge, we'll jump.*
> *She'll get it by hook or ladder.*

HUMOR AND TURNING YOUR SORROW UPSIDE DOWN

We find in play the possibility for new growth. If we are open to the odd angle, the skewed perspective, we are relieved to find that life is not just drama. With enough distance, it can be melodrama, or even farce. And, for a time, we can become willing actors in our own exaggerated comedies. In Woody Allen's films, his characters bumble through precisely because they are able to laugh at their own vulnerabilities and frailties. Humor underscores our humanness, accepts it—and prevails in spite of it.

Letting Go

Laughter is akin to turning the world upside down for a time. In my own Word Sculptures, I experimented with the other side of darkness by sketching my initial configurations upside down on the page, turning the page right side up and then embellishing them. (See Figure 7.3.) One change I noticed was their "floating" effect; they didn't have their usual base. Re-

If only we'd stop trying to be happy, we could have a pretty good time.

EDITH WHARTON

Men who are unhappy, like men who sleep badly, are always proud of the fact.

BERTRAND RUSSELL

Figure 7.2

create a sense of turning your darkness upside down through an upside down Word Sculpture in your Feeling Sketchbook. Number and date your entry, then turn your Sketchbook upside down, drawing a quick configuration of lines. In a sense you are standing your shape on its head. Turned right side up, it will simply look different. Now experiment with two things that may create further unexpected angles.

1. Embellish right side up, but use shapes you've not used before. For example, if you haven't ordinarily used wavy lines, or little circles, or egg shapes, try that. Use whatever comes to your hand. Omit any embellishing features you've used before. Several of mine took the shape of faces (Figure 7.3).

We don't stop playing because we grow old, we grow old because we stop playing.

SATCHEL PAIGE

A tragic preoccupation only serves to rob us of the immediacy of our participation in the playfulness of life.

SHELDON KOPP

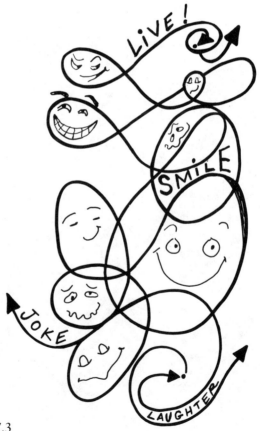

Figure 7.3

Figure 7.4

To say that play is essential to the human species is to corroborate what creative scientists, artists, and the great saints have understood as central. Play, fantasy, imaging, free exploration of possibilities: these are the central powers of human beings.

BRIAN SWIMME

2. When a word or phrase crosses your mind, let your mind flow to its opposite and make it part of your configuration. For example, should you think "depression," write "exuberance"; if "heaven," write "hell," and so forth. My own Word Sculpture (Figure 7.4) surprised me into awareness of how far I had come: I see at least five words that evoke music or song, not counting the implied music of laughter.

Exploring the Act

Be aware of where this shape-making has led you. You want to be open to experimentation, to improvisation, to the unexpected, to the cosmic frame of reference. You are creating receptivity by triggering conscious awareness of polarities. Like sudden laughter, awareness of polarities is a way of jogging yourself out of accustomed grooves. The mind-leaps you make may lead to insight. They also may seem to lead you to nothing, but remember that the mind processes and stores connections that you may not be immediately aware of. If something emerges from this Word Sculpture, move into writing a Word Sketch, numbering and dating your entry.

HUMOR AND THE SERIOUS PLAY OF OXYMORONS

We've seen that there is pattern in chaos, a random order. Likewise oxymorons seem incompatible on the surface but they speak of deeper human truths. A good example is the "darkness visible" in Styron's description of clinical depression (a phrase he borrowed from Milton). The word *oxymoron* comes from the Greek, literally meaning "cleverly stupid" suggesting purposeful absurdity. If oxymorons point us to deeper truths, they also let us smile at the lighter truths. Think of "death benefit," "flexible freeze," "tight slacks," "loose tights," "open secret," or "amicable divorce."

Letting Go

In your Feeling Sketchbook play a little by choosing one or more of the oxymorons below, cluster them, and see where the combined potential of their light side and your lightening up takes you.

ACCIDENTALLY ON PURPOSE   SWEET HELL

CONSTRUCTIVE CRITICISM   LIVING END

CREATIVE SUFFERING   HAUGHTY HUMILITY

MELANCHOLY MERRIMENT   PRETTY UGLY

ELOQUENT SILENCE   CONFIDENTLY SCARED

STRONG WEAKNESS   SPLENDID FOOL

LIVING DEATH

MELODRAMA: TURNING DRAMA
INTO COMIC DRAMA

One way to play with melodrama is to use the idea of the Bulwer-Lytton Contest created by Scott Rice, who also happens to be my office-mate at the university at which I teach. In this contest competitors write incredibly bad opening lines for imaginary novels. The model is an opening line actually written by author Lord Bulwer-Lytton, an infamously awful nineteenth-century novelist. The line, "It was a dark and stormy night," is used frequently by artist Charles Schultz' cartoon character and aspiring writer, Snoopy. The openings are so dreadfully clever or so cleverly dreadful that they surprise us—and bring on a smile. Scott collected them in a book called *It was a Dark and Stormy Night.* Here are some samples.

"The sun rose slowly, like a fiery furball coughed up uneasily onto a sky-blue carpet by a giant unseen cat."

"Patrick had the kind of personality that put my intestines on fast forward."

"Writer's block gripped him like the sphincter muscle of an anal retentive."

Letting Go

Unlike the people who enter this contest, you may not feel like working hard to manufacture intentionally unintentional funnies, but you can open your own stories from a playful perspective—without wasting much time! Risk a smile by contextualizing your story of crisis in momentary absurdity. Play a little by writing the opening sentence of a novel about yourself. Give your personal story an incongruous opening, as though you were writing the beginning of a bad novel. Write only one sentence of it. Play with it. Make it as awful as possible. You may want to write several versions of an opening sentence until one of them makes you chuckle, or at least smile. Let it be as ludicrous as you can make it. If you're enjoying your "story," give it a silly title. As you write, think about reading your sentence to a friend. Imagining their reactions can help make it funnier, and can certainly make you receptive to chuckling inwardly, even to working up to a genuine belly laugh.

Exploring the Act

- Notice anything in either your sentence or title that provides an insight.
- Notice to what extent you were absorbed in this playful exploration. Note whether the doing made you feel different—lighter, sillier, more open. Perhaps it made you feel heavier than before. If so, cluster (HEAVY) to see if it will throw some light on your response.
- Notice whether your exaggeration into melodrama or farce had a rueful quality. When we cling to unhappiness or pain longer than necessary, we can be sure that it is serving some purpose. That's precisely when the ridiculous can throw light on your views of yourself here and now.

At some point you will notice something to light your way past your usual ways of seeing. Our own familiar, unexamined patterns are our biggest blinders to creative breakthroughs in personal struggle. Naming and framing from a playful perspective brings your feelings out in the open in a way that is safe but creates distance. Playfulness can move your feelings into delicious melodrama, stories we can tell about ourselves that are likely to make us smile or laugh even if they more often seem to make us cry.

A recent letter from one of my older sisters, a first-time grandmother and an inveterate traveler, depicted such melodrama that I called her and read her last paragraph back to her. She wrote in anger; now the laughter was infectious:

> I am going nuts trying to figure out what to wear in New York. I look hideous, plain and simple. Hideous. I am reading a guide book, and, instead of making me feel better, I'm spooked! They paint a picture of a Manhattan peopled by the most chic, outrageous human beings who don't get up until noon, then "go" through the night. I am terrified. Even IF I had a dress or

two, I don't have a jacket to go with them. I went to a Mall and wandered around like a lost dog. Even IF I wanted to pay the price at Macy's, the colors this year are gaggingly awful, designed to make EVERYTHING else in your wardrobe unfit to wear with it. I have stuff in my closet I wore ONCE. Either I got too fat, or it is just not right. I have ugly pants that would gag a Goodwill employee. I HAVE looked for a jacket and the JUNK they offer in those JUNKIE MALL SHOPS are APPALLING. I am NOT a punker, for God's sake. I always look fine in Truckee, but when I see myself in a window in Sacramento, I look AWFUL. I tried the skinny stirrup pants. No respectable grandmother wears them, and those who do, even IF skinny, still look silly—and once YOU are a grandmother, you will, too! Dots are in—I tried them. I look like a circus clown in purple polka dots. And MOST pants with elastic in the waist make me look like I have diapers on. It is HOPELESS! Love, H.

Letting Go

As you have been playing with your awful opening sentence to your own life story, little lightning flashes of connections may have been triggered in your brain. Follow up with a Feeling Sketchbook entry, by writing and clustering the phrase SOMEDAY I'LL LAUGH ABOUT.

Issues you've been struggling with may surface in the Cluster. Go with the one that resonates emotionally. Imagine yourself in the future, looking back, and write a Word Sketch about that issue as though it had happened ten years ago.

Exploring the Act

- Notice any new perspectives that arise from this imagined hindsight. What does the distance in time tell you about your response of today?
- Note whether you found fantasizing about your future reactions easy or whether you resisted it.

New research shows that fantasy, far from being harmful, is actually healthy. It allows you to think about or imagine, in your mind's eye, what you would never do in actuality. Among the beneficial effects of fantasizing are release of tensions, merriment, moments of flow, and radically altered perspectives. In fantasy, by adopting different perspectives, you can see your place in the world, the world's place in your life, your place in the lives of others, their places in your life, and the effects of your ongoing transformation. In the process, you may not die laughing, but you may learn to live laughing.

COMEDY AND INCANTATIONS

Infinite players are not serious actors in any story, but the joyful poets of a story that continues to originate what they cannot finish.

J. P. CARSE

Yet another way to live laughing is to find an odd phrase to play with as a refrain for a few days, weeks, or months. In former times, family or folk sayings in some way significant were used as incantations to keep evil spirits away. Incantation comes from the Latin *incontar* 'to enchant.' One I recall from my childhood reading of fairy tales is "Open, Sesame!" Another recalls the flow experience researched by University of Chicago's Mihaly Csikszentmihaly: the incantation "let it flow" calls up the image of a river, life as a flow. Laughter is a flow of feelings, as are tears, both of which trigger release.

We can still use incantations to keep our spirits up in the face of the absurdity of modern life. An incantation that has become a favorite personal phrase and triggers immediate laughter in tense moments for me is "O Kinky Turtle!" *Time Magazine* journalist Gregory Jaynes tells the story. One Sunday, just before moving to New York City, Jaynes was attending church in Ohio with his daughter. The pastor announced to the congregation: "Now we shall all rise and sing hymn number 508, *Lead On, O Kinky Turtle.*" With some glee, Jaynes reports:

> At that, my fellow parishioners fell to mumbling. The good Reverend then blushed crimson and admitted that title stuck in his head because his own child called it that. Recovering his composure, to say nothing of his solemnity, our guide instructed us to stand and "sing hymn number 508, *Lead On, O King Eternal.*"
>
> Well, in the days since, the phrase "Lead on, O Kinky Turtle" has assumed a profound significance in the course of my wanderings. I use it in a kind of incantatory fashion, muttering "Lead on, O Kinky Turtle" whenever I feel shorted, stiffed, put upon by outside forces. I keep it handy, as you would a rabbit's foot.

The pastor's mistake became an incantation for Jaynes, whose retelling of the story made it available to me.

Letting Go

Cluster any silly words or funny sayings you remember from your childhood, a phrase you associate with a parent, a friend, a spouse, or one of your own personal jokes that makes you smile just to think of it. Then write a Word Sketch with this as its subject. See what surfaces.

Exploring the Act

- Experiment with using whatever resulted from your Word Sketch as an incantation. See if it sparks a grin. Repeat it for a day, perhaps a week, even more. Let it grow on you. It will slow down your adrenaline, provide a kind of balance. Play with incantations as they cross your mind. Write down any that sound pleasurable or useful from radio, TV, books, magazines, friends. The very awareness of potential in incantatory phrases invites playfulness.

WORDPLAY

Language provides so many opportunities for humor, it is hard for me not to imagine that the first speakers and writers were also the first tellers of puns and jokes. Word play is universal. Word play involves our emotions. It is a latent resource of our feelings, a way to relieve tensions harmlessly. We play with, and laugh at, many aspects of language: mispronunciation, mistranslation, odd connections and more. Wordplay can overpower customary usage and return a sense of the fertile chaos that is the ground of language. Picasso once wrote "I don't search, I find." In other words, he was receptive. Likewise, we can't search for humor, we can only be open to finding it. Language is both coded and loaded, but we won't see its funny side unless we are receptive.

Psychiatrist Sheldon Kopp tells the story of his attempts

to teach his children responsibility through linguistic reframing. Each time they used the passive construction, he corrected them as in "My milk spilled."

> They were quick to adapt, saying "I broke my bike," instead of "my bike broke." One day, one of his sons ran inside, soaking wet from a sudden downpour: "He must have seen on my face some readiness to blame him. "I was just going to tell you, Dad," he rushed. "I'm sorry. I guess I rained all over myself."

Language has such potential for humor because it is shot through with ambiguity and paradox. We use this potential both intentionally and accidentally. We create word play and discover it all around us. Witness this collection of authentic hotel signs whose "almost English" point to the humor inherent in the way the human race quite unintentionally miscommunicates.

Sign in a Paris hotel elevator:
> *Please Leave Your Values at the Desk*

On the menu of a Swiss cafe:
> *Our Wines Leave You Nothing to Hope For*

Sign in a Copenhagen airport:
> *We Take Your Bags and Send Them in All Directions*

Sign in a Budapest zoo:
> *Please Do Not Feed Animals. If You Have*
> *Any Suitable Food, Give it to the Guard on Duty*

Sign in an Acapulco hotel:
> *The Manager Has Personally Passed All the Water Served Here*

Air conditioner information in a Japanese hotel:
> *Cooles and Heates. If You Want Just Condition of Warm in*
> *Your Room, Please Control Yourself*

As good comedians know, humor is the art of capitalizing on life's sorrows. Humor requires a spontaneous openness before others, the ability to change perspective, to stand back from yourself and pick the odd angle. Humor is the sign of flexibility toward your life, toward yourself, toward others, toward the world in which you live. In humor the naturally playful attitude of the child reasserts itself.

For several years now, I have been unearthing a side of me that was so deeply buried I didn't even know it existed. Five years ago I became a reluctant participant in "Humor Night" at a major academic conference. I was convinced I couldn't possibly be funny. But I took the risk anyway and that risking opened me to playfulness. The first three years were sheer terror. The past two have been pure pleasure. Now I see the possibility of humor everywhere; collect whatever I find funny wherever I can.

Nothing is better than the unintended humor of reality.

STEVE ALLEN

Some of the best humor, as we've already seen, comes from unintentional word play, available to all of us if we are open to it in signs, in newspaper headlines, in people's mouths. A wonderful source of humor lies in student essay examinations. These innocent errors allow you to see in the juxtaposition of what is said and what was meant a burst of healing laughter.

> *Three kinds of blood vessels are arteries, veins, and caterpillars.*
> *To be a good nurse, you must be absolutely sterile.*
> *In many states murderers are put to death by electrolysis.*
> *In the Renaissance Martin Luther was nailed to the church door at Wittenberg for selling papal indulgences. He died a horrible death, being excommunicated by a bull.*
> *Gutenberg invented the Bible. Sir Walter Raleigh invented cigarettes. Sir Francis Drake circumcised the world with a hundred-foot clipper.*
> *George Washington married Martha Curtis, and, in due time, became the Father of our Country.*
> *Benjamin Franklin invented electricity by rubbing cats backwards and declared, "A horse divided against itself cannot stand."*
> *Lincoln's mother died in infancy, and he was born in a log cabin which he built with his own hands.*
> *Beethoven wrote music even though he was deaf. He was so deaf he wrote loud music.*

The very ways we word excuses and rationalizations—our own and others'—to avoid blame can be hilarious. *The*

Toronto Sun published the following examples, taken from insurance forms, of how various accidents were supposed to have happened.

> *A pedestrian hit me and went under my car.*
> *The guy was all over the road. I had to swerve a number of times before I hit him.*
> *I had been shopping for plants all day and was on my way home. As I reached an intersection, a hedge sprang up, obscuring my vision. I did not see the other car.*
> *I had been driving my car for forty years when I fell asleep at the wheel and had an accident.*
> *My car was legally parked as it backed into the other vehicle.*
> *The telephone pole was approaching fast. I was attempting to swerve out of its path when it struck my front end.*
> *An invisible car came out of nowhere, struck my vehicle, and vanished.*

Newspaper headlines are a dependable source of inadvertent word play. Here are a few of my favorites, collected from various papers over the years.

> *Fried Chicken Cooked in Microwave Wins Trip*
> *Doctor Testifies in Horse Suit*
> *Egg-Laying Contest Won by Local Man*
> *Defendant's Speech Ends in Long Sentence*
> *Stiff Opposition Expected to Casketless Funeral Plan*
> *Local Man Takes Top Honors in Dog Show*
> *Police Begin Campaign to Run Down Jaywalkers*
> *Jerk Injures Neck, Wins Award*

Classified Ads are another marvelous source of unintentional humor and cleansing laughter.

> *No matter what your raincoat is made of, this miracle spray will make it really repellent.*
> *Dog for sale: eats anything and is fond of children.*
> *Four poster bed, 101 years old. Perfect for antique lover.*
> *Man, honest. Will take anything.*
> *Wanted: Man to take care of cow that does not smoke or drink.*

These quotes from famous people have struck me as funny largely because they point to uncomfortable truths:

Vladimir Nabokov on psychoanalysis: "Why should I tolerate a perfect stranger at the bedside of my mind?"

Abraham Lincoln: "When you have got an elephant by the hind legs and he is trying to run away, it is best to let him run."

Oscar Wilde: "The advantage of the emotions is that they lead us astray."

Woody Allen: "More than any time in history, mankind faces a cross-roads. One path leads to despair and utter hopelessness, the other to total extinction. Let us pray we have the wisdom to choose correctly."

Franklin P. Jones: "Honest criticism is hard to take, particularly from a relative, a friend, an acquaintance, or a stranger."

Mark Twain: "Part of the secret of success in life is to eat what you like and let the food fight it out inside."

Anywhere, anytime, I'd sacrifice the finest nuance for a laugh, the most elegant trope for a smile.

EDWARD ABBEY

Finally, simply listen with receptive ears for malapropisms. Collect your own examples, and enjoy them.

That's just putting the gravy on the cake!
That's the whole kettle of fish in a nutshell.
I wish someone would make a decision; I'm tired of
   hanging in libido!
Here's the crutch of the matter.
Don't put your umbrella and goulashes away just yet!

I have stopped waiting for the world to become less threatening, less painful. I have become an active seeker of humor in the serious. I have discovered that, in being receptive to it, it is all around me ready to let me smile and, if I'm lucky, to let me laugh whole-heartedly several times a day.

LOOKING AHEAD

The strange attractor of the princess with a glass heart pops up. I liked her when I was too small to grasp the real import of the story. I like her even better as I close this chapter on the role of humor in healing.

Something impels me to search for the story on my book-shelves; it is in one of the few books to have survived the flames of war. I find it between Bruno Bettelheim's *The Uses of Enchantment* and Grimm's Fairy Tales. She would like her place there, my princess. As I reread her story, what I remembered is true: despite the jagged crack in her heart, she developed a marvelous sense of humor. She taught others to laugh. And she laughed—genuinely. One day, I want to translate this story into English.

In chapter 8 we will examine the subtle processes of reflection, which help us to fill in the blanks and hollows of our lives by learning how to reconcile polarities.

Reflection: Filling Blanks and Hollows

As you continue to heal, there is a time for reflection on what has been, what is now, and what is yet to be. The word *reflect* has multiple meanings. It suggests a casting back, a pensive contemplation. Even its literal meaning, "the bending or folding back of a part upon itself" recalls the nature of fractals, the recursive nature of our lives, the patterns we create in—and of—our lives, all too often without recognizing them.

When we reflect, we look inward. The more aware we become, the richer our vision. The delicate patterns in life's fabric reflect our experience and suffering, our disappointments and growth, our dyings and transformations.

RECURSIVE PATTERNS: THE STRANGE ATTRACTORS OF OUR LIVES

Reflecting on the recursive patterns impinging on our awareness creates an ever-expanding orbit of personal growth, a healthy spiral of healing. In clustering my own strange attractors, I have been surprised by the shift from the obvious images I carried with me from childhood to less obvious but much more powerful nuances of feeling. For example, the moment of realization in the cemetery was more shattering than the bombing itself. Briggs and Peat note that nuances of meaning "exist in the fractal spaces between our categories of thought."

Seemingly isolated images in memory are amplified by feelings which, when experienced rather than denied, generate new self-organizing patterns. The dominant sensations in those few moments at my mother's grave were physical: a liquid heat flooding my body, and an unbearable sense of light, juxtaposing a dawning reality against the incongruous May sun.

But memory is under ongoing revision to help us endure—and prevail—even when we understand little of our pain. As I look back I see the child's mind searching out its own frail thread of meaning in the meaninglessness of war and dying. Death demands expression of grief. As a child, I had no avenue for grieving. I now know there was a funeral which the two smallest children were not allowed to attend. I now know that the older grieving children, only twelve and thirteen themselves, couldn't handle the funeral in addition to their youngest, uncomprehending siblings. I now know their father could not make it in time to be with his children to see his wife, their mother, buried.

I now know that, after that long walk back from the graveyard, I took my blocked grief to the night sky. In a mind-leap born of necessity, I saw it: the constellation Orion, with its belt of three stars. Call it a child's fantasy or an emotional need, but the center star seemed to pulse as if its light were for me alone. "That star is Mutti!" I whispered.

We ask ourselves, we say unto ourselves. And, listening in, we come, if we are watchful and reflective, to know shade by shade, though never wholly, the persons we have been and are and are becoming.

WENDELL JOHNSON

Our wondering, uncertainty, and questioning are full of nuance. In experiencing nuance we enter the borderline between order and chaos, and in nuance lies our sense of the wholeness and inseparability of experience.

JOHN BRIGGS AND
F. DAVID PEAT

Figure 8.1

For me, the light was alive; it sent signals. From that night on I felt her presence and all through that blossoming spring in the midst of rubble I knew I could find her. That center star became a mental measure of safety in the time following loss and the after-effects of war. Then, after crossing the Atlantic by ship, I was amazed to find she had followed me to America. I never shared my odd secret. I was ashamed of it. Writing about it now helps me see it as a necessary survival strategy. In filling these blanks and hollows, I understand that memory is not fixed but undergoes continual revision. An entry in my Feeling Sketchbook presents a different angle—a pensive, adult look at a mother whose image has changed for me (see Figure 8.2).

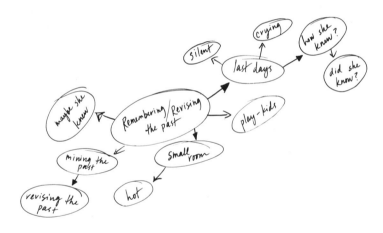

Figure 8.2

Water mists the pane you stare at. Water clouds your vacant eyes, looking inward at some unfathomable sorrow. You sit all day. We play. You weep without sound. We quarrel over an empty spool of thread. You stare at nothing. We beg for our cereal. I squeeze your cheeks with thumb and forefingers as if to say: "Look at us; see us; nourish us." You look through me. I hurt but don't know why. The clock ticks. Your small son, more persistent, whines. Our tiny room shut tight against the March cold, is suffocating. It will be your coffin. The mist of your shallow breathing makes runnels on the glass. You know what I don't know. You will die.

In the course of our life we leave and are left and let go of much that we love. Losing is the price we pay for living. It is also the source of much of our growth. Making our way from birth to death, we also have to make our way through the pain of giving up and giving up and giving up some portion of what we cherish.

JUDITH VIORST

Lasting gains can be achieved by flights of imagination. Particularly during periods of stress caused by depression or by change over which the individual has no control, the mind is often at work composing and demolishing imagery that floats to the surface of consciousness because the human being needs to reacquire confidence that life has meaning. . . . The self explores its own capacities for growth and change.

DIANE MIDDLEBROOK

I ask myself, "What is the point of this Word Sketch?" Specifically, its words reflect images I have carried with me since I was seven. More generally, the writing from this new angle has enabled me to let go of the focus on myself and to imagine how she felt. I see her in a new light. In the naming, I transform buried, nonspecific fear into a sense of curiosity and wonder. The old, unfocused fear has become a phantom. As long as it had no form, it could not be contained.

Other previously unexamined images unfold into new patterns; for example, Orion's belt, saturated with nuances of feeling, has not only stayed with me, it has expanded to encompass the growing orbits of my life. Although an occasional glance still recalls a mother, it has also come to reflect my three daughters in their own emerging light. Patterns—similar but not identical, evolving patterns which speak profoundly to me: Child and mother; death and life; mother and daughters; silence and sound. I see how my early silences have been transformed, small step by small step, into genuine dialogue.

In the real (as opposed to the ideal) world, a tender heart needs to be balanced by a tough mind; good feelings, by a willingness to struggle. Those who want love without anger, relationship without conflict, harmony without contradictions, are forced to create an illusory world of unambivalent love . . .

SAM KEEN

MAKING OUR SEPARATE PEACE: OPENING TO OTHERS

My three daughters simultaneously suffered from and flourished despite my pain. In my own role as mother, the uncompromising silences of my childhood were transformed into a storm of dialogue. Paper and pen became natural vehicles of expression in our household. Sometimes angry, sometimes loving, sometimes serious, sometimes funny, our communiqués channeled feelings into constructive avenues of expression.

Stephanie, my oldest daughter, at eighteen wrote her way through some of the insecurities of her early adolescence (see Figure 8.3).

"Well, bird. . . ." That's Mike, talking to me in a flat in London. "Bird," the English equivalent of "chick" in the U.S. Why are we birds? Am I a bird? I always thought of myself as a wolf, a loner, apart from others. Especially in Jr. High.

All the birds were flocked together. How I wanted to be a

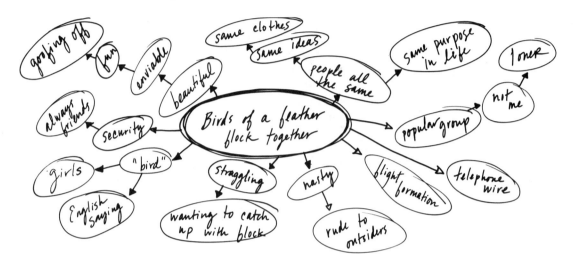

Figure 8.3

bird, to fit in, to be part of that flock. I tried to be a bird, but somehow, I was just a straggler, an outcast, always fluttering on the fringe of things, not daring to plunge into the thick of the flock for fear of ridicule, fear I'd be pecked at, stared at, or, most frightening—ignored. I felt like the wolf under the lamb's skin in the Grimm's fairytale—except that I was harmless and only pretending to be a bird who could fly.

No! I'm not a bird. I did wish to be a bird, part of the flock; they all had the "in" clothes, the "cool" look, the latest hair-do's. They even flocked with boys, flew in bird formation, perched together on telephone wires to gossip.

"Hey, bird! What's wrong?" Mike again.

"I'm not a bird!" I growl, showing my teeth.

Suzanne, at thirteen, I now see, was steeped in a rage whose reasons one can only infer from the context of a long note I found on the kitchen table after work. The normally impermissible use of swear words was apparently part of a great catharsis. I only recall that her writing through the anger dissolved the anger.

January 10, 1978
Mom:

I always have to say sorry or give in and I'm so goddamn sick of it I could scream. You always think you're better than me and you're not and the reason you think you are is because all your friends tell you you're great and fill you up with shit about how great a speaker you are.

I'm just not good enough to wear your clothes. I'm too piggy. Is that it? Well, if that's your moto (sic) you just think that way all you goddamn want to. When Steph was thirteen she went out all the time but she never got into trouble. In fact we all went looking for her; when I do for fifteen min. you give me hell when I come home. You don't remember when you were thirteen, do you? Because it's harder than you think it is. I get crap from you all the time but I never hear you bitchen at Steph or Simone. You *never* give me a chance. If Steph messes up something 1st then *I* don't get a chance. You make me *sick* when you say you understand everything—because you don't.

If I'm not good enough for you then let me know because I'm getting sick of your conceitedness. Also, you *know* it makes me mad when you don't answer me so you do it to see me mad. You *love it* when I'm mad because you like to see me cry because you think it's the laugh of the month; well, I don't. It *hurts* me when I cry but it's just a big *joke* for you. Remember that next time you want someone to talk to.

from:
Not Good Enough for You

Simone, my youngest, quietest, most rebellious daughter, and my greatest puzzle, posed a real communication problem. The most inward, independent, and solitary of the three, at thirteen she was hypersensitive to the smallest emotional fluctuations around her, particularly tone of voice. Discussions with her were out of the question. In a last-ditch move to keep doors open between us, I offered her a red, cloth-bound "Mom's and Simone's Sharing Book." I wrote a first entry and left it for her. To my surprise, she responded. I wrote back. She answered again. Sometimes the book would disappear for months, only to reappear on my bed during a crisis. It became the fragile thread that kept us emotionally connected through difficult years. It gave us a voice. It allowed each of us to be heard by the other, to make our own interactive music. The emotional turbulence was the strange attractor. One of her entries at age seventeen—and my response—gives a flavor of our tentative steps toward, rather than away from, one another.

> Mamalein:
>
> It's 3:20 A.M. and I can't sleep. There are a few things I have to get off my chest: I want to get my brain back in order. Sometimes I know I'm wasting so much by watching the tube or sitting around. It seems much easier than reading a good book. I need to develop my skills, and that takes time and practice. I'll probably need a little help, so if you could just remind me once in a while . . . Help me realize that even the smartest person needs to put time, energy, and practice into what they do . . . Let's keep up our Sharing Book.
> I love you, Sim-1

6:30 A.M. I was in a rush to leave for the East Coast when I discovered the Sharing Book, but I knew it was imperative to respond immediately.

> Simone:
>
> You at 3:30, me at 6:30. You, remembering our Sharing Book and me, still not quite sure how we were able to start it in the first place, though we needed it badly—and glad your impulse is to keep it up, even now. Someday we'll read around in it through the lens of time and laugh at how smart we were to take time to work things out in writing—and how thoughtful we could sound even in the middle of our ugliest struggles . . . The need that made you reach out at 3:30 is also the unnameable thing that bonds us. I know you are a very private person, and I try to respect it.
>
> Let's *do* keep up our Sharing Book. It's a record of two human beings caring enough to make contact now and then, wanting to learn about the other, trying to figure out the puzzling world. . .
>
> How lucky you are to be seventeen and aware *for yourself* that your life is essentially in your hands and that control over it is *internal*. I'll be glad to give you an external nudge now and then.
> Dein Mamalein

Writing had become a way of receiving and expressing; dialogue, not monologue. Clashes were transformed into learning from each other and growth for both of us. The writing unlocked the door of silence to the room of sound—today we are fast friends.

RECONCILING POLARITIES

Upon reflection we can see how polarities converge in our lives. The dictionary tells us that polarities are contrasting or opposite qualities: up and down, in and out, empty and full. Indeed, we usually think of polarities as opposites; *either* something is inside *or* outside. But there is another way to look at them. A cup is *both* half full *and* half empty, depending on which condition we want to call attention to. Full and empty are polarities. But we can think of them as *both/and* as well as *either/or*, depending on our point of view. When we perceive them as connected, we reconcile what seem to be opposites and regain significant power for self-healing. In the upward spiral toward wholeness, we gradually learn to move from seeing our lives in an either/or perspective to a both/and perspective.

The goal of this chapter is reconciliation. As we free ourselves of the unbearable bind of either/or, which inevitably sustains and prolongs needless emotional pain, we feel more and more at home in a both/and perspective.

As we learn to be receptive we see more readily the two sides to every emotional coin. In Chinese, the phrase is *fan mien* 'the reverse face.' In a both/and perspective we accept uncertainty. When something doesn't turn out the way we imagined it ought to be, we may grieve or be sad or frustrated, but we do not drown in regret, or burn in anger. We experience the two sides of the coin as connected.

Reconciling polarities means seeing light *and* shadow, accepting yes *and* no. As we continue to fill in our emotional blanks and hollows, learning more about feelings we have denied, we need to look at the complete picture, accepting that, as poet Howard Nemerov wrote, "running and standing still at once is the whole truth." It makes sense to me. Part of the truth is running; part of the truth is standing still. Together, they form the whole truth.

Reconciling polarities has played a powerful role in my gradual transformation of self. Ken Wilber in *No Boundary* articulated with grace what for so long I only vaguely felt.

> There are many kinds of lines and surfaces in nature—outlines of leaves and skins of organisms, key lines and tree lines and lake lines, surfaces of light and shade, and lines setting off all objects from their environment. Those lines are actually there, but these lines, such as the shore line between land and water, don't merely represent a *separation* of land and water, as we generally suppose. They equally represent precisely those places where the land and water *touch* each other. That is, lines *join* and *unite* just as much as they divide and distinguish.

So what? you say. What do lines dividing or joining have to do with my difficulties? Everything. When we can perceive only one side of the equation, our emotional lives list so badly we often capsize. Rebalancing means letting go of our arbitrary boundaries. The essential ambiguity of life suggests a connection of possible meanings. We begin to think of cycles, vortices, winding spiral paths. In fact, life is a rhythmic movement among opposites, an ebb and flow of wave patterns containing within itself the seed of its opposite.

If our emotional boundaries are too rigid, we lose the flexibility necessary to balance life's losses. And so we are bound to experience nameless dread, terror, desperate clutching, and obsession with ultimate order. Poet Richard Frost satirizes the understandable fear of possible dangers letting us see for ourselves the self-imprisoning effect of such an extreme.

Some Important Advice

There isn't any way to be perfectly safe.
Something terrible is possible
every time you touch the refrigerator
or flush the toilet. A long porcelain sliver
may ruin one kidney or destroy your liver
when you slide into the bathtub. If the pipes
get crossed,
you can be scalded when you wash your face.
You can get knocked down, squashed, swallowed,
or even lost.

You can be careful. When you sit anyplace,
watch for hidden scissors. Be wary
of poisonous banquets. If you cross the tracks
Keep your ankles far enough from the switch,
which will mangle you even if the train does
miss.
Be normally alert. Watch out for pets.
If a cat's nail scratches, you know what the
germs can bring.
Don't fondle dogs. And never kiss anything.

Yes, it is true that the world is inherently uncertain, but it is also true that we can let our fear of risk cripple our lives. When we internalize the dynamic rhythms of both/and, we don't need to cling so hard. We can remember that failure makes success possible, pain makes pleasure possible, loss makes gain possible.

Letting Go

Explore some of the blanks and hollows of your reflections on your own life by clustering DANGER/SAFETY. Number and date your entry. Write a series of these if you feel the impulse— or only one.

Exploring the Shift to Shape

- Notice any images of danger that emerged. Some you may have known you were holding, but there will be some you weren't aware of.
- Notice what images of security, safety, or pleasure emerged.
- Recognize that you can turn images that were once dangerous into images of security. The ability to make this change is in the mind.

Once we internalize the knowledge of how to reconcile polarities, we can take steps to transform negative qualities in our lives into constructive ones. Writing our way into both/and connections instead of either/or divisions leads to insights—little ones, big ones, and sometimes, life-changing

ones. Every single one of them, big or small, makes a difference. A wonderful example of reconciling polarities is this
piece by writer Jacqueline Werth.

She

There are still times when, in the half-sleep of early morning's darkness, I nudge closer toward a warm spot on the other
side of the bed that is no longer there. It is in these dark dawn
hours that I cry (softly, so I don't wake our sons) about the fact I
am no longer married to you.

The times that my days begin in this remorseful way are
fewer and farther between, but they not all gone. Six years
haven't erased them. New loves, a new life, and new feelings
haven't dispelled them. Divorce is difficult enough without
doggedly carrying around decade-old feelings. Why can't I just
be over and done with you?

After you left, you found another woman to replace me,
and soon after I found others to replace you somewhat. But in
that leaving, you left behind more than just a half-filled
hamper, an empty favorite chair, power tools, and some wide
ties. You securely fashioned body parts, body movements, and
identical heavily-lashed blue eyes onto two sons who look like
they popped out of your mouth. Constant walking advertise-
ments that *Mark slept here.*

That's a whole lot more than a warm spot in a double bed.
As I find myself deeply in love and on the threshold of commitment, I'm terrified of making the same mistake twice. And
then wonder: Did I really make a mistake in falling in love with
you and marrying you all those years ago? When we were both
so young and full of hope and plans and new furniture? When
sleeping together every single night in our own bed was the
greatest dream that could come true? And did I make a mistake when I knew I was pregnant with our first son, way before
we could financially afford it? Were those mistakes?

I now choose to weed out the crummy things you did to
me and selfish things I did to you. I would rather not remember
I never put you first in the marriage and often spent more time
with friends than with you. I'll tuck away the fact you seldom
called when you went out of town and lay on the couch watching football instead of spending lazy Sunday afternoons with
me.

Instead, I'll remember how you got down on your hands
and knees and searched all over for my engagement ring after

I, at 19, had thrown it at you during an adolescent tantrum and then put it back on my finger instead of walking out with it. I'll remember knowing (even if only for several years of my life) that, when you did love me, you unequivocally loved me.

How can I put time and space and a legal document between that?

You were a rat for leaving me when you did—with a brand-new baby in a snowstorm in February, no less! But I can see now the courage it took because things had gotten so bad and so sad and neither one of us knew how to fix it.

Maybe I've finally come to know you as a person and not just as a failure as a husband. I see what a good human being you are (even though my mother will always maintain what a creep you are). You are sociable, outgoing, and intelligent. Contrary to my telling you for years that you were loudmouth, showoff, know-it-all.

You are an ex-husband to be proud of in an age of deadbeats and skip-outs who never pay a dime in child support and truly bail out on their children. Though I wouldn't nominate you for Father of the Year, I have felt a softening taking place, and it both amazes and confuses me. There were days when you really did boil my blood.

Experts say that as time goes by you forget the bad and remember only the good. Wrong. I'll remember the bad, all right, but maybe now I'm able to forgive you for it—and hope you can forgive me, too.

Don Herod said, "Marriage is a mistake of the young—which we should all make."

I'm glad I made my mistake with you.

The strength of this piece lies in its unsentimental, unwavering look at the conflicting feelings about her failed marriage. As she writes, Werth sees self and other in perspective—and writes of the thin line that joins and unites as much as it divides and splits. The result is reconciliation without whitewashing; acceptance of uncertainty, and the inescapable overlap of love and hate. She acknowledges the both/and qualities of her feelings.

Sy Safransky, author of *New Men, New Minds,* gives voice to the profound interconnectedness of our hurts and loves.

I dreamt last night my father had died. Waking up, I felt thankful it was only a dream. I reached out to him, across that twilight space that separates dreaming from waking. Then I opened my eyes. Fully awake now, I realized he *was* dead. I wept, reliving the pain of his dying four years ago. When I was a teenager, we were each other's best friends. When I fell in love at nineteen, we began drifting away from one another. No, drift is the wrong word; it suggests indifference, but our new inability to communicate bound us as passionately as our camaraderie. Not having a vocabulary for my new emotions, nor he for his sadness that I no longer idolized him, we watched our closeness die like a beloved animal neither of us knew how to save. Eventually, I found the words, but I was nearly thirty then, and he was dying.

Absorbed in the battle between the light and the dark (either/or thinking), we rarely glimpse the myriad of potentialities that lie between.

SAM KEEN

To let our parents be, to accept them as people, human, and therefore imperfect, rather than as gods—that is the challenge. They *were* gods for us when we were small, their approval and disapproval roping us in, their love our meat and bone. How hard to let go, in all the cells of the body and folds of the mind.

We live out the dramas that most compel us—being powerful; being powerless; being *someone*. Pain itself can become an identity easier than joy to bear, because it's familiar, a lumpy old mattress shot through with knives, but with *our* name on it, and therefore more to be trusted than the unknown . . .

Letting Go

Number and date your Feeling Sketchbook entry. Cluster IMPERFECT/PERFECT and let it lead you to parts of yourself, or to a relationship. Your cluster will let you know where it is necessary to go. Write a Word Sketch that follows that intuition.

Exploring the Act

- Notice any new perspective in what emerged.
- Notice any physical sensation of lightness or of release resulting from your awareness that something no longer has to be perfect. Conversely, notice a heaviness if the need for perfection has not yet let go.

RECONCILING AND THE BODY

One of our most important boundaries is our skin. Our bodies can tell us much about how we have dealt with polarities. As we explore the relationship between our minds and bodies, we discover that, as dance therapist Gabrielle Roth says so beautifully,

> . . . your body is the ground metaphor of your life, the expression of your existence. It is your Bible, your encyclopedia, your life story. Everything that happens to you is stored and reflected in your body. Your body knows; your body tells. The relationship of your self to your body is indivisible, inescapable, unavoidable. In the marriage of flesh and spirit, divorce is impossible, but that doesn't mean the marriage is necessarily happy or successful.

Indivisible. How well I know! Yet body and spirit are often at war. As we go about relearning the language of cooperation between mind, heart, and body, we may strike a truce that is uneasy at best. But it is a necessary truce.

The fact that unease comes, that anxiety comes, is not the issue here, is not the fact that we cannot necessarily pinpoint its cause. The only issue worthy of attention is that we have tools at hand with which to deal with what comes—to accept, understand, and let go. Breathing is a stabilizer, grounding you in your body, making you aware of your own life rhythms, the blanks of not breathing, the hollows of breathing so shallowly that your nerves and muscles turn into invisible knots.

Letting Go

Sitting or lying comfortably, focus on your breathing. Inhale deeply. Be sensitive to the moment of in-between, the moment of stillness between inhale and exhale. Exhale deeply. Now return to normal breathing rhythms, but with awareness of doing both.

As we travel beyond the emotional trap of either/or thinking, we come to realize that even our illnesses are signposts. Physical health is part of the both/and truth of our lives. Sometimes our bodies simply reflect the nicks and scratches inherent in living. Sometimes our bodies reflect low self-esteem. And sometimes our bodies reflect the wrong-headedness of the belief that all illness is harmful. In a sense, you cannot have health without having had it tested. Without testing your health, you may be caught in the illusion that you are exempt from sickness and death. Not one of us is exempt. No one. Never.

I found it utterly shocking to realize that being truly whole might depend on acknowledgment of my damage. The *whole* truth lies in reconciliation, a coming to terms with the polarities of our lives—illness and health, damage and intactness, which builds resiliency despite the setbacks and disasters life brings.

I knew a man, proud of his logical approach to life who became ill with cancer. With deadly calm, he said: "I've been held hostage by the AMA (American Medical Association) for almost a year now, and I *resent* their control of my body, of my life."

"Wait!" I said. "Is the AMA really holding you hostage? Are you choosing your treatments?"

"Yes, but . . ."

"Are you aware of other options?"

"Yes, but . . ."

"Then, at best, you can say your illness is holding you hostage, not the AMA."

"They've kept me from doing the things I planned to do."

"Who has?"

"The AMA!"

"No, your illness."

"Are you blaming the illness on *me*?"

And so it went. The issue is not one of blame. The issue is that in this man's frame of reference, his boundaries were too rigid. The blame, he was convinced, lay with the institution. As long as he clung with steel rigidity to the control of which he was so proud, he was unable to reconcile the interconnectedness of control and surrender.

POWER IN HELPLESSNESS

Psychiatrist Sheldon Kopp writes that one of the truths of life is that "we must learn the power of living with our helplessness." An interesting paradox: power in helplessness.

Letting Go

We all leave childhood with wounds. In time we may transform our liabilities into gifts. The faults that pockmark the psyche may become the source of a man's or woman's beauty. The injuries we have suffered invite us to assume the most human of all vocations—to heal ourselves and others.

SAM KEEN

Cluster THE POWER OF HELPLESSNESS and go into free flow, letting connections spill out, no matter how absurd they may seem. As soon as something resonates, play with it in language. Write a Word Sketch without worrying about how good it is. Just get thoughts down. You can always revise later if what you are getting down feels important.

Exploring the Act

- Notice what images seem to strike a chord;
- Notice what image suggests *both* power *and* helplessness. That is the image you want to explore in writing.

If the essence of living is change and flexibility, then human beings who are too set in their ways will stagnate. Becoming aware of the convergence of polarities is learning to adapt to changed circumstances—learning to reframe, redefine, recognize, and reconcile.

I know a man who has said, again and again, "I know who I am." He says it with set jaw. Well and good. But the lines of being and becoming are constantly blurred. If we are growing, who we are shifts the boundaries of who we once were, and who we are becoming. There may be similarity, but not sameness. We cannot possibly stay the same if we are living creatures. Each unpredictable turn, each surprise, produces unexpected shifts, the potential for new insights, and new resilience. A willingness to change is a prerequisite for openness to life. Being closed to life means being stuck in the expectation of stability, fixity, certainty.

The more receptive we become, the more open we are to the expression that carries the seeds of our own healing. Reread what you have written. Now, simply pull out one thought from your Word Sketch that feels like one of those seeds. Write it as a nutshell statement or a question at the bottom of the same page—a single sentence—a compressed awareness of your own evolving awareness.

GIVING AWAY UNNEEDED BAGGAGE

In filling our blanks and hollows, we sometimes want to look at the other end of the spectrum. Sometimes, instead of reconciling, we need to discard something we may not have realized we've outgrown. Like last year's clothing on this year's child, we may be trying to squeeze ourselves into categories that no longer fit.

Removing the superfluous, the unnecessary, the destructive, or the outlived from our mental attics is a vital part of making room for new possibilities, as poet Miller Williams wrote in his poem "Sale."

Sale

Partnership dissolved.
Everything must be sold.
Individually or the set
as follows:
Brain, one standard, cold.
Geared to glossing.
Given to hard replies.
convolutions convey the illusion
of exceptional death.
Damaged.
think. think of me. but you are not thinking
One pair of eyes. Green. Like new.
Especially good for girls and women walking,
wicker baskets,
paintings by Van Gogh,
red clocks and frogs, chicken snakes and snow.
look at me, but you are not looking at me
One pair of ears, big. Best offer takes.
Tuned to Bach, Hank Williams, bees,

the Book of Job.
Shut-off for deans, lieutenants and
salesmen talking.
listen. listen please, but you are not listening
Mouth, one, wide.
Some teeth missing.
Two and a half languages. Adaptable to pipes
and occasional kissing.
Has been broken but in good repair.
Lies.
tell me. tell me please. why won't you tell me
Hand, right and left.
Feet. Neck. Some hair.
Stomach, heart, spleen and
accessory parts.
come. come quickly. there is only a little time
Starts tomorrow
what you've been waiting for
and when it's gone it's gone
so hurry
hurry

Letting Go

Numbering and dating your entry in your Feeling Sketch-book, cluster FOR SALE. Experiment with objects, feelings, persons you might be willing to—or need to—let go of. Sell off something you don't want: a job, a grudge, a hurt, an out-lived assumption, an outworn *must* or *ought*. Spill out the possibilities. After clustering, go with the one that becomes a strange attractor for you. Write a Word Sketch in the form of a "For Sale" ad. Let it be whimsical, serious, abbreviated, or lengthy. Let it take whatever form it wants to.

Exploring the Act

- How did it feel to recognize what you would be willing to let go of? Did you feel more powerful or less? Relieved or regretful?

- Whether it is painful or fun, look at what you are choosing to let go of through the safety valve of words: A person? A part of yourself? A material object? A desire? An impossible dream? An obsession? An injury? You name it.

After reading your Word Sketch, restate, at the bottom of the page in a single sentence what you are willing to part with. Should this act trigger a veritable "garage sale" of ideas, write down as many of these as want to come. Each is part of a pattern which makes up an emotional whole: what you were, are now, and are willing to become.

Letting Go

Selling off outworn emotional baggage is not the only way to build on your new insights. Another way is to play with a pattern such as William Stafford's "How to Build an Owl."

How to Build an Owl
    1. Decide you must

    2. develop deep respect for feather, bone, claw

    3. Place your trembling thumb where the heart will be: for one hundred hours watch so you will know where to put the first feather

    4. stay awake forever. when the bird takes shape gently pry open its beak and whisper into it: "mouse"

    5. let it go

Stafford approaches the polarity of holding on/letting go from yet another direction: that of defining the necessaries in our life. Think of the cliché question: If you were to be left indefinitely on a desert island, what would you take with you? Some of us list our favorite companions, others might name foods, books, or a guitar. Whatever we may choose, such thinking allows us to pare our lives down to the essentials, to the things we feel life would not be worth living without.

Letting Go

Reread the poem, cluster (HOW TO BUILD . .) Play with
what emerges, number and date your entry in your Feeling
Sketchbook, and write a Word Sketch using Stafford's poem
as a model.

Exploring the Act

- Notice what in your Cluster attracted you to build.
- Notice what ways the building of this thing is a metaphor of where you are at the present moment.
- Notice whether your building project is a reflection of
  your emotional state.
- Notice whether this building is a part of the evolving
  pattern of your reflections. Certain images will recur.
  This writing is all part of the reconciling process, of filling the blanks and hollows for your feeling life. Partici-
  pate. Allow yourself to play. Enjoy the surprises when
  they appear.

Your diverse paths through pain to possibility are fashioned by your own ongoing decisions. Refusing to decide is
impossible—for that refusal too is a decision.

Letting Go

Wishes. What a potent word resonating from our childhoods.
Read author Robert Fulghum's "Wish list."

> I do know what I want someone to give me for Christmas:
> Wind-up mechanical toys that make noises and go round and
> round and do funny things. No batteries. Toys that need me to
> help them out from time to time. . . . Well, okay, that's close,
> but not quite exactly. It's delight and simplicity I want. Foolish-
> ness and fantasy and noise. Angels land miracles and wonder
> and innocence and magic . . . But what I *really, really, really*
> want for Christmas is just this:
> - I want to be five years old again for an hour.
> - I want to laugh a lot and cry a lot.
> - I want to be picked up and rocked to sleep in someone's arms,
>   and carried up to bed just one more time . . .

Notice that his impossible wishes are stated as "just one more time" and "again for an hour." Not for all time. Fulghum is willing to confront his real world. But his middle wish to out of time: "I want to laugh a lot *and* cry a lot."

Cluster (THREE COSMIC WISHES.) You may get nine or nineteen, but choose the three that mean most to you here and now.

Exploring the Act

- Notice whether your wishes reflect a time constraint or wether they are "out of time."
- Reflect on what might have triggered your wishes.
- Become aware of any recurring patterns; for example, were there any connections between your wishes and other Sketchbook entries?

RECONCILIATION: CLIMBING BY SMALL STEPS

Awareness of the polarities of life helps us remember that the solution to a complex problem is always a series of improvisations, approximations, and experiments. Reconciling helps us become flexible. There are no absolutes in the business of living. Downs have ups; ups have downs. In facing the ups and downs we learn resilience.

Frances Lear in "Color Me Blue" looks back on one of her recurring depressions, and sees that the upward spiral is made of tiny steps.

> One morning long ago I woke up down. And so I went back to sleep, the depressive's reflexive refuge from the blues. I re-awakened to the sound of ancient ghosts—childhood traumas—gathering at my bedside. They did not make chit-chat. Effortlessly, they took away my approval of myself firmly felt the day before and, as if it were an afterthought, ushered in my helplessness—the despot of downs. My depression snapped into place. My limbs were leaden. My sense of size was altered. I had no eyes. Dimly remembering what was possible from other downs, I got up. I defrosted a lemon cake and ate it whole.

Again, the warning signs had gotten past me: the irascibility, the pressure building up behind my belt, my dark view of tomorrow. I dressed myself in black to be unseen.

One's impulse in depression is to crawl inside it, to drown out consciousness, to be so rooted in defeat as to lose all hope of ever being up. To think one *can* do anything is to be up. One *cannot* think "up" when one is down. The command to "pull yourself together," spoken by someone who is reasonably pulled, only serves to compound the depressive's guilt for failure to improve. Orders to feel better can only be heard from one's own inner voice—mine too faint to reach on that day.

Downs are keen on worsening, and do worsen by escape into mind-altering substances, food, or the transient approval of a stranger. I drank water to diffuse the lemon cake, and as the day went by searched, against the odds I thought, for some history upon which to pattern my recovery. The determination to do battle with my mood changed my position some, although pessimism, inherent in depression, kept me listening for the other shoe to drop. Healthfully, I recalled a lesson from the past: Time spent listening for the other shoe will certainly produce one. Shoes are dropping all the time. The point is to be agile and move on to something else.

Agility—exercise—sets off a reaction in the body that prods the psyche. I took a coldish shower and dressed this time in green, my mother's favorite color on me because my eyes are green. My mirror was less bitchy. Glancing at it, I muttered, "That woman has a certain character." *Did I say that? Did I hold an approving thought of me?* If so, I am surely on my way back up.

Not so fast, I warned myself. Downs have a fierce tenacity. One moment of self-love may tremble them, but more, much more—consistent self respect—is needed to render them benign.

Piece by piece, I gathered up my whole self, as if it were a string of pearls, and returned myself to me. My chemistry began to right itself. The past was now less with me. I walked into the bathroom and turned sideways to the mirror. The lemon cake did not show much.

On that long-ago evening, I understood at last that the tiny voyage I had just taken—which seemed to me a thousand treks to the moon—would someday be less arduous. Yes. I was certain of it.

Figure 8.4

Figure 8.5

Experience, which destroys innocence, also leads one back to it.

JAMES BALDWIN

Two of the Word Sculptures (Figure 8.4 and Figure 8.5) from a time of reflection look slightly different to me than others I have created. They speak more of a quiet awareness of my mind's ongoing patterns. These Word Sculptures reflect not only the world's unpredictability we experience in the radical discontinuities of periods of crisis but also the awareness that life does exhibit relatively stable patterns which sustain us when we consciously become aware of them. If the polarities of predictability and unpredictability are powerful forces in our daily lives, not to mention crisis, we can reconcile these opposites by understanding that our minds are so constructed that we simultaneously seek stability *and* novelty. Pain may be as much a part of reflection as the pleasure gleaned from seeing an outworn pattern from a different angle. Both hindsight and foresight are under constant revision. Acceptance of both leads to new ways of being. Flow, new meaning.

LOOKING AHEAD

In moving through this chapter, we have been filling in emotional blanks and hollows. We have become increasingly open to the nuances of feeling carried in our recursive images. We have discovered more of our personal patterns. We have seen examples of the power of reconciliation and of coming to terms with whatever damage our psyches or bodies may have suffered. Now we are letting go of the superfluous in our lives, needless baggage weighing us down. We are gradually coming to recognize what is essential to our well-being. As we recognize our options through naming and framing, we are growing into resilience.

The focus of our final chapter is to complete the spiral and rejoin the ever-flowing streams of our lives. We do so by learning to discover the beginnings of wisdom, our awareness of a wider spectrum of options.

The Wisdom of the Glass Heart: Reconnecting with the World

And so we begin to come full circle; to emerge from the depth of the spiral of personal crisis and return to its upper, outer edge where we entered it—but now with the clarity of vision we have gained along the way. Now we know that chaos has pattern, that turbulence provokes the discovery of strange attractors, that emotional turbulence, when accepted and not avoided, leads to growth. We understand the spirals of our life for the first time because we accept what is, rather than struggle for what we think should be. We recognize ourselves as living, breathing, dynamic, changing beings, always in process. We have begun to value flexibility and adaptability, qualities necessary for wholeness.

Our goal in this chapter is to return to healthy participation in the world. In becoming receptive to and expressive of who we were, who we are, and who we may become, we are engaged in an ongoing process of self-healing. We could call this process of the mind at play *wisdom*.

Living with wisdom is learning both to hold on and to let go. In time, as we confront our feelings, and learn to welcome uncertainty, our lives take on new depth and breadth. The movement toward wisdom is both serious and playful, and it depends less on our outward circumstances than on a new way of looking at the world.

What we call the beginning is often the end And to make an end is to make a beginning. The end is where we start from. And every phrase And sentence is right . . . Every phrase and every sentence is an end and a beginning. Every poem an epitaph.

T.S. ELIOT

My increased awareness of the patterns and paradoxes of my life has eased me through difficult transitions. This awareness still moves me toward something I can only call wholeness. Still, when I am overtired or overworked, I reexperience the familiar symptoms of anxiety. I no longer fight them. Instead, I listen to what they have to say. I focus on my breath. I do a quick Word Sculpture, just to see what patterns my mind is occupied with at the moment. Then I write my way into discovery of their meaning. Having named and framed, I no longer feel so overwhelmed. An image or a single word or phrase becomes a signpost that tells me where I am.

Wisdom is knowing you cannot separate pain and pleasure, although you can distinguish between them. Wisdom is facing real fear as well as embracing real joy. Wisdom is knowing, as poet Peter Meinke put it, that "beauty without the perishable pulse/is dry and sterile."

The spiral of wisdom, like that of pain, is organic. Each time we rediscover its still center, we move into the possibility of change. We can reach the calming core of the spiral as often as we wish—or need to—with the tools of Aware Breathing, naming and framing through the Word Sketches resulting from clustering, or through the deceptively simple designs of Word Sculptures. Computer scientist Clifford Pickover noted that, no matter how you sample chaotic processes, they will exhibit unique patterns. Not only do different people's voices create recognizably different fractal patterns, but so do the sounds of their hearts. So do our feelings. The configurations of my occasional Word Sculptures these days reflect an emotional shift as do the words that embellish them: greater balance, wholeness, a sense of participation in life's rhythms.

WISDOM AND OUR EXPANDING STORY

Writing our stories puts our suffering in context. Expression is at the heart of this book. To create personally meaningful patterns is a fundamental function of the human brain. Each of us has a unique story to write. Yet, each of us also reflects universal emotional patterns of feelings. That is our human story— the story simultaneously unique and universal.

Figure 9.1

Figure 9.2

Long intrigued by the stories pouring from the pens of my workshop participants, triggered by a deep hunger for meaning, I looked up the many definitions of *story*. The first definition was predictable: "The narrating of an event or series of events, whether true or fictitious." Yes, but there is more to the idea of *story*, having to do with coherence, patterns. The collective human story subsumes all individual stories. They echo with the commonality of feeling, begun in infancy with our most fundamental differentiation between pleasure and pain, between yes and no, and all the gradations in-between. Wisdom lies in creating patterns of meaning. To create stories is to create patterns of meaning. Psychobiologist Renee Fuller in *In Search of the IQ Correlation* suggests this need to create coherent meaning may be the ultimate "deep structure" of cognition, so fundamental to mind that she calls it "the lost engram":

> The human need to make life coherent, to make a story out of it is fundamental to human thinking . . . because for us, a mind without a story is a mind without meaning. And meaning is the essence of our consciousness. Our story-engrossed brain seems to believe that, in Cartesian fashion, we exist because we tell the story of our existence.

Philosopher Sam Keen has said that we can only read the world story through the lens of our own autobiography. We define ourselves in our stories. Yet, no matter how exhaustive, we can never write or tell our *whole* story. Any of us can only perceive a part of reality. In effect, our stories are always fractal patterns of aspects of our lives with the greatest emotional resonance. Events with little emotional punch don't strike in our memory. Our stories—past, present, and future—are colored by feeling: what hurts, what brings joy. What we are today may not be at all what we were yesterday. What we feel today will not be what we felt yesterday. Some feeling we didn't acknowledge yesterday may explode into expression today.

Unless we constantly use our tools, there can be little growth; and stunted growth invites the body's revenge. Without expression our stories remain unborn, locked inside to wreak their private havoc on our physical selves.

Writing and story-telling contextualizes our suffering. In context, we can envision a larger picture, and glimpse moments of wisdom. In those moments our unique personal stories and the larger human story merge.

The nature of human being can only be defined by recounting the history of what we are becoming.

SAM KEEN

[Stories reflect our] continuities and discontinuities, themes that appear and disappear, references, comparisons, similes and metaphors, intimations and suggestions, moods and mysteries, contours of coherence and spells of impenetrability. . . . 'Their story, yours, mine—it's what we all carry with us on this trip we take, and we owe it to each other to respect our stories and learn from them' (R. Coles telling about what William Carlos Williams told him.)

ROBERT COLES

John Donne wrote, "No man is an island." Modern poet Linda Pastan insisted there was only one human story: ". . . but what storms I could describe/swirling/in every thumbprint." And so it is. Our stories are both universal *and* unique. Our own personal experiences of human feeling are part of the larger tapestry of human emotion.

You have taken time to read this book because you had a need. You have explored and experienced a period of pain and suffering. You have chosen to face your emotions instead of running from them. You have dared look at your own moments of unbearable turbulence. You have faced the kind of feelings none of us is exempt from: restlessness without apparent cause, internal struggle without apparent reason, plain misery without provocation, helplessness, profound grief during which you felt as though you would never be whole again—and facing them is allowing you to move to deeper levels of integration.

You have discovered that tools of transformation are accessible and simple. With only a small notebook and a pen you can awaken, acknowledge, express the full range of your emotional being. You have learned one secret of wisdom: to know the power of reconciling life's polarities. You can't make them go away. You can't separate black from white, up from down, in from out, pain from possibility. You can only externalize, express, and transform your hunger for absolutes. Reconciling polarities happens within; it cannot be imposed from without. It is the shift in the angle of your perception, a shift you can achieve when you write.

Leafing through Alastair Reid's volume of poems, I rediscovered "Weathering," a poem about the growth of trees in which he makes a metaphoric leap to his own life, ending with the line, "Weathering is what I would like to do well." Weathering is what I, too, would like to do well. I leafed further and chanced on his poem "The Spiral"—the same metaphor we have used throughout this book.

> The seasons of this year are in my luggage.
> Now, lifting the last picture from the wall,
> I close the eyes of the room. Each footfall
> clatters on the bareness of the stair.
> The family ghosts fade in the hanging air.

We remember sadness so that we can ignite and enhance life. What we eventually discover in our passionate remembering of the galactic, terrestial, biological, and human stories is that a study of the universe is a study of the self.

BRIAN SWIMME

Mirrors reflect the silence. There is no message.
I wait in the still hall for a car to come.
Behind, the house will dwindle to a name.

Places, addresses, faces left behind.
The present is a devious wind
obliterating days and promises.
Tomorrow is a tinker's guess.
Marooned in cities, dreaming of greenness,
or dazed by journeys, dreading to arrive—
change, change is where I live.

For possibility,
I choose to leave behind
each language, each country.
Will this place be an end,
or will there be one other,
truer, rarer?

Often now, in dream,
abandoned landscapes come,
figuring a constant theme:
Have you left us behind?
What have you still to find?

Across the spiral distance,
through time and turbulence,
the rooted self in me
maps out its true country.

And, as my father found
his own small weathered island,
so will I come to ground

where that small man, my son,
can put his years on.

For him, too, time will turn.

Only you can map out your own "true country," and that
is exactly what you have been doing as you worked your way
through this book. You were willing to risk, you yearned for
creative expression, and you began to trust in something
beyond pain. That something is the possibility of change and
the promise of wisdom.

WISDOM, SELF, AND WORLD

Wisdom is as ambiguous a concept as humor. It is as impossible to say "I have learned humor!"—and foolish—as to say to ourselves, "I have achieved wisdom!" Yet sometimes we recognize wisdom in someone else. I sensed wisdom born of suffering in psychiatrist Sheldon Kopp's books, several of which were written during his struggle with a brain tumor. His wisdom was framed in a tongue-in-cheek list of "truths," he called "An Eschatological Laundry List." The list originated in play. He describes in *Even a Stone Can Be a Teacher* how he wrote

> . . . during one of those uncluttered spaces when I took time out to enjoy the pleasure of writing to a loved friend far away, an unobligated letter born wholly out of abundance. The subject of this letter was the foolishness of pontificating in my profession.

Although his list began as a joke, in light of all we have learned about being receptive to feelings, Kopp's description of how his list emerged speaks volumes.

> I did not have to search for them. They arose . . . as in a dream, taking form almost more quickly than I could write them down. This was to be a zany private spoof, a way of tenderly making fun of myself. Instead, what emerged was a fragment of a cosmic joke, a visionary list of truths which, at my best, shape my life, provide answers to unasked questions, and give insights too powerfully simple to be grasped finally and forever.

Kopp's "Laundry Lists" (he later wrote a second) strike me as wise and rich. I return to them again and again. Often, as I reread them, I find them a fertile source for new patterns of insight, hindsight, throughsight. They speak to me most when hindsight connects one of them with slivers of my own life story. They continue to expand the boundaries of my seeing, to soften the rigid lines I once drew around what seemed to be absolutes.

Letting Go

Here are some of my favorites from both of Kopp's lists. They are taken from *Even a Stone Can Be a Teacher* and from *Who am I . . . Really?* Some will speak to you more than others. Choose one that touches you, write it in a circle on a page, and quickly cluster as many specific, personal examples of events, feelings, or incidents which are suggested by this truth.

By holding your breath you lose life, by letting go you gain life.

ALAN WATTS

An Eschatological Laundry List: A Partial Register of the 927 (or was it 928?) Eternal Truths

5. Nothing lasts!
8. You only get to keep what you give away.
10. The world is not necessarily just. Being good often does not pay off, and there is no compensation for misfortune.
11. You have a responsibility to do your best nonetheless.
14. You can't make anyone love you.
21. All of you is worth something, if you will only own it.
28. The most important things, each of us must do for ourselves.
29. Love is not enough, but it sure helps.
31. How strange that, so often, it all seems worth it.
32. We must live within the ambiguity of partial freedom, partial power, and partial knowledge.
36. You can run, but you can't hide.
38. We must learn the power of living with our helplessness.
39. The only victory lies in surrender to oneself.
41. You are free to do whatever you like. You need only face the consequences.
42. What do you know . . . for sure . . . anyway?
43. Learn to forgive yourself, again and again and again and again.
46. None of us is what we were taught we are supposed to be.
48. Instead of spending so much of my life trying to fight off depression, overcome anxiety, deny inadequacy, I can willingly experience just how sad and scared and helpless I sometimes feel.

51. Victory requires only that I learn to survive repeated defeats.

54. Revealing myself to others is taking a chance. But hiding out can be just as risky.

60. When I succeed in deceiving others, I am left isolated and unknown.

63. If no one knows me, who can love me?

Exploring the Act

- Notice any similarities or differences between those items that spoke most strongly to you. Noticed any recurring patterns reflective of your emotional turbulence or plateaus.

- Whatever items in the list that you responded to signal where you are today. What emerged in your cluster reflects your ongoing transformation. Follow up by writing a nutshell statement of what strikes you as significant. If you want to, write several statements.

- If nothing struck you as significant, try asking yourself "What is *not* there?" That question often reveals more than the first. If necessary, try reverse clustering. Draw a circle, leaving it blank, then cluster the not-there's until you sense a focus for them. Name and frame this not-there awareness by writing a Word Sketch in your Feeling Sketchbook. Follow up by writing a nutshell statement at the bottom of the page.

Over the past twelve years I have learned that a tree needs space to grow, that coyotes sing down by the creek in January, that I can drive a nail into oak only when it is green, that bees know more about making honey than I do, that love can become sadness, and that there are more questions than answers.

SUE HUBBELL

When you become receptive, you cannot help but change. You are learning truths you never expected to learn and will gradually internalize the bits of wisdom encapsulated in each of these insights. By personalizing these truths you create your own.

Letting Go

Over time, you will be able to identify your own truths. The statement "Today is the first day of the rest of your life," can be a cliché or profound wisdom, depending on your point of view. Today's feeling may mark an imperceptible movement or it may be a major shift in whole-seeing, whole-being. Be open to it. Name it; frame it. Then, one day, look back on it and cherish it or laugh at it or play with it or elaborate on it. If a new pattern of feeling follows a downward spiral of negatives, invite it; let it have its say. You will learn from it; it is part of the spectrum of feeling nuances that constitute *you*.

AFFIRMING AND RENOUNCING

Living a life of wholeness demands both affirmation and renunciation. There is a time and a place to affirm with the sacred *yes* and there is a time and a place to renounce with the sacred *no*. The small child learns the power of *no* at an early age. It is the beginning of a sense of self, of empowerment. The forthright negative allows us to let go, to renounce.

Workshop participant Marla Johnson clustered NO (see Figure 9.3), enabling her to name and frame a new understanding of her difficulty with decisiveness.

Let us think of two people who have been together in a warm and truthful relationship. . . . They have taken the risk of loving each other with no guarantees or superficial promises. Our relationship to life can be the same: Joy and pleasure enrich it; pain may mold and deepen it.

PIERO FERRUCCI

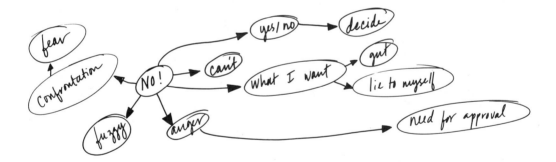

Figure 9.3

I have never had the knack for No. To be noisy about knowing what I really want has never been as easy as just being nice. I go back and forth between fuzzy and clear, lies and gut—and the timeless anger of avoided confrontation makes me nod my head yes when I really mean no. Do you want to go? Well, I don't know. Do you? Ultimately, I say I don't really care. I am needy of the nubby knit of approval on my cheek and ever unwilling to release myself from kneeling at the sacrificial altar of decision.

In this Word Sketch we see the beginnings of a transformation, the recognition of what *is*, not what *ought* to be. That is the beginning of change, of wisdom. We can't make changes if we are not aware. When we are, we can ask questions of ourselves, becoming seekers of personal meaning.

Letting Go

Find out where you are in this time and space. Begin by breathing evenly, listening to the rhythm of your breath. Add the sound of *no*, letting the word wash over you. Say it tentatively, quietly, then assertively. Try it on for size. Say it until you can cluster (NO.) Then be open to whatever comes and write a Word Sketch involved with what you have discovered in your Cluster.

Exploring the Act

- Notice how your *no* sounds as you reread your response. Is it hesitant, tentative, angry, confident?
- Notice what you said *no* to, whether it surprised you, how it felt in your gut.
- Follow the same process with *yes*. Hear its sound, cluster it, write a Word Sketch that uses that *yes*.

Our responses of *yes* and *no* are like water faucets that control the flowing currents of our lives. Completion of our spiral and acceptance of new challenges and joys will depend on our willingness to affirm *and* renounce by listening to our inner limbic *yes* and *no*. It does not lie.

WISDOM AND OUR PROJECTS

We are all travelers to uncertain destinations, yet despite our uncertainty, we have an inborn need to make commitments to projects, people, and ideas.

Commitment, J. Ruth Gendler tells us in *The Book of Qualities*, ". . . is such a simple man, and yet he is mysterious. He is more generous than most people. His heart is open. He is not afraid of life. He is married to Joy."

Genuine travelers travel not to overcome distance but to discover distance.

J. P. CARSE

One discovers that destiny can be directed, that one does not have to remain in bondage to the first wax imprint made on childhood sensibilities. Once the deforming mirror has been smashed, there is a possibility of wholeness. There is a possibility of joy.

ANAIS NIN

Joy is possible precisely because of our awareness as one end of a continuum. Poet William Bronk in his poem "I Am" says it somewhat mysteriously.

I Am
Joy
which is neither
because
nor in spite of
but is
joy

and despair
which neither
was
nor will be
but is all.

Doing work which has to be done over and over again helps us recognize the natural cycles of growth and decay, of birth and death, and thus become aware of the dynamic order of the universe.

FRITJOF CAPRA

Bronk's poem "I Am" is as enigmatic as poet Alan Dugan's "Morning Song" is pragmatic.

Look, it's morning, and a little water gurgles in the tap.
I wake up waiting, because it's Sunday, and turn twice
    more
than usual in bed, before I rise to cereal and comic strips.
I have risen to the morning danger and feel proud,
and after shaving off the night's disguises, after searching
close to the bone for blood, and finding only a little,
I shall walk out bravely into the daily accident.

Despite the chances of accident or the certainty of uncertainty, we are the principal actors of our lives. The Letting Go activities of this book have made us even more aware of the responsibility and choices inherent in this role. "My life is the only creation I am sure is my own." wrote Jeanann Collins, one of my students.

As imperative as the exploration of our interior emotional landscapes may be, it is not, in itself, enough to make a full life. As challenging as our duties to those around us may be—our jobs, our family roles, our relationships and community services—neither are they enough. Unless we give ourselves the gift of something which engages our attention purely for our own private and personal joy, we have disenfranchised ourselves from our own lives.

It is never too late to grow into whatever you choose to be and become. Engaging in projects *personally* meaningful to you is another big step toward wisdom.

I have mentioned earlier my adolescent lack of understanding for Martin Luther's statement that even if he knew the world would end tomorrow he would still plant an apple tree today. Luther's statement has nothing to do with reason. It has everything to do with attitude, with a way of being and acting in, and on, the world, with yes and no, with *will*, as neurologist Oliver Sacks pointed out in a speech in Washington, D.C.:

> It seems to me will is the deepest thing in our being. Even in profound dementias, when the slate seems to have been wiped clean, there's this urge—something I equate with life itself—that is suggested in the last words of Samuel Beckett's novel, *The Unnameable*: "You must go on, I can't go on, I'll go on."

Wisdom, or however close to it we can come, depends on that will, that going on. Without the constant challenge provided by our projects, without the spur of personal interest and enjoyment that keeps us involved with our projects, even wisdom becomes sterile and bleak, a negative renunciation. Involvement that springs from the self expands the life spiral. But refusal to go onward, an unwillingness to chance risky outcomes, may be a vestigial desire to hold onto our pain or to hide from ourselves and from the world.

Letting Go

In your Feeling Sketchbook, cluster (HUNGER.) Be open to whatever feelings come. You may be surprised to discover that you have hungers you haven't dared to acknowledge before. Be free to acknowledge them.

Do you know that disease and death must needs overtake us, no matter what we are doing? What do you wish to be doing when it overtakes you? If you have anything better to be doing when you are so overtaken, get to work on that.

EPICTETUS

The torch of doubt and chaos, this is what the sage steers by.

CHUANG TSU

Exploring the Act

- To help you in your exploration, notice—just notice, nothing more—the tone of what emerged. Were you moving mostly into the past with regretful "if only's"? Into the future with "oughts"? Was there a despairing sense of the present, as in "What difference does it make"? Most of all, notice any unfulfilled hungers that can be actually satisfied if you have the *will* to satisfy them.

You may gain a handle on whether you are feeling ready for a personal project. If not, go on with other things and allow yourself more time to heal. Come back to this question at another time by reclustering HUNGER. Remember that you are not a static but a dynamic system and do not step into the same river twice. On another day the emotional landscape of your life will look different.

WISDOM AND AGING

While age is never a guarantee of wisdom—a person can be wise or unwise at any age—as we accumulate more and more experience in life's spirals, something changes. Perhaps it gets easier to look in the spaces *between* our usual categories, to grasp emotional nuances like those "powerfully simple" insights Kopp described.

Mennet Jacob, the correspondent I have quoted before, is a growing person. The seven years during which I've known her have not been easy. She has followed the spiral both up and down and up again. She has taken on projects which define her. She is vitally alive, despite loss. Read her implicit yes to life in a Word Sketch she sent me.

> The day I became seventy I crossed the bridge from today to tomorrow. I feared senility. I met enlightenment. Although I was afraid in body and soul of coping with and weeding out the painful past and made jokes about official "senility," deep down I knew I had hit a brick wall—the wall of me, my life, my future, my mortality, my death. Seventy—an official OKness

to be senile if I choose. Let me fracture my bones of wisdom. It is OK. But I'd come a long way, Baby. I wasn't about to sit out the rest of the unexpected in Rocking-Chair Land. No, that isn't my style. True, I'd been crippled by my past. But I believe I have severed several umbilicals, faced some "necessary losses," moved through and beyond, [and] remember what Goethe said, "The only way out is through." I remember because I have done it! So seventy is just the beginning for me. At last I understand I am gloriously free—at least for now.

Joy, amazement, pleasure in the face of life's relentless uncertainty is yet another part of wisdom.

Margaret Thompson, whom I have never met, recently wrote me about her own experiences in naming and framing. Insisting she had never had a bent for—or interest in—writing, she admits:

> Let me say right now this writing has been an adventure. It has been like opening Pandora's box. I've gone through the brambles of memories and what has filtered through them is a strong potion of pain. I've cried, I've been amused, and I've experienced catharsis.

The experience of surprise is a sign of one's readiness to grow. Amazement and wonder signify that one's concepts of self and of the world and of other people are ready to be re-formed. When we can be dumbfounded at what comes out of us or what others are capable of disclosing, we are growing persons.

SIDNEY JOURARD

Our shifting nuances of feeling are best evoked with our own language. Paradoxically, wisdom is also the realization that some feelings cannot be named. It may seem odd in a book about writing to suggest that not all lessons of wisdom can be articulated, and that perhaps they need not be.

As I write this, the mail arrives, and with it, a note from Mennet which begins:

> Where is my music, you ask—I'm not making any, I guess—except for positive living and enjoying positive experiences . . . enjoying the simple joy of appreciating being together forty-eight years. How we needed this time alone . . . don't feel as though I have to be the best at anything—just happy. Just remember, I, too, will write when I can and when I want to. But my music is my spirit right now . . .

The Mexican philosopher Octavio Paz called this peaceful place, where not even naming and framing is a necessity, "momentary fixity." It may not last—nothing lasts—but it is a point of liberation.

And it didn't last. Mennet faced another tailspin after that letter. But her projects sustain her. Her last New Year's letter made me smile, picturing this seventy-five-year-young woman at her desk, foresight in high gear, writing.

> So the goals are ahead, at hand, also behind, but always within a possible circle . . . The 1990s are a decade to move out and up and beyond, and I know I'm doing it!

Wisdom is not fully realized without the saving grace of humor. Louise Canby, eighty-seven and a self-described old lady, wrote for the *Washington Post* about her guilty secret.

> I must dress young. I may look like mutton but I must get myself up as lamb. Independence, did I say? Independent as a sheep! In my dogged pursuit of youthfulness I have embraced youth's weakness: I have yielded to peer pressure. I have been a sap. Why should I make myself keep up with the swim when what I really want to do is slump? What harm in idle moments? I want just to sit for a bit, look out the window at the buds bursting, the snow falling, the squirrels robbing the bird feeder. To label old family photographs. To reread *War and Peace* and finish *The Decline and Fall* . . . diluted with whodunits . . . I shall do what is natural to my age, and be a Natural Old Lady.

I think of the wisdom of others. I think of watching Pablo Casals and Arthur Rubinstein, both in their eighties, performing the music they loved and had made their life's work. I think of a German sculptress Elisabeth Kronseder, who came into my life shortly after my mother's death. Now at one-hundred-one, she wouldn't miss a second of her life. At ninety-seven she wrote:

> You won't believe how ancient I am; I am sooo ancient. I am through carving six-foot crosses. Now I want to paint flowers, those soft, vibrant creatures that please me so. And then, then I will learn to type, so you won't have to struggle with this crinkly handwriting.

The lessons of wisdom are not the invisible, they are the unsaid residuum; they are not the other side of reality but, rather, the other side of language, what we have on the tip of our tongue and that vanishes before it is said, the other side cannot be named because it is the opposite of a name.

OCTAVIO PAZ

Figure 9.4

Figure 9.5

Figure 9.6

The wisdom of age can be a gift, a "nude and secret silence" as Sandra Hochmann says. Too often in this youth-oriented culture we've forgotten how to accept it—a serious oversight. Like it or not, we are all on that same road through time. What we can learn from those ahead of us underscores the importance of continuing to grow, to dare, to expand the spirals of our lives. Such growth helps us to remain accepting and flexible in the face of wisdom's greatest challenge: dying.

WISDOM AND DYING

On my morning run today, I had an insight. If "living" is nothing more than ongoing learning, then even the process of dying can reveal—and demand—much new learning. The recent spate of books on dying, from Elisabeth Kubler-Ross's *On Death and Dying* to Gerald Jampolsky's *Love is Letting Go of Fear*, indicates a real hunger to learn how we may approach death more constructively. Poet Michelle Murray died barely having reached middle age. Her writing is eloquent testimony to the idea that constructive dying is another form of learning.

Death Poem

What will you have when you finally have me?
Nothing.
Nothing I have not already given
freely each day I spent
not waiting for you
but living
as if the shifting shadows of grapes
and fine-pointed leaves in the shelter
of the arbor would continue to tremble
when my eyes were absent
in memory of my seeing,
or the books fall open where I marked them
when my astonishment overflowed
at a gift come unsummoned, this love
for the open hands of poems,
earth fruit, sun soured grass, the steady

outward lapping stillness of midnight
snowfalls, an arrow of light waking me
on certain mornings with sharp wound
so secret that not even you
will have it when you have me.
You will have my fingers
but not what they touched. Some gestures
outflowing from a rooted being, the memory
of morning light cast on a bed
where two lay together—
the shining curve of flesh!—
they will forever be out of your reach
whose care is with the husks.

"Sharp wounds so secret" that not even death can claim them. This is a powerful *yes*. As Michelle Murray's dying was transformed into words, so too can the fear of death be transformed into new possibility for appreciating life. In a similar vein, poet Stanley Kunitz, an octogenarian, moves from the one-sidedness of absolutes and their resulting fear to their reconciliation. In *Next-to-Last Things* he transforms pain into possibility in one short passage.

The first grand concept I had was of death, my death, everyone's death. Through the circumstances of my childhood it was the fox at my breast, wrapped under my coat, a consuming terror. I could not sleep at night, thinking about dying. And then I realized that if I wanted to retain my sanity I had to learn how to live with this dreadful knowledge, *transforming it into a principle of creation instead of destruction* [italics mine]. The first step toward salvation was the recognition of the narrowness of my world. My affections had to flow outward and circulate through the natural order of things. Only then did I understand that, in the great chain of being, death as well as life has its own beauty and magnificence.

In recognizing the power to transform our understandable fear of death into a "principle of creation," we can respect what both Murray and Kunitz have achieved. Another poet, James Laughlin, approaches death obliquely, through tongue-in-cheek humor. Nevertheless, his tone of bittersweet emotion is sufficiently playful to make his point: We all have reasons for not wanting to die some terminally serious, some facetious, some whimsical. Lightness and grace are indicators of wisdom.

The Junk Collector

Those who fear death are those who enjoy life least.

EDWARD ABBEY

what bothers me most about
the idea of having to die
(sooner or later) is that
the collection of junk I
have made in my head will
presumably be dissipated
not that there isn't more
and better junk in other
heads always will be
but I have become so fond of
my own head's collection.

Letting Go

Just as one person's material junk is another person's treasure, wisdom is knowing to cherish our own mental "junk" because it is ours and because we value it as a reflection of our uniqueness. Just for the lightness of it, do a quick Word Sculpture of the junk collection in your head. Number and date your shape, and embellish it with all the words, ideas, and things that are part of your personal collection of junk.

Exploring the Act

- Be aware of the shape your junk took. Does the pattern jibe with anything else in your Feeling Sketchbook?
- How were you feeling as you word sculpted your junk—regretful? playful?
- Look for surprises in what you called your junk. Note the presence of anything unexpected.

If the Word Sculpture of your mental junk produced insight or pleasure, you may wish to follow it up with naming and framing it in a Cluster or Word Sketch. You can write about your junk in general, or you can zero in on something that turned out to have particular significance.

BOUNDARIES: LIFE AT DEATH

Death is also a boundary, one we have no choice but to acknowledge and with which we must reach a compromise. In
Finite and Infinite Games, James P. Carse describes death as
one of the limits we must take into account. In doing so, we
can then play whatever games we choose within life's boundaries. How clear and simple! Yet how hard to grasp—until
someone names and frames it for us. Some boundaries are
worth respecting as we play out the course of our lives. Other
boundaries can be shifted and moved about. Some can even be
erased or knocked down. And there lies the essence of the flexibility so fundamental to moving toward wisdom: our ability
to sense when compromise is necessary or when, perhaps, a
fervent *no* represents a breakthrough to new possibility.

*Compromise is the
essence of the adult.*

SAM KEEN

Letting Go

Now cluster

PLAYING WITHIN
PLAYING WITH BOUNDARIES

We have worlds of possibility here. This activity may enable you to see what boundaries you have imposed on yourself, or what boundaries you once thought you *had* to live
within, yet didn't. It may also enable you to see what boundaries you *can* play with. Number and date your entry as usual.
As you move into and through new or altered perspectives, it
will be interesting to explore where you've been and where
you are heading. Remember, simplicity is the key to insights.

Exploring the Act

- Notice which side of the Cluster Seed Word attracted
  more of your attention—PLAYING WITHIN or
  PLAYING WITH?
- If you found yourself stuck, or if you want to play, try a
  quick Word Sculpture. See if drawing the shape of your
  own boundaries or any particular boundary produces
  anything interesting. Embellish with the details of the
  boundary you drew. Don't force.

You can cluster PLAYING WITHIN / PLAYING WITH again and again, each time discovering new boundaries you thought were fixed or absolute. Each time you do it, you will see which boundaries you can play with, break, or shift. As transpersonal psychologist Ken Wilber describes so well, we live in worlds of boundaries that both separate and connect simultaneously. Some are of our own making, some we feel are imposed on us by others. Sometimes these boundaries are part of the nature of being alive.

Facing the boundary of death often stimulates difficult feelings. Uneasiness, uncertainty, and restlessness are not reserved for the classic midlife crisis or the confusion of adolescence. Such feelings can hit us at any time for any number of reasons—some identifiable, some mysterious. The poet W. S. Merwin chronicles such a momentary feeling. Through his naming and framing of a profound foresight, it becomes conscious thus, shareable.

For the Anniversary of My Death

Every year without knowing it I have passed the day
When the last fires will wave to me
And the silence will set out
Tireless traveller
Like the beam of a lightless star
Then I will no longer
Find myself in life as in a strange garment
Surprised at the earth
And the love of one woman
And the shamelessness of men
As today writing after three days of rain
Hearing the wren sing and the falling cease
And bowing not knowing to what.

A part of wisdom lies in that "bowing not knowing to what." Another part is moving with the spiral. Wisdom lies ultimately in trusting the inevitable patterns of chaos without needing to control them.

The recursive flow of the natural order of things is reminiscent of the spiral and Chaos science metaphors with which we began this book. The spiral moves, up as well as down. It expands as well as contracts. Like the unpredictable patterns discovered in chaos, the natural order is a process that *con-nects* polarities. It allows us to perceive them, to *feel* them as connected. The connection we feel intuitively tells us that even life and death are reconciled in possibility.

AN EMOTIONAL WILL

Death may be the ultimate boundary, but we can learn to face it with trust, to prepare for it in a deeply personal way. In doing so, we discover how much of our fear is transformed into a new capacity for the enjoyment of living. Let's look at an illustration of this new angle. Linda Pastan has written a poem I would call an *Emotional Will*—a kind of last will and testament, but dealing in feelings instead of objects. She expresses, in words on a page, what are, for most of us, only ephemeral, uncomfortable thoughts, quickly pushed aside. An Emotional Will represents a checkpoint in the moment, here, today, at this juncture in our lives. It creates a momentary boundary, paradoxically letting us look over the entire vista of our life, both backwards and forwards. An Emotional Will is an assertion of self intended to reach out to others. It validates the writer by offering a projection of self, of will, of desire, into a future in which we are no longer members of the cast. It is similar to letters buried in the cornerstones of buildings or time capsules, signifying an awareness of the continuity of life and the people in it, from grandparents to grandchildren, of the interconnectedness of past and future from one civilization to another.

Last Will

Children
when I am ash
read by the light of the fire
that consumes me
this document
whose subject is love.
I want to leave you everything: my life
divided into so many parts
there are enough to go around; the world

from this window: weather and a tree
which bequeaths
all of its leaves each year.

Today the lawyer plans
for your descendants,
telling a story
of generations
that seems to come true
even as he speaks.
My books will fill your children's shelves,
my small enameled spoons
invade their drawers. It is
the only way I know, so far,
to haunt.

Let me be a guest at my own funeral
and at the reading of my will.

You I'll reward first
for the moments of your births,
those three brief instants
when I understood my life.
But wisdom bends as light does
around the objects it touches.
The only legacy you need was left
by accident long ago:
a secret in the genes.
The rest is small change.

Note that the word *will* implies intention, the taking of an action for some purpose. It implies the future, something that will happen later. It implies connection to the past as well as a future disconnection, because you will be relinquishing something you once possessed. It also implies the here and now since you are writing in the present. What do you leave? And to whom? Whatever you put into an Emotional Will today may not be what you would put in the one you write next year. You will be a different person then whose experiences will have had an additional impact on your life story. "Wisdom bends as light does," Pastan writes.

Letting Go

Risk writing an Emotional Will. It is only for today. At this moment what would you bequeath to whom, and what do you want your legacy to be? In what ways would you like to "haunt" constructively?

Begin with Aware Breathing to help you be receptive, perhaps playful, or sad in the bittersweet way which comes with insight. Next, make a Word Sculpture. Its quick, easy arabesque will invite images, memories, which in turn will invite words and phrases. The process is one of opening to your deepest feelings. Now cluster EMOTIONAL WILL. Date and number your entry and write. Write quickly and without worrying about what you are leaving out, what you *should* include. Remember you can change it, erase it, throw it away and start again another day. This page of your Feeling Sketchbook is not etched in stone. It is part of the process of wisdom, inviting you to consider what in your emotional life is important enough to *you* to express.

Exploring the Act

An Emotional Will, done again and again whenever you are moved to, enables you to experience playing with one of life's most profound boundaries. it helps to build emotional muscles. You could continue to play with this idea by clustering whatever comes, followed by a simple listing of your initial impulses. From there on, you may write an Emotional Will for specific people, for yourself, for the world. Don't feel you need to do it all in one sitting. Beginning with one entry will provoke thoughts and feeling. These are likely to move you to add to your list periodically. It is fitting that this should be an ongoing, dynamic process, like life itself. You may not touch it for months, then, suddenly, a new feeling pops up, one you have the urge to name. If you choose, you can periodically rewrite your jottings into a Word Sketch, a poem, a manifesto. Address it to yourself, to someone you love, to someone imaginary, to humanity.

Ultimately, writing is giving witness to the "wealth of self," as poet David Ignatow tells us in "Witness":

Witness

We can't write ourselves into eternal life
and that is the sorrow and waste of writing,
but those who would write in this knowledge
have found a subterfuge by which to let
themselves be prompted, in heady confidence
of meaning: the wealth of self
spread among the readers who themselves
will read for reasons of earth:
that they have been witness
to their birth, growth and death
and shared the earth with earth.

The metaphor of Chaos I have used throughout to explore the brain/mind's complexity, particularly that of our emotional lives, is reflected in a passage by Dane Rudhyar in *The Pulse of Life:*

> Chaos is the path to greater wholeness of being and consciousness: a path, a transition, a process. The Sage is the one who, first of all, understands this process, feels its rhythm, realizes the meaning of its polar attractions and repulsions. It is the human being who sees all nature as a cyclic interplay of energies between "lesser wholes" and "greater wholes."

Dane Rudyar observes that, in complex dynamic systems, the patterns across scale from individual pain to universal pain, can be transformed into fulfillment ultimately through understanding the bigger picture of the inevitable recursiveness of pain, which also ensures its transformation into possibility.

FINAL THOUGHTS—AND LOOKING AHEAD

The fifteen seconds of wild shaking during California's 1989 earthquake were instantaneous attractors for my childhood memories of war. Logically, intellectually, I said, "It could be worse." But physically, all my old symptoms spread through my body like lightning. Instead of trying to control them, my former habitual reaction, I picked up my Feeling Sketchbook. I had made no entry for some time.

First I quieted my breath by becoming aware of it until it was even. Then I repeated the word *fear*: "Fear! Fear, fear, fear, fear, fear, fear, fear, fear, fear. . . ." until my adrenaline flow slowed. I wrote quickly, calming as I named and framed. I did a Word Sculpture (see Figure 9.7), which led to a cluster (see Figure 9.8), which in turn led to a dialogue with my own fear, the paradoxical, life-preserving, and life-destroying fear now once again lodged in my muscles and nerves like shrapnel.

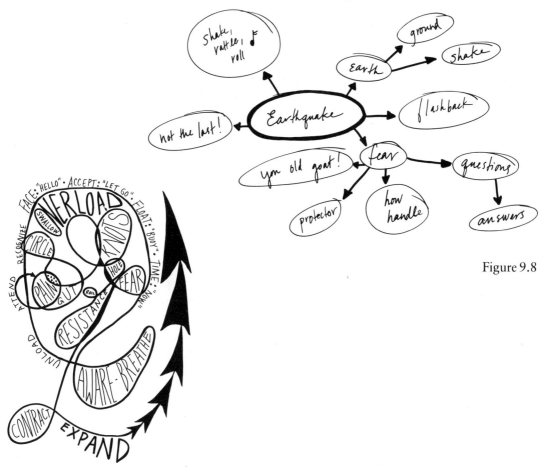

Figure 9.8

Figure 9.7

We cannot put off living until we are ready. The most salient point of life is its coerciveness; it is urgent, here and now without any possible postponement.

JOSE ORTEGA Y GASSET

Hello, Fear, old friend, I see you found me again.
* I always know where you are; I've never lost you.
You spread like a stain in my muscles, clog up my throat
    as though you had squatter's rights.
* That's only to remind you to attend to my knocking,
    But I'm Busy. Time is short!
* All in its own time. Shortchange me, and I'll take *your*
    time—I'll paralyze you so you *have* to wait, slow
    down, stop.
So, what do I do now—I mean, today?
* Let go. Go slow. Flow with the shock.
I can't! Too much to do.
* You can. Because you must. You mean, you won't!
But I've wasted time and energy!
* Cut your but's. You can only unpack one box at a time.
Wait! Where are you going? I have more questions.
* I'll check with you tomorrow. By then, you'll have some
    answers of your own.

Wisdom is not asking, "How can I get rid of this depression?" It is not asking, "What can I take to calm this anxiety?" It is not asking, "Why, why did this happen to me?" Wisdom is shifting from a passive stance to dynamic involvement with one's own healing by asking, "What can I learn from this loss?" "What signals have I ignored to make me so anxious?" "What is my depression trying to tell me?" "How can I learn to acknowledge my imperfections to let me live into a combination of the me I was, the me I am, the me of possibility?"

The very questions permit us to acknowledge the recursiveness of the life of feeling. Receptive, we can begin to rephrase our questions: "If this is, how can I tune into the unique music of my feeling self instead of struggling against it?" The princess of the fairy tale not only had a glass heart; she had a hairline fracture. She thrived in spite of it.

It is a metaphor so powerful it spoke to me when I was seven; it speaks to me today. We are all damaged. The very act of living is sustaining damage. Living is also remembering to smile at the absurdity of it all.

My glass princess might have said: God grant me the serenity to accept the things I cannot change, the courage to

change the things I can, the wisdom to know the difference—
and a sense of humor when I can't.

Damaged, yes, Broken, no. These delicate cracks in our
glass hearts render us simultaneously vulnerable and strong.
That is the price of being alive, of being human, of being feeling, as well as thinking, creatures. By opening to our range of
feelings, by giving them shape, we open to our self and others.
We reconnect with the world. We reconcile its polarities instead of getting mired in a false one-sidedness.

Process. Cooperation. Cosmic laughter at the incongruous, paradoxical wholeness of life.

I shall not forget my ongoing learning. It is rooted in reconciling polarities: fear and laughter, pain and joy, closing and
opening, vulnerability and strength.

Fear contracts, letting go expands. One-sided seriousness
shrinks into fear and hopelessness. Cosmic laughter expands
into a willingness to go with the flow of living. We no longer
need to wait until all is perfect—because if we do we will wait
a long time. We can live "in a wealth of self" despite suffering
and pain.

*The universe is a story. It's
not a place, it's an event.*

BRIAN SWIMME

*Just as zero is both plus
10 and minus 10 at the
same time, we are
composed of
complementary
properties. If we seek
ultimate order or
ultimate chaos, we create
a monster.*

FRED ALAN WOLF

Surgeons must be very careful
When they take the knife
Underneath their fine incisions
Stirs the culprit—Life!

EMILY DICKINSON

I am; therefore, I continue.

THEODORE ROETHKE

Human writing reflects that of the universe.
It is its translation, but also its metaphor:
it says something totally different and it says the same thing.

OCTAVIO PAZ

The greatest and most important problems of life
are all fundamentally insoluble.
They can never be solved but only outgrown.

CARL JUNG

The reverse side also has a reverse side.

JAPANESE PROVERB

Bibliography

Abbey, Edward. *A Voice Crying in the Wilderness.* NY: St. Martin's, 1989.

Auden, W. H. *Collected Shorter Poems: 1927–1957.* NY: Random House, 1966.

Babbitt, Natalie. *Tuck Everlasting.* NY: Bantam, 1975.

Barth, John. *The End of the Road.* NY: Avon, 1958.

Benson, Herbert. *The Relaxation Response.* NY: Avon, 1975.

Berry, Wendell. *Collected Poems: 1957–1982.* SF: North Point Press, 1985.

——. *Sabbaths.* SF: North Point Press, 1987.

Bhaerman, Steve. *Driving Your Own Karma.* VT: Destiny Books, 1989.

Bick, C. H. *International Journal of Neuroscience* 47 (1990):31-40.

Bloomfield, Harold, M.D., and Robert Kory. *Inner Joy.* NY: Playboy Paperbacks, 1980.

Bly, Robert, ed. *Neruda and Vallejo.* Boston: Beacon Press, 1971.

Bogen, J. E. "One Brain, or Two, or Both?" In *Two Hemispheres, One Brain?* ed. F. Lepore, et. al. NY: Allan Liss, 1990.

Bogen, J. E. "The Dual Brain." In *The Dual Brain.* eds. D. F. Benson and E. Zaidel. NY: The Guilford Press, 1985.

Bogen, Joseph, and Glenda. "The Other Side of the Brain: An Appositional Mind." In *The Nature of Human Consciousness,* ed. Robert Ornstein. SF: W. H. Freeman, 1968.

Bohm, David. "Parts of a Whole." Interview by Michael Thoms, 1984. New Dimensions Radio, San Francisco.

Bombeck, Erma. *If Life is a Bowl of Cherries—What Am I doing in the Pits?* NY: Fawcett, 1978.

Bradbury, Ray. *Dandelion Wine.* NY: Alfred A. Knopf, 1978.

Branden, Nathaniel. *The Psychology of Self-Esteem.* NY: Bantam, 1969.

Briggs, John. *The Looking-Glass Universe.* NY: Harper and Row, 1984.

Briggs, John, and F. David Peat. *Turbulent Mirror.* NY: Harper and Row, 1984.

Bronk, William. *That Tantalus.* London: The Press of Villiers Publications Ltd., 1971.

Brown, Barbara B. *Supermind: The Ultimate Energy.* NY: Harper and Row, 1980.

Brown, Norman O. *Love's Body.* NY: Vintage, 1966.

Calvin, William. *The Cerebral Symphony.* NY: Bantam, 1990.

Campbell, Jeremy. *Grammatical Man.* NY: Simon and Schuster, 1982.

——. *Winston Churchill's Afternoon Nap.* NY: Simon and Schuster, 1986.

Campbell, John, M.D. "Functional Organization of the Central Nervous System With Respect to Orientation in Time" *Neurology,* 4, 4 (1954): 295-300.

Capra, Frijof. *The Tao of Physics.* Boston: Shambhala, 1983.

Carse, James. *Finite and Infinite Games.* NY: Macmillan, 1986.

Churchland, Patricia Smith. *Neurophilosophy: Toward a Unified Science of the Mind/Brain.* Cambridge: MIT Press, 1986.

Ciardi, John. *Live Another Day.* NY: Twayne, 1949.

Coles, Robert. *The Call of Stories.* Boston, MA: Houghton Mifflin, 1989.

Cousins, Norman. *The Healing Heart.* NY: Avon, 1984.

Csikszentmihalyi, Mihaly. *Flow: The Psychology of Optimal Experience.* NY: Harper and Row, 1990.

Cumes-Rayner and J. Price. "Understanding Hypertensive Behavior." *Journal of Psychosomatic Research* 33:63-74. 1989.

D'Arcy, Paula. *Song for Sarah.* Wheaton, IL: Harold Shaw, 1979.

Davies, Phyllis. *Grief: My Climb to Understanding.* San Luis Obispo: Sunnybank, 1988.

De Bono, Edward. *Lateral Thinking* NY: Harper and Row.

De Chardin, Pierre Teilhard. In *The Creative Imperative,* ed. Charles Johnston. Millbrae, CA: Celestial Arts, 1986.

——. *Activation of Energy.* NY: Harcourt Brace Jovanovich, 1963.

Didion, Joan. *Play It as It Lays.* NY: Farrar, Straus and Giroux, 1970.

Dinnerstein, Dorothy. *The Mermaid and the Minotaur.* NY: Harper and Row, 1983.

Dossey, Larry, M.D. *Space, Time and Medicine.* Boston: Shambala Press, 1982.

Dugan, Alan, *Poems 4.* Boston: Little, Brown, 1972.

Dunn, Stephen. *Between Angels.* NY: W. W. Norton, 1989.

Ferguson, Marilyn. *The Aquarian Conspiracy.* LA: Jeremy Tarcher, 1980.

Ferrucci, Piero. *Inevitable Grace.* LA: Jeremy Tarcher, 1990.

Field, Edward. *Variety Photoplays.* NY: Grove Press, 1967.

Field, Joanna. *A Life of One's Own,* and *An Experiment in Leisure.* LA: Jeremy Tarcher, 1981 and 1987.

Fontana, Alan. "Cynical Mistrust and the Search for Self-Worth." *Journal of Psychosomatic Research,* 33:(1990) 449-456.

Foucault, Michel. *language, countermemory, practice: Selected Essays and Interviews.* ed. D. F. Bouchard, tr. D. F. Bouchard and Sherry Simon, Ithaca, NY: Cornell University Press, 1977.

Fraser, J. T. *Time the Familiar Stranger.* Redmond: Tempus Books of Microsoft Press, 1987.

Frost, Richard. *The Circus Villains.* OH: Ohio University Press, 1965.

Fulghum, Robert. *All I Really Need to Know I Learned in Kindergarten.* NY: Villard, 1988.

Fuller, Renee. *In Search of the IQ Correlation.* NY: Ball-Stick-Bird Publications, 1977.

——. "Teaching with the Story Engram." *Journal of the Society for Accelerated Learning and Teaching.* 15, nos. 1 and 2 (1990): 19-36.

Fuster, Joaquin M. M.D. *The Prefrontal Cortex: Anatomy, Physiology, and Neuropsychology of the Frontal Lobe.* 2nd. ed., NY: Raven Press, 1990.

Gardner, Howard. *The Shattered Mind.* NY: Knopf, 1975.

Gaylin, Willard, M.D. *Feelings: Our Vital Signs.* NY: Ballantine, 1979.

Gendler, J. Ruth. *The Book of Qualities.* NY: Harper Collins, 1987.

Ghiselin, Brewster. *The Creative Process.* NY: New American Library, 1955.

Gilman, Charlotte. "The Yellow Wallpaper." NY: Feminist Press reprint of 1899 by Small, Maynard, Boston, 1973.

Gleick, James. *Chaos: The Making of a New Science.* NY: Viking Books, 1987.

Gordon, Barbara. *I'm Dancing as Fast as I Can.* NY: Bantam, 1980.

Gould, Stephen Jay. *Time's Arrow, Time's Cycle.* MA: Harvard University Press, 1987.

Gray, William. "Understanding Creative Thought Processes: An Early Formulation of Emotional-Cognitive Structure Theory." *Man-Environment Systems* 9, no. 1 (1980).

Hageseth III, Christian, M.D. *A Laughing Place.* Fort Collins, CO: Berwick, 1988.

Hansel, Tim. *You Gotta Keep Dancin'* Elgin, IL: Cook, 1985.

Hardison, O. B. *Disappearing through the Skylight.* NY: Viking, 1989.

Haviland, Jeanette and Mary Lelwica. "The Induced Affect Response: 10 Week Old Infants' Responses to Three Emotional Expressions." *Developmental Psychology* 23, (1987): 97-104.

Hermann, Steffi. *Elisabeth Kronseder: Bildhauerin und Malerin Am Samerberg.* Grabenstaett, Germany: Drei Linden Verlag, 1983.

Hoffer, Eric. *The Ordeal of Change.* NY: Harper and Row, 1963.

Hooper, Judith and Dick Teresi. *The 3-Pound Universe.* NY: Dell, 1986.

Houston, Jean. *Life Force.* NY: Dell, 1980.

Houston, Jean. *The Possible Human.* LA: Jeremy Tarcher, 1982.

Hughes, Langston. *Selected Poems.* NY: Alfred A. Knopf and Harold Ober Assoc., Inc., 1959.

Huizinga, Johan. *Homo Ludens: A Study of the Play Element in Culture.* Boston, MA: Beacon Press, 1955.

Jacob, Mennet. *Mastectomy Write-Out: Anatomy of a Loss.* Menomonee Falls, WI: McCormick and Schilling, 1990.

James, William. *Varieties of Religious Experience.* Cambridge, MA: Harvard University Press, 1985.

Jampolsky, Gerald. *Love is Letting Go of Fear.* NY: Bantam, 1982.

Janov, Arthur. *The Primal Scream.* NY: Dell. 1970.

——. *Prisoners of Pain.* Garden City, NY: Anchor Press, 1980.

Jaynes, Gregory. "Lead on, O Kinky Turtle." *Time Magazine,* 12 January 1987.

Jefferson, Lara. *These Are My Sisters.* Garden City, NY: Anchor Press/Doubleday, 1974.

Johnson, Wendell. *Verbal Man: The Enchantment of Words.* NY: Collier Books, 1965.

Johnston, Charles. *The Creative Imperative.* Berkeley, CA: Celestial Arts, 1986.

Jong, Erica. *Half-Lives.* NY: Holt, Rinehart and Winston, 1973.

Jourard, Sidney. *Ways of Growth.* NY: Grossman, 1968.

Joyce, James. *Portrait of the Artist as a Young Man.* Reprint. NY: The Viking Press, 1956.

Kanner, L. "Irrelevant and Metaphorical Language in Early Infantile Autism." *American Journal of Psychiatry,* 103 (1946): 242-246.

Keen, Sam. *Apology for Wonder.* NY: Harper and Row, 1969.

——. *The Passionate Life.* NY: Harper and Row, 1983.

——. *To A Dancing God.* NY: Harper and Row, 1970.

——. "Stories We Live By." *Psychology Today,* (December, 1988).

——. *What to Do When You're Bored and Blue.* Wyden Books, 1980.

Keen, Sam and Anne Valley-Fox. *Your Mythic Journey.* LA: Jeremy Tarcher, 1989.

Keleman, Stanley. *Your Body Speaks Its Mind.* NY: Simon and Schuster, 1975.

Keller, Helen. *The Story of My Life.* Garden City, NY: Doubleday, 1954.

Kinnell, Galway. *Mortal Acts, Mortal Words.* Boston: Houghton Mufflin, 1982.

Klee, Paul, *The Thinking Eye.* Ed. Juerg Spiller, tr. Ralph Manheim. NY: George Wittenborn, 1961.

Koestenbaum, Peter. *Is There an Answer to Death?* NJ: Prentice-Hall, 1976.

Koestler, Arthur. *The Act of Creation.* London: PAN Books, 1970.

Kopp, Sheldon. *This Side of Tragedy.* Palo Alto, CA: Science and Behavior Books, 1977.

——. *Who Am I, Really?* LA: Jeremy Tarcher, 1987.

Kübler-Ross, Elizabeth. *On Death and Dying.* NY: Macmillan, 1969.

Kumin, Maxine. *The Retrieval System.* NY: Penguin Books, Inc., 1978.

Kunitz, Stanley. *Next-to-Last Things.* NY: Atlantic Monthly, 1985.

La Violette, Paul A. "Thoughts about Thoughts about Thoughts: The Emotional Perceptive Cycle Theory." *Man-Environment Systems* 9, no. 1 (1979).

Lamendella, John. "The Limbic System in Human Communication." In *Studies in Neurolinguistics,* ed. H. A. Whitaker. NY: Academic Press, 1977.

Langer, Ellen J. *Mindfulness.* Reading: Addison-Wesley, 1989.

Langer, Susanne. *Problems of Art.* NY: Scribner's, 1976.

——. *Philosophical Sketches.* Baltimore, MD: Johns Hopkins, 1962.

——. *Mind: An Essay on Human Feeling.* 2 vols. Baltimore, MD: The Johns Hopkins University Press, 1967–72.

Lashley, Karl. "In Search of the Engram." *Physiological Mechanisms in Animal Behavior.* No. 4: 454-82.

Laughlin, James. *Selected Poems, 1936–1985.* SF: City Lights Books, 1985.

Lederer, Richard. *Anguished English.* NY: Dell, 1987.

——. *Crazy English.* NY: Pocket Books, 1989.

Lewis, C. S. *A Grief Observed.* SF: Seabury Press, Inc. and Faber and Faber, Ltd., Publishers, 1961.

Lorde, Audre. *The Cancer Journals.* Argyle, NY: Spinsters, 1980.

Lorde, Audre. *Claims for Poetry.* ed. Donald Hall. Ann Arbor: University of Michigan, 1982.

Loye, David. *The Sphinx and the Rainbow.* NY: Bantam, 1984.

Luria, A. R. *Higher Cortical Functions in Man.* Plenum Pub., NY: 2nd ed., 1980.

Luria, A. R. *Human Brain and Psychological Processes.* NY: Harper and Row, 1966.

MacLean, Paul D. "On the Evolution of Three Mentalities." In *New Dimensions in Psychiatry: A World View.* Vol. 2, eds. Silvano Arieti and Gerard Chrzanowski. NY: Wiley, 1977.

MacLean, Paul, M.D., *The Triune Brain in*

Evolution. NY: Plenum Press, 1990.

Mairs, Nancy. *Remembering the Bone House.* NY: Harper and Row, 1989.

Mandelstam, Osip. *Stone.* Princeton, NJ: Princeton Press, 1981.

Mann, Thomas. *A Sketch of My Life.* NY: Alfred A. Knopf, 1960.

Maslow, Abraham. *The Farther Reaches of Human Nature.* NY: Viking, 1971.

Meinke, Peter. *The Night Train and the Golden Bird.* Pittsburgh, PA: University of Pittsburg Press, 1977.

——. *Trying to Surprise God.* Pittsburgh, PA: University of Pittsburgh Press, 1981.

Merwin, W. S. *Carriers of Ladders.* NY: Atheneum, 1970.

Middlebrook, Diane. *Worlds into Words.* NY: W. W. Norton, 1980.

Miller, Jonathan. *States of Mind.* NY: Pantheon, 1983.

Moffat, Mary Jane, ed. *In the Midst of Winter.* NY: Vintage, 1982.

Murray, Michelle. *The Great Mother and Other Poems.* Kansas City, MO: Sheed and Ward, 1974.

Nabokov, Vladimir. *Speak, Memory.* Middlesex, England: Penguin, 1966.

Nachmanovitch, Stephen. *Free Play.* LA: Jeremy Tarcher, 1990.

Navarre, Jane Piirto. *Postcards from the Upper Peninsula.* Pollock, SD: Pocasse Press, 1983.

Neider, Charles. *The Autobiography of Mark Twain.* Reprint. NY: Harper and Row, 1959.

Nemerov, Howard. *Poets on Poetry Series.* Ann Arbor, MI: University of Michigan Press.

Nisker, Wes. *Crazy Wisdom.* Berkeley, CA: Ten Speed Press, 1990.

O'Hanean, Bernard. "The Lost Words of Joseph Chaikin," *Hippocrates,* Ja.–Feb. 1989: 74-80.

Olds, Sharon. *The Gold Cell.* NY: Alfred A. Knopf, 1987.

——. *The Dead and the Living.* NY: Alfred A. Knopf, 1987.

Ornish, Dean, M.D. *Dean Ornish's Program for Reversing Heart Disease.* NY: Random House, 1990.

Ornstein, Robert, and David Sobel, M.D. *Healthy Pleasures.* Reading, MA: Addison-Wesley, 1989.

Pastan, Linda. *A Fraction of Darkness.* NY: W. W. Norton, 1985.

——. *PM/AM: New and Selected Poems.* NY: W. W. Norton, 1982.

Paz, Octavio. *Alternating Currents.* NY: Viking, 1973.

——. *The Monkey Grammarian.* NY: Seaver Books, 1981.

Pelletier, Kenneth, M.D. *Mind as Healer, Mind as Slayer.* NY: Delacorte, 1977.

Percy, Walker. *Lost in the Cosmos.* NY: Pocket Books, 1983.

Piirto, Jane Navarre. *mamamama.* Ashland, OH: Sisu Press, 1979.

Polanyi, Michael. *The Tacit Dimension.* Magnolia, MA: Peter Smith, 1983.

Prigogine, Ilya. *From Being to Becoming.* NY: W. H. Freeman, 1980.

Purce, Jill. *The Mystic Spiral.* NY: Thames & Hudson, 1974.

Restak, Richard, M.D. *The Brain.* NY: Bantam, 1984.

——. *The Mind.* NY: Bantam, 1988.

Rice, Scott. *It Was a Dark and Stormy Night.* NY: Penguin, 1985.

Richards, M. C. *Centering: Poetry, Pottery, and the Person.* Middletown, CT: Wesleyan University Press, 1964.

Rico, Gabriele L. "Educating the Emotions." *International Brain Dominance Review.* Ned and Margy Hermann, 1989.

——. "Writer: Personal Patterns in Chaos." In *Teacher's Craft, Writer's Art,* ed. Mimi Schwartz. Portsmouth, NH: Boynton/Cook, 1991.

——. *Writing the Natural Way.* LA: Jeremy Tarcher, 1983.

Robbins, Anthony. *Unlimited Power.* NY: Random House, 1986.

Roethke, Theodore. *Words for the Wind.* NY: Doubleday, 1958.

——. *The Collected Poems of Theodore Roethke.* NY: Doubleday, 1964.

——. *On the Poet and His Craft,* ed. Ralph J. Mills, Jr. Seattle: University of Washington, 1965.

Ross, Elliot, M.D. "Aprodosia." *The Sciences* 22, no. 2 (1982).

Rothenberg, Jerome. *The Emerging Goddess.* Chicago: University of Chicago Press, 1979.

Sacks, Oliver. *The Man Who Mistook his Wife for a Hat.* NY: Summit Books, 1985.

——. *Seeing Voices: A Journey into the World of the Deaf.* Berkeley: University of California Press, 1989.

Safransky, Sy. *New Men, New Minds.* Freedom, CA: Crossing Point, 1988?

Sapirstein, Milton R. *Paradoxes of Everyday Life.* Greenwich, CT: Fawcett, 1955.

Sartre, Jean-Paul. *The Words.* Greenwich, CT: Faucett World Library, 1964.

Schaeffer, Neil. *The Art of Laughter.* NY: Columbia University Press, 1981.

Schwenk, Theodor. *Sensitive Chaos.* London: Rudolf Steiner Press, 1965.

Selzer, Richard. *Confessions of a Knife.* NY: Simon and Schuster, 1979.

Sheehy, Gail. *Spirit of Survival.* NY: Bantam, 1987.

Siler, Todd. *Breaking the Mind Barrier.* NY: Simon and Schuster, 1990.

Singer, June. *Seeing through the Visible World.* NY: Harper and Row, 1990.

Sinnot, E. W. *Matter, Mind and Man.* NY: Harper and Brothers, 1957.

Sperry, Roger W., "Hemisphere Disconnection and Unity in Conscious Awareness." *American Psychologist* 23, no. 10 (1968): 723-733.

Sperry, Roger, and Laura Franco. "Hemisphere Lateralization for Cognitive Processing of Geometry." *Neuropsychologia* 15 (1977): 107-14.

Stafford, William. *Writing the Australian Crawl.* Ann Arbor, MI: The University of Michigan Press, 1978.

——. *Allegiances: New Poems by William Stafford.* NY: Harper and Row, 1970.

Steele, Shelby. *The Content of Our Character.* NY: St. Martin's Press, 1990.

Stevens, Wallace. *The Collected Poems of Wallace Stevens.* NY: Alfred A. Knopf, 1982.

Stone, Ruth. "Interview with Ruth Stone" *AWP Chronicle.* (October/November 1990).

Styron, William. "Darkness Visible." *Vanity Fair,* December, 1989.

Swimme, Brian. *The Universe is a Green Dragon.* Santa Fe: Bear and Co., 1984.

Vallejo, Cesar. *Neruda and Vallejo,* tr. Robert Bly. Boston: Beacon Press, 1971.

Viorst, Judith. *Necessary Losses.* NY: Ballantine, 1986.

Vonnegut, Kurt. *The Sirens of Titan*. NY: Dell, 1977.

Vygotsky, Lev S. *Selected Psychological Investigations*. Moscow: Academic Pedagogical Science, RSFSR Press, 1956.

Wagoner, David. *Who Shall Be the Sun?* Bloomington, IN: Indiana University Press, 1971.

———. *First Light*. Boston: Little, Brown.

Walker, Alice. *Good Night, Willie Lee, I'll See You in the Morning*. NY: Dial Press, 1979.

———. *The Temple of My Familiar*. NY: Hascourt, Brace, Jovanich, 1989.

Ward, Milton. *The Brilliant Function of Pain*. NY: Optimus Books, 1977.

Watts, Alan. *The Wisdom of Insecurity*. NY: Vintage, 1951.

Watzlawick, Paul. *Ultra-Solutions: How to Fail Most Successfully*. NY: W. W. Norton, 1988.

———. *How Real Is Real?* NY: Vintage, 1977.

———. *The Situation is Hopless, but Not Serious*. NY: W. W. Norton, 1983.

Weekes, Claire. *Peace from Nervous Suffering*. NY: Bantam, 1972.

Wigan, A. L., M.D. *The Duality of the Mind*. 1844. Reprint, with Foreword by Joseph Bogen, M.D. Malibu, CA: Joseph Simon, 1985.

Wilber, Ken. *No Boundary*. San Francisco, CA: Shambala Press, 1981.

Williams, Miller. *Halfway from Hoxie*. NY: E. P. Dutton, 1973.

Wilson, Stephen. *Eat Dessert First*. Pickerington, OH: Advocate Pub Group, 1990.

Winnicot, Donald. *Playing and Reality*. London: Tavistock, 1971.

Winokur, Jon. *The Portable Curmudgeon*. NY: New American Library, 1986.

———. *A Curmudgeon's Garden of Love*. NY: New American Library, 1989.

———. *Zen to Go*. NY: New American Library, 1989.

Witkin, Robert. *The Intelligence of Feeling*. London: Heinemann Educational, 1974.

Wolff, Tobias. *This Boy's Life*. NY: Atlantic Monthly Press, 1989.

Zaidel, Eran. "The Elusive Right Hemisphere of the Brain." *Engineering Science* (September/October 1978)

Zohar, Danah. *The Quantum Self*. NY: William Morrow, 1990.

Zukav, Gary. *The Seat of the Soul*. NY: Simon and Schuster, 1989.

Index